HOW FFAW-UNIFOR CONFRONTED POWER AND SHARED THE WEALTH

BOULDER
BOOKS

Library and Archives Canada Cataloguing in Publication

Title: A match to a blasty bough : how FFAW-Unifor confronted power and shared the wealth / Earle McCurdy.
Names: McCurdy, Earle, author.
Description: Includes bibliographical references and index.
Identifiers: Canadiana 20210314451 | ISBN 9781989417447 (softcover)
Subjects: LCSH: Fish, Food and Allied Workers (N.L.)—History. | LCSH: Fishers—Labor unions—
  Newfoundland and Labrador—History. | LCSH: Labor unions—Newfoundland and Labrador—History.
Classification: LCC HD6528.F652 F576 2021 | DDC 331.88/139209718—dc2

© 2021 Earle McCurdy

Published by Boulder Books
Portugal Cove-St. Philip's, Newfoundland and Labrador
www.boulderbooks.ca

Design and layout: Tanya Montini
Editor: Stephanie Porter
Copy editor: Iona Bulgin

Printed in Canada

Excerpts from this publication may be reproduced under licence from Access Copyright, or with the express written permission of Boulder Books Ltd., or as permitted by law. All rights are otherwise reserved and no part of this publications may be reproduced, stored in a retrieval system, or transmitted in any form or by any means, electronic, mechanical, photocopying, scanning, recording, or otherwise, except as specifically authorized.

We acknowledge the financial support of the Government of Newfoundland and Labrador through the Department of Tourism, Culture, Arts and Recreation.

Table of Contents

Author's Note 5
List of abbreviations 11
Milestone Events 1970–2020 13
1. Pre-existing Conditions 25
2. "A Match to a Blasty Bough" 37
3. "Never Again Will We Beg" 48
4. Goodbye Co-Adventurer System, Hello 20th Century 57
5. 1980: United We Stand 69
6. "Some People Might Have to End Up on Welfare" 77
7. "Dog Eat Dog and Vice Versa" 88
8. "How Are We Going to Feed Our Children?" 108
9. "A Famine of Biblical Scale: A Great Destruction" 117

10.	Troubled Waters: The Onslaught of the Foreign Fleets ... 138
11.	Restoring Hope to Coastal Communities 153
12.	LFUSCo—A Lifeline for the Labrador Coast 165
13.	The Yellow School Bus. 172
14.	The Endless Attack on Employment Insurance 185
15.	"We're the Women of the Union" 198
16.	Working in the Plants: "Some Good Times and Some Hard Times" 210
17.	What's That Got to Do with the Price of Fish?. 226
18.	RMS: "Any Independence We Had Would Be Gone" 242
19.	Owner-Operator: Linking the Resource to Coastal Communities 252
20.	Promoting Safety in a Dangerous Industry 271
21.	"More Than Just a Union" 282
22.	A Comprehensive Science Program 297
23.	Lobster: Creative Solutions to Difficult Problems. 305
24.	"Where the Power Comes From". 318
25.	That Blasty Bough Is Still Burning 328
Appendix A 338	
Appendix B 341	
About the author. 351	

Author's Note

This is a story about people. It's about communities, about solidarity, about struggle, about hard work, about money, and about power.

This is the story of the people who work in the Newfoundland and Labrador fishery, and the organization they built from the ground up.

Dismissed by many in its early days as bound to fail, the organization now known as FFAW-Unifor turns 50 in 2021. For decades, it has been firmly entrenched as a force to be reckoned with in the political life of Newfoundland and Labrador. In the half-century since its founding convention, the union has faced market crashes, corporate restructuring in the industry, reorganization of the union itself, ongoing corporate campaigns to break the link between coastal communities and adjacent fish stocks, climate change, scandalous levels of foreign overfishing, and fish stock collapses that threatened the union's very survival.

The union was initially called the Northern Fishermen's Union

(NFU), which transitioned into Newfoundland Fishermen, Food and Allied Workers Union (NFFAWU). It later became known at various times as Fishermen's Union-UFCW Local 1252, NFFAW Local 465, FFAW-CAW, and FFAW-Unifor, its current name. But it was always essentially the same people. There is a straight line from 1971 to 2021. In this book, rather than confusing the reader by using the various names in effect at a particular time, I refer to "the union" or "our union" or occasionally "FFAW." I'm talking about the same people.

In a similar vein, terminology has changed over the years. To be inclusive of the growing number of women who were fishing for a living, in the 1990s we changed our union's official name and started using the term "fish harvester" instead of "fisherman," but in this book I haven't tampered with quotes and comments that reflect the common usage at the relevant time.

This book is not a documentary; it's not being narrated by an impartial third party. I've been part of this race for most of the union's 50-year existence.

It's not exactly a memoir either. In writing this book, I rely heavily on my recollections and my own extensive handwritten notes, files, correspondence, and written documents that I accumulated over 37 years of involvement in this extraordinary piece of history, as well as on various reference books, source documents, and news clippings. More importantly, I conducted dozens of interviews with current and former union officers, staff, and rank-and-file members whose recollections and viewpoints are vital to the telling of this story. Of these, at least half a dozen are now in their 80s and one—Bill Short—has turned 90, while others span a range of ages, as young as in their 20s. It's our story, not my story; I'm the one holding the pen, who happened to have a front-row seat for many of the main events.

FFAW has members in industries other than the fishery—hospitality, brewing, and metal fabrication, among others—but this story is primarily about those who work in the fishery. That fishery is widely misunderstood and often poorly managed, but it is the lifeblood of the hundreds of small communities that dot the coastline of our province and is deeply embedded in our sense of ourselves as Newfoundlanders and Labradorians. For a few years in the 1980s, the union membership included bargaining units in Nova Scotia and Prince Edward Island, but this ceased at the time of the affiliation with the Canadian Auto Workers in the late '80s, when these bargaining units established separate CAW locals. Except for that interval, the union membership has consisted entirely of Newfoundlanders and Labradorians.

I'd like to thank the 50-plus people who took the time to meet with me (or talk on the phone when the COVID-19 pandemic ruled out face-to-face meetings), answer my questions, and help fill out the picture of the past 50 years. Most are (or were) union activists—the executive board, council, and committee members, who are the guts of any trade union. They don't show up on the audited balance sheet, but elected rank-and-file leadership are any union's greatest asset. Hundreds of these activists have contributed to building the union. Appendix B lists many of these rank-and-file leaders who were involved in building the union. It is also important to recognize the contribution of their spouses and families, who had to put up with the phone ringing at all hours and with a family member frequently away from home helping to build the union. To those I missed because of inadequate records or faulty memories, please accept my apologies.

In particular, I would like to acknowledge Richard Cashin, both for his bold vision in launching the union in the first place, and for sitting down with me for several hours to talk about the highlights and challenges of his term as president.

I extend my sincere thanks to those who helped me with interviews and ideas, in particular Rick Williams and Ged Blackmore, who took the time to read multiple drafts of the book and forward their suggestions. Thanks also to the current officers and executive board members of the union, who authorized and supported this venture. Any mistakes in reporting are my responsibility.

In addition to those I interviewed, many others would have had so much to add to this story, but they are no longer alive. Prominent among these are Father Desmond McGrath, Ray Greening, and Kevin Condon, all of whom played central roles from the beginning. Luckily, there is published material available—notably former Memorial University anthropology professor Gordon Inglis's excellent book *More Than Just a Union: The Story of the NFFAWU*, which was published in 1985—that provides insight into their recollections and views about the union's formation and its early years.

Continuity in key leadership positions has been a strength of FFAW. Richard Cashin held the position of president for the first 23 years, before I took over in 1993, having served as secretary-treasurer for the previous 13 years. In November 2014, it was my turn to pass the torch, after 21 years. I was succeeded by Keith Sullivan, who came from a fishing family and worked as my assistant for several years. Growing up, Keith didn't have to go any further than the kitchen table to learn about the union; his father, Lloyd, was a cod-trap fish harvester on the Southern Shore who served for many years on the union's inshore council and later the executive board, and his mother, Linda, worked in a fish plant. Keith spent his summers during his school and university years fishing on his father's boat.

The FFAW has two full-time elected executive positions, as there are with many unions: president and secretary-treasurer. In the initial year or so of the union's existence, Kevin Condon served as secretary-treasurer as a volunteer, until Ray Greening took over on a full-time basis in 1972. Ray, who had worked in a Canada Packers plant in St. John's, then as a union staff representative, remained as secretary-treasurer until his death in 1980, when I succeeded him.

I was fortunate to have two capable and dedicated first mates during my years as skipper. Reg Anstey moved up through the industrial sector after working as a jackhammer operator at the fish plant in Harbour Breton. After stints as industrial/retail director and later secretary-treasurer of FFAW, Reg served several terms as president of the Newfoundland and Labrador Federation of Labour. When Reg moved on, he was succeeded as secretary-treasurer by David Decker, who grew up in Ship Cove on the tip of the Northern Peninsula, where he fished in a small boat before coming to work for the union in 1990. He served as staff rep, then inshore director until moving up to secretary-treasurer when Reg left. The most recent change at the secretary-treasurer position occurred in October 2020, when Dave stepped down after 17 years. He was succeeded by Robert Keenan, who had worked with the union for six years as a projects officer, following several years with Municipalities NL.

It's not sensible—or even possible—to try to relate between the covers of this book all the events that occurred over the past 50 years; there's too much material. I have focused on highlights, turning points, themes, and values. What is clear throughout is that progress is never handed to workers and their unions.

Richard Cashin had great respect for Kevin Condon, a fish harvester from Calvert on the Southern Shore who was prominently involved in the union from the beginning. Condon, a principled man, always spoke his mind. In an interview more than 35 years ago with Gordon Inglis, Condon concluded that a fisheries union was inevitable: "It had to come. We needed it and we were ready for it. If it hadn't come one way, it would have come another. [But] if it hadn't been for Richard, and Father Des, and Ray Greening, we wouldn't have got it when we did. And it wouldn't be the same union we've got now."

Fortunately, Richard and Father Des and Ray *were* involved from the early days.

They saw the need to break down the notorious truck system in the inshore fishery and the dominant position of the merchant class, to recognize the importance to the industry of people who work in fishing boats and fish plants, and to give them a strong voice. Their vision was to build a strong, militant, democratic organization that would fight for increased prosperity in fishing communities and a fairer sharing of the wealth of our fishery.

This is the story of how their vision of what was possible unfolded over the next 50 years.

List of Abbreviations

AIB	Anti-Inflation Board
APPQ	Alliance des Pêcheurs Professionels du Québec
ASP	Association of Seafood Producers
CAFSAC	Canadian Atlantic Fisheries Scientific Advisory Committee
CAW	Canadian Auto Workers
CBRT	Canadian Brotherhood of Railway, Transport and General Workers Union.
CCPFH	Canadian Council of Professional Fish Harvesters
CEP	Communications, Energy and Paper Workers
CFAWU	Canadian Food and Allied Workers
CLC	Canadian Labour Congress
CUPW	Canadian Union of Postal Workers
DFO	Department of Fisheries and Oceans
DTI	Deepsea Training Inc.
EEC	European Economic Community

ERCO	Electric Reduction Company
FANL	Fisheries Association of Newfoundland and Labrador
FFAW	Fish, Food and Allied Workers
FOS	Final Offer Selection
FPI	Fishery Products International
FPU	Fishermen's Protective Union
FRC	Fish Harvesters Resource Centre
ICNAF	International Commission for the Northwest Atlantic Fishery
IRO	Industrial-Retail-Offshore Council
IWA	International Woodworkers of America
LFUSCo	Labrador Fishermen's Union Shrimp Company
LIFO	Last in-first out
NAFO	Northwest Atlantic Fisheries Organization
NCARP	Northern Cod Adjustment and Recovery Program
NFF	Newfoundland Federation of Fishermen
NFFAWU	Newfoundland Fishermen, Food and Allied Workers Union
NFU	Northern Fishermen's Union
NLFHSA	Newfoundland and Labrador Fish Harvesting Safety Association
NRDA	Northern Rural Development Association
OCI	Ocean Choice International
PFHCB	Professional Fish Harvesters Certification Board
PIIFCAF	Policy for Preserving the Independence of the Inshore Fleet in Canada's Atlantic Fisheries
POWA	Program for Older Worker Adjustment
RMS	Raw Material Shares
TAC	Total Allowable Catch
TAGS	The Atlantic Groundfish Strategy
UFCW	United Food and Commercial Workers

Milestone Events
1970–2020

This book follows chronological order, to the extent possible. Some chapters are issue-based, covering events that took place over several years, and in some cases, decades. The following chronology summarizes landmark events in this remarkable 50-year history.

1970   Founding meeting of Northern Fishermen's Union (NFU) in Port au Choix. Structure modelled on constitution of United Fishermen and Allied Workers Union in British Columbia. Membership is open to fish harvesters and fish plant workers.

1971   Founding convention of Newfoundland Fishermen, Food and Allied Workers Union (NFFAWU) in St. John's, combining NFU with units of fish plant workers previously organized in the province by Canadian Food and Allied

Workers Union. Richard Cashin elected president; Kevin Condon, secretary-treasurer.

Provincial government passes *Fishing Industry Collective Bargaining Act*, giving fish harvesters collective bargaining rights for the first time.

Labour Relations Board certifies union as bargaining agent for plant workers employed by Burgo Fish Industries. Employer refuses to recognize union. Strike ensues.

1972   After bitter strike in Burgeo, employer pulls out. New Frank Moores government buys Burgeo Fish Industries and settles strike, signing collective agreement with union.

Ray Greening elected secretary-treasurer.

1973   Breakthrough collective agreement with B.C. Packers in Harbour Breton brings major improvements in wages, benefits, and contract language for fish plant workers. Agreement sets pattern for other unionized plants.

1974   Inshore fish harvesters on Northern Peninsula strike for higher fish prices.

South coast trawlermen tie up in support, then remain tied up to push their own demands.

To get trawlers back to sea, provincial government appoints conciliation board chaired by Dr. Leslie Harris to investigate dispute between trawlermen and trawler operators. Harris writes comprehensive report recommending fundamental change to relationship between trawlermen and companies.

1975   Trawlermen vote 450 to 5 to strike to achieve recommendations of Harris conciliation board report and refuse to sail after Christmas tie-up. Strike settled in March with breakthrough terms for trawlermen.

Federal support helps finance trawler settlement. Union president Richard Cashin successfully lobbies federal government to have equivalent amount (2.5 cents per pound for groundfish, and similar amount for crab) paid directly to inshore fish harvesters. Previous price supports had been paid to companies only, with no guarantees it would be passed on to primary producers.

For first time, union successful in negotiating inshore prices with buyers on systematic basis.

1977   January 1, 1977: federal government extends Canada's Exclusive Economic Zone to 200 miles (200-mile limit).

Union negotiates province-wide inshore collective agreement with significant price increases, expanding coverage of collective agreement to all areas where union is active, certified or not.

1978   Union successfully lobbies federal government to have offshore shrimp licences set aside for people of Labrador coast. Union holds public meeting in Labrador that leads to the creation of Labrador Fishermen's Union Shrimp Company (LFUSCo).

First over-the-side sales provide important outlet and millions of dollars of sales for inshore harvesters for mackerel and squid.

1980   Province-wide inshore strike/lockout shuts inshore fishery for five weeks in peak of season.

   Fishery Products plant workers make major gains in wages and benefits after three-month strike. Agreement sets the pattern for other plants.

1981   Union launches major campaign to win workers' compensation for fish harvesters. Provincial government agrees to union demands and designates fish buyers as employers of fish harvesters for purposes of *Workers' Compensation Act*.

1981–83   Financial crisis in deep-sea fishery. Industry totters on brink of bankruptcy. Federal government sets up Kirby Task Force to make recommendations on Atlantic fishery generally and to devise plan to assist deep-sea sector.

1984   Union launches Unity '84 campaign to activate and unify members of all sectors and defend threatened communities, as high interest rates and weak markets batter the industry.

   Kirby restructuring plan leads to creation of Fishery Products International (FPI), which immediately becomes largest employer of fish plant workers and trawlermen and largest buyer of inshore fish in province.

   FPI demands major rollbacks in wages and benefits for plant workers and trawlermen. Trawlermen strike for six months until new management team is brought in at FPI and demands for concessions removed.

Mid-1980s   First warning signs of significant decline in inshore catch rates on northern cod. Scientific advice points to increasing stock. Concerns of inshore sector dismissed as "anecdotal."

1987   Lack of Canadian autonomy within United Food and Commercial Workers (UFCW) leads to crisis. Newfoundland and Labrador local pulls out of UFCW and announces affiliation with Canadian Auto Workers (CAW).

Founding convention held in St. John's for Fish Food and Allied Workers (FFAW/CAW).

1987–88   Sign-up into FFAW/CAW conducted bargaining unit by bargaining unit. Dozens of applications for certification filed with Labour Relations Board.

1988   Certification votes continue in various bargaining units.

CAW constitution amended to formally recognize status of FFAW.

First collective agreement under CAW banner negotiated with FPI plant workers' bargaining unit. Major gains in wages and benefits.

1989   Scientific advice for northern cod abruptly adjusted to biomass index less than half the previous estimate.

1990   Resource crisis in deep-sea fishery, as well as many inshore areas.

Plant closures begin.

1992   Union plays lead role in protest at sea to focus public attention on foreign overfishing. Massive rally on St. John's waterfront.

Widespread failure of northern cod fishery, both in- and offshore.

Federal government announces two-year closure of northern cod fishery. Union opposes compensation program. Significant improvements achieved within two weeks under Northern Cod Adjustment and Recovery Program (NCARP).

1993   Severe cuts to south coast and Gulf cod quotas, as well as other groundfish stocks.

Richard Cashin steps down after 23 years as FFAW president, replaced by Earle McCurdy. Reg Anstey elected secretary-treasurer.

1994   Further closures of groundfish stocks.

New Liberal federal government announces five-year, $1.9 million Atlantic Groundfish Strategy (TAGS) to replace expiring NCARP program.

1995   Federal government engages in "turbot war" with Spain as heavy foreign overfishing continues. Union organizes major protest to meet arrested Spanish trawler in St. John's harbour.

Union launches sentinel cod program, in collaboration with DFO.

Union plays lead role in formation of Canadian Council

of Professional Fish Harvesters.

Union fights back against planned cuts to TAGS benefits.

<35-foot fleet gets first access to snow crab in 2J3KL and 3Ps.

1996   Provincial House of Assembly gives legal authority to formation of Professional Fish Harvesters Certification Board (PFHCB) following strong lobby from union. Board formed in 1997.

1997   Breakthrough northern shrimp management plan gives access to northern shrimp for <65-foot fleet, creating fishing opportunities for fleet and hope for plant workers and communities.

Access to crab for small boats expanded. Temporary permits issued to all <35-foot core enterprise owners in 2J3KL and 3Ps (Labrador coast, northeast coast, southern Avalon, and south coast).

Lengthy strike in crab fishery. Eleventh-hour settlement salvages season.

Union protests reported elimination of fifth year of TAGS program by demonstrating at an event in Bull Arm involving prime minister and premier.

1998   Federal government cancels fifth year of TAGS program. Union stages two-day protest at Revenue Canada at income tax filing deadline. Union and provincial government intervene with prime minister's office. Federal government announces $760 million post-TAGS funding.

Provincial government establishes independent task force to study and make recommendations on dispute-settlement options in the inshore fishery.

1999 *Fishing Industry Collective Bargaining Act* amended to provide for settlement of price disputes via independent arbitrators instead of strike/lockout. System based on final offer selection.

Union opposes proposed takeover of FPI by NEOS, a partnership involving Clearwater Seafoods, Barry Group, and Icelandic participant. Proposal eventually withdrawn.

2001 John Risley of Clearwater Seafoods spearheads another takeover bid at FPI, this time by shareholder revolt at FPI annual meeting. Bid is successful; old board of directors and management team replaced by new group. Thousands of union members potentially affected.

2002 Fisheries Association of Newfoundland and Labrador (FANL) gives notice of intention to withdraw from arbitration-based dispute settlement mechanism for inshore fish negotiations. Provincial government extends program for one year.

2003 Federal government announces long-term closure of northern Gulf cod fishery. Union stages multi-day protest, tying up Gulf ferry service in Port aux Basques. Closure lifted after 2003. Modest commercial cod quotas in place ever since.

Fish plants close doors partway through crab fishery. Union claims illegal lockout, successful in obtaining injunction from the Provincial Supreme Court. Processors resume buying.

Processors disband FANL. Successor organization, Association of Seafood Producers, set up with no collective bargaining mandate.

Reg Anstey steps down as secretary-treasurer, replaced by David Decker.

2004   Province-wide collective bargaining for shrimp only. Union negotiates with buyers individually in other species. Attempt to terminate bargaining in inshore sector fails; Association of Seafood Processors eventually adds collective bargaining mandate.

Provincial fisheries minister advises industry detailed consultations will take place on proposal for plant production quotas in processing sector. Union strongly opposes scheme. No consultations held.

2005   Despite absence of promised consultations, provincial government announces two-year "pilot project" plant-production quota system called raw material sharing (RMS). Union reacts strongly with major fightback campaign. Government eventually gives Richard Cashin authority to decide the matter. He advises government to drop RMS unless agreed to at the bargaining table. He recommends permanent price-setting panel be given authority to resolve fish price disputes, with panel decisions binding on all buyers. Government accepts Cashin's recommendations.

2006–7 Management puts FPI for sale. Premier Danny Williams offers to invest public money to retain FPI marketing arm as asset of provincial fishery. Union supports this position, but processors opposed. Marketing arm eventually sold to High Liner Seafoods of Nova Scotia and plant and trawler operations taken over by Ocean Choice International (OCI).

2008–9 Seafood markets rocked by global economic recession. Difficult bargaining in all sectors of industry.

2009 Union stages four-day lobster tie-up and occupation of federal offices leading to commitment from federal government for targeted financing for projects aimed at conservation, rationalization, and value added in lobster fishery.

2010 Union and PFHCB open new office building in St. John's, named Richard Cashin Building after union founding president.

2011 Union negotiates plan for joint federal-provincial-industry lobster licence buyout. Both levels of government commit $9 million to the program.

Standing Fish Price-Setting Panel adopts price-to-market formula for lobster proposed by union and binding on all lobster buyers. When buyers refuse to buy, union buys lobster from harvesters and ships across Gulf to mainland buyers. Provincial buyers eventually resume buying.

2012   Union provides strong leadership in formation of Canadian Independent Fish Harvesters' Federation, a national voice for owner-operator fisheries.

Union key partner in formation of Newfoundland and Labrador Fish Harvester Safety Association.

2013   New union, Unifor, created from former memberships of CAW and Communications, Energy and Paperworkers Union of Canada. FFAW name changed accordingly to FFAW/Unifor. New union is largest private sector union in Canada.

2014   Earle McCurdy steps down as FFAW president, succeeded by Keith Sullivan.

2015   Union accelerates campaign against last in-first out (LIFO) policy in northern shrimp fishery.

2016   Federal government abolishes LIFO policy in northern shrimp fishery in favour of permanent proportional sharing arrangement, preserving place for inshore shrimp sector.

Union plays lead role in formation of Newfoundland and Labrador Groundfish Industry Development Council, aimed at managing cod and other fisheries to maximize value.

2017 Federal court upholds protection of owner-operator and fleet separation policies for inshore fleets by the Department of Fisheries and Oceans (DFO). Decision upheld in 2019 by Federal Court of Appeal.

2019 Union mounts strong pushback against DFO plan to significantly reduce crab quotas, in significant break from collaborative efforts of previous years. DFO reverses most rollbacks.

Federal government passes Bill C-68, giving DFO minister the power to make regulations to protect independence of licence holders in commercial inshore fisheries. Regulations required to give this provision weight.

2020 COVID-19 pandemic. No direction from government for opening fishery. Union insists on safe opening protocols. Fishery eventually opens after five-week delay, as COVID levels in province diminish.

David Decker retires as secretary-treasurer, replaced by Robert Keenan.

Pre-existing Conditions

One bad season could place a fisherman hopelessly in debt, and by refusing him further credit the merchant had it in his power to destroy a fisherman's livelihood.

—Sidney Noel

Nearly 60 years later, Cyril Dalley recalls the indignity as clearly as if it had just occurred.

"We sold salt cod to a merchant," Dalley says. "I was about 12 years old at the time. On a hot day in August, my brother and I helped with the fish. My father said he'd give us a Dixie cup [an ice cream treat]—something to look forward to on a hot day. He went to the merchant after we finished up. I can see my father now, coming back to the wharf with no Dixie cups."

That was the kind of power merchants had in the early 1960s. Dalley's father had no cash; his only recourse for buying his boys Dixie cups was credit, at the sole discretion of the merchant. The merchant said no.

Looking back over a lifetime in the fishery, Dalley says, "At a very early age dealing with merchants, I knew something had to be done relative to the way fishermen were treated."

It had been that way ever since European settlers came to Newfoundland to exploit her bountiful fish stocks. In his book *Politics in Newfoundland*, Sidney Noel talks about the powerful position of St. John's merchants in the 19th century:

> With the decline of the English west country influence, virtually the entire export and import trade of the country (Newfoundland) had fallen into the hands of a small group of St. John's merchants, who with the government officials, churchmen, and others they supported, formed the dominant social class. They were invariably English and protestant. And not only were they wealthy, they were also immensely powerful, for the financial structure of the fishery had become totally dependent upon their capital ...
>
> A middle class of small traders and artisans was numerically insignificant.... The lower class, which included the vast majority of the population, consisted almost entirely of fishermen, roughly half of whom were Roman Catholic. Over this class the merchants held practically unlimited power, based upon the operation of a truck system of credit trading. Under it, the merchant set both the price of the goods he supplied to the fishermen on credit and the price of the fish he accepted in payment of their debts. In consequence, the use of cash was practically eliminated from the transaction.

Other than occasional localized flare-ups that were put down mercilessly by the authorities, there was no meaningful effort to do anything about the fish harvester's lot from the early settlement days until William Coaker (later Sir William) called a meeting of fish harvesters in the Orange Hall in Herring Neck on November 2, 1908, which was attended by about 200 people. Coaker urged those who wished to form a union to remain in the hall after the meeting. As Noel put it, "Only 19 were sufficiently convinced and sufficiently courageous to risk the merchants' wrath to do so."

But those 19 brave souls, together with Coaker, were enough to get the Fishermen's Protective Union (FPU) started, and there followed a remarkable period of organizing, expansion, and political influence. In his book *A Class Act: An Illustrated History of the Labour Movement in Newfoundland and Labrador*, Bill Gillespie summarizes the scope of the FPU's achievements:

> At its height, the FPU had 20,000 members, elected 13 of its own members to the House of Assembly, founded its own trading company with 40 branch stores doing business of $3 million a year; had its own electric company, a shipbuilding company, steamships, a daily newspaper, and even its own town.

The FPU had tremendous momentum in its early years, with Coaker serving as minister of fisheries in a coalition government during World War I. In that capacity, he brought in sweeping and ambitious fisheries reforms. But the post-war economy was a mess, and adverse changes in exchange rates in Europe resulted in a collapse in salt fish prices early in 1921. As Noel put it, "By March, Coaker's plan lay in ruins. The regulations were withdrawn by proclamation."

Salt codfish, the foundation of the rural economy for centuries.

By the early 1920s, except for some of its commercial operations, the FPU was a spent force. Meanwhile, the truck system kept on trucking.

In *The Story of Newfoundland*, historian A.B. Perlin describes the formation in 1936 of the Newfoundland Salt Codfish Association, with an executive that reads like a who's who of the Water Street merchant class of the day. Perlin said that the chief function of the executive of this association "was to act as an advisory council to the Newfoundland Fisheries Board, and it had also the right to request information from the Board and to make recommendations to it in relation to any subject connected with the production, marketing and export of codfish."

In 1949, this powerful, well-connected association expanded to embrace members of other branches of the fishery, including frozen, pickled, and canned fish producers, as well as seal producers, and reconstituted itself as the Newfoundland Fish Trades Association (later Fisheries Association of Newfoundland and Labrador [FANL]), and became affiliated with the Fisheries Council of Canada.

Thomas Lodge, one of the Commissioners of Government who ran Newfoundland when the political class renounced self-government from 1934 to 1949, said that the Newfoundland fishery is almost unique as an industry in that the class which owns the capital employed in it has managed, somehow or other, to throw the whole risks, or very nearly the whole risks, which capital normally takes and on which it bases its abstract claim for reward, onto the shoulders of the working classes. Moreover, it is a striking example of an industry in which the real capitalist has gone very far towards making profit the first charge on the proceeds of the sale of a manufactured article, taking precedence even over bare subsistence for the primary producer."

Many undoubtedly hoped that this would change with Confederation. In April 1951, the new province's premier, Joseph R. Smallwood, brought 200 fish harvesters to St. John's at government expense to form what he termed a fishermen's union, known as the Newfoundland Federation of Fishermen (NFF). Although it was structurally similar to the FPU, according to Gillespie, "The NFF had none of the FPU's independence or sense of mission. Smallwood hand-picked its chief executive officer ... and financed the organization with an annual government subsidy."

The labour legislation Smallwood's government brought into effect in 1950 did not confer collective bargaining rights on fish harvesters, so the NFF was a toothless tiger. Nothing of significance changed with respect to bargaining rights for fish harvesters, or to the truck system, for 20 years following the NFF's inaugural meeting.

Unlike the harvesting sector, fish plant workers were covered as employees under the 1950 *Labour Relations Act*, and over the next 20 years, workers at about a dozen plants organized themselves into small local unions, many of which came directly under the umbrella of the Trades and Labour Congress, later the Canadian Labour Congress (CLC).

But the Congress is an umbrella organization, not a trade union. Organizing workplaces is not its primary mandate. In hopes of avoiding conflict and duplication of effort between member unions, the CLC had a practice of awarding jurisdiction over a particular economic sector to a single national or international union. In 1967, the Congress gave jurisdiction over the fishing industry in Atlantic Canada to the United Packinghouse Workers of America, which a year later was absorbed into the Amalgamated Meatcutters and Butcher Workmen of North America, based in Chicago. The

Canadian division of the Meatcutters was known as Canadian Food and Allied Workers (CFAWU).

By 1970, CFAWU represented several fish plants in the province, primarily on the south coast. But up to that point, as Gillespie points out, "Even though the CFAWU had jurisdiction over the entire fishing industry, it concentrated on organizing plant workers rather than inshore fishermen or trawlermen."

David MacDonald's *Power Begins at the Cod End* cites provincial government data showing that, in October 1969, the average hourly rate for fish cutters—the highest paid production line workers—was a meagre $1.34: "Plant workers often lacked benefits common in other industries, such as statutory holidays with pay, or vacations other than those called for by legislation at 4 per cent, and overtime pay."

A Royal Commission on labour legislation found that wages were, as Gordon Inglis notes in *More Than Just a Union: The Story of the NFFAWU*, "considerably below Canadian averages for the fish-processing industry, and most fish plant workers earned less than such traditionally low-paid workers as shop clerks."

Some fish plant workers received wage increases when the minimum rate went up, because the new minimum wage eclipsed what they were being paid under the collective agreement. The minimum wage legislation openly discriminated against women. In 1970, the legislated minimum was $1.25 an hour for men and $1 for women; in 1972, the gap widened when the male rate went to $1.40 and the female rate to $1.10. It would be January 1, 1974, before the provincial government implemented a single minimum wage of $1.80 an hour, irrespective of gender.

Writing about the labour scene in 1969, the Royal Commission commented: "It is clear that, for the majority of employees in the province, the collective bargaining system has had little direct effect upon their wages and working conditions."

In the inshore sector during the 1960s, prices and incomes were also very low. There wasn't a single year in that decade when the average price of cod reached 4.5 cents a pound, according to statistics compiled by the DFO. Bill Broderick, who later became inshore vice-president and then inshore director of the union, was one of many people from the northeast coast of the province who went to Labrador to fish.

"If you had a successful voyage," Broderick reported, "a shareman might get $700 or $800 or $900 for three months' work." In 1969, when he and his family stayed home to fish out of their hometown of St. Brendan's, they were paid 2.5 cents a pound for their fish. People were being paid a pittance compared to the value they were creating. Long after the 19th-century stranglehold on fish harvesters by the St. John's merchants that Noel describes, little had changed, except for a declining participation rate in the fishery as other employment opportunities opened up.

In the late 19th century, the fishery employed 90 per cent of the male workforce in the province. By 1970, the industry represented about 6 per cent of its gross domestic product (GDP), employed 15 per cent of the total workforce, and was the mainstay of hundreds of communities.

But incomes remained extremely low. Even by 1973, DFO reported that 60 per cent of Atlantic Canadian fish harvesters had less than $5,000 in total income, with the poorest-off being in Prince Edward Island and Newfoundland and Labrador.

In *From Traps to Draggers*, Peter Sinclair reports on local boycotts of fish companies that flared up in 1968 in Trinity Bay, Conception

Although there is a lot of salt fish on this busy wharf, harvesters didn't get paid much for it.

Bay, and the northwest coast after the companies dropped the price for cod from 3.75 to 2.5 cents per pound. "The boycott in 1968 showed that fishermen could overcome competition among themselves and act collectively. It also gave fishermen an idea of the strength of collective action," Sinclair commented.

Inglis elaborates on the changing attitudes in rural Newfoundland and Labrador:

> In 1967, a report to the provincial government recommended that no public investment be made in communities throughout the entire northern part of the island and in Labrador—above a line drawn from Cape Bonavista to Bay of Islands—unless they had some other economic activity than inshore fishing. Government assistance to the fishery was to be concentrated in the offshore sector and the south coast. This approach was repeated in another planning document in 1970, but by then public attitudes to development were beginning to change. The mega-projects were failing.... There was growing rural resentment of centralization projects and a movement to demand improvement, rather than abandonment, of rural areas—as expressed, for example in the Northern Rural Development Association (NRDA) and the Fogo Island Co-op.

But something of a remarkable and fundamental nature would have to occur, or the lot of the fish harvester would remain essentially unchanged from the 19th century, and fish plant workers would continue to be paid minimum wage-level earnings.

"A Match to a Blasty Bough"

I wouldn't be surprised if we're not after starting something.
—Delegate, Bonavista Bay, at the end of the founding convention of the NFFAWU

Something of a remarkable and fundamental nature did occur. That something had its origins in the 1950s when two young Newfoundlanders—Richard Cashin and Desmond McGrath—headed off to St. Francis Xavier University in Antigonish, Nova Scotia, where they were influenced by the Antigonish Movement. Spearheaded by Father Jimmy Tompkins and Dr. Moses Coady, this movement was recognized worldwide for its leadership in promoting co-operation and community development. In the late 1920s, Tompkins and others became actively involved in the struggle to break the hold of local merchants over the lives of small-scale fish harvesters in the Diocese of Antigonish. The ideas of the Antigonish Movement had a profound influence on the two young Newfoundlanders, who became friends, a friendship which would change the course of political life in their home province years later.

Richard Cashin and Desmond McGrath were an unlikely team of

Left to right: Kevin Condon, Father Des McGrath, and union supporter Gus Dalton sign up fish harvesters to the new union.

union visionaries and organizers. In 1962, at the age of 25 and just out of law school, Cashin was elected Member of Parliament for St. John's West, at the time the youngest person ever elected to Parliament. He held the seat until 1968. Cashin came from a politically active family; his grandfather, Sir Michael Cashin, was once the prime minister of Newfoundland, and his uncle, Major Peter Cashin, was the leader of the anti-Confederate forces in the build-up to the vote on Confederation with Canada. Richard Cashin was widely touted as a potential future premier of the province, including, when it suited him, by Premier Joseph Smallwood in his latter years.

Desmond McGrath—"Father Des" to many—grew up in Corner Brook, then went to university in Antigonish and on to Toronto to study theology. He spent his first seven years as a priest at the

Cathedral parish in Corner Brook before taking over the parish on the St. Barbe coast. There he had his first contact with fish harvesters and realized that they were at the mercy of the fish companies.

The fishery Cashin and McGrath set out to organize was characterized by the consolidation of wealth and power in the hands of the few, and hard work, low incomes, and no power as the circumstances of the many. Reflecting on his role in challenging the dominance of the fish companies, Cashin said he was driven, above all, by "paternalism and the truck system. Everything was controlled by an elite from St. John's."

The events that gave rise to the formation of a province-wide industrial union in the fishery occurred in a time of profound change in rural Newfoundland. In the post-Confederation years, government plans, both provincial and federal, focused on centralization, industrialization, and moving away from the traditional inshore fishery, although one report described the inshore fishery as "an astonishingly durable operation."

An example of Smallwood's "develop or perish" approach to the economy occurred in Long Harbour, Placentia Bay, where he had used cheap power and lax pollution control standards to lure the Electric Reduction Company (ERCO) into establishing a phosphorus plant. The term *red herring* is usually employed as a metaphor for a smoke screen or distraction, but it took on a literal meaning in Placentia Bay when bright red herring, with red, bulging eyes and other symptoms consistent with phosphorus poisoning, turned up in fishing nets. The fishery was closed, and the harvesters lost income.

By this time, Cashin was practicing law in St. John's. Several fish harvesters from Placentia Bay, many of them former constituents from his days as Member of Parliament, engaged Cashin to represent them. On behalf of several hundred harvesters, he filed a legal action against ERCO. The action was settled on the courthouse steps in what was, at the time, the largest court settlement in the province's history. It also gave Cashin a taste of working with fish harvesters.

"At the time," Cashin recalled 50 years later, "I was reading about movements like NRDA and Fogo, and felt I was interested in working for fishermen. I wrote to Des [McGrath] in the fall of '69. I got a call from him in January 1970 asking me to come to Port Saunders ... He said, 'How about a fishermen's union?'"

In an interview nearly 20 years later for a CAW video, Cashin called it "a magnificent idea." Cashin headed to the Northern Peninsula, where he and his old university friend met with 15 or 20 fish harvesters from Port Saunders and Port au Choix. They had additional meetings in Port au Choix and Anchor Point. Then they went public.

Cashin later described the response to the union as being "like a match to a blasty bough." A key meeting was with Kevin Condon, an influential figure who was vice-president of the NFF.

Another influential fish harvester who became an executive board member and strong advocate of the union, Levi George Norris of Bay de Verde, described the truck system this way: "Men fished all their lives, and got nothing, only gear and groceries." He was all in for a union, and, like Condon and many others, spent countless hours campaigning on the union's behalf.

At about the same time, Cashin was contacted by the Bonavista North Fishermen's Association, who were looking for provincial government help for harvesters who had experienced a total failure in the Labrador fishery. That matter was successfully resolved with Cashin's assistance, and these men joined the union.

"They invited Des [McGrath] and me to a meeting in Centreville (in Bonavista Bay). It was a tremendous meeting. It was the first time I heard Newfoundland's greatest orator—Lester Kean. He was magnificent. One of the fish harvesters said, 'A priest and a lawyer in an Orange Hall. This is going to work.'"

Inglis reported that a group of fish plant operators, concerned about this activity, met with Smallwood, who told them: "Don't worry about Cashin. He'll never stick with it. In six months, he'll be doing something else."

Joey was off by about 22 years.

The premier's reassurances notwithstanding, fish plant owners would undoubtedly have been rattled by the thrust of a letter to the editor of the *Evening Telegram* from McGrath published on June 26, 1970. The letter was pointed:

> One of the great weaknesses of Newfoundland society is the lack of acceptance of the importance of collective action. The Northern Fishermen's Union is a real attempt on the part of fishermen of the northwest coast to influence events in the industry that gives them a livelihood. The fishermen have long known of the need for such action.

The letter pointed to the absence of collective bargaining legislation as a major barrier preventing fish harvesters from making meaningful progress:

> How will fishermen become more informed and more involved and participate in a more mature way if they

are denied the right to collective action? It is a fearsome thing in this day and age to see so much power in the hands of so few. The old fears and suspicions and uncertainties associated with the fishery will multiply. It is a direct challenge to the dignity of these men to deny them the right of meaningful collective action, to deny them the right to participate as equals in the industry that is their very livelihood.

The present relationship of fishermen to both government and industry constitutes a serious social injustice, a serious social imbalance.

Meanwhile, the hard work of starting a union from scratch continued. Cashin contacted, among other people, Homer Stevens, president of the United Fishermen and Allied Workers Union in British Columbia and obtained a copy of that union's constitution. He used it as a model for what was to become the Northern Fishermen's Union (NFU), founded at a meeting in Port au Choix in April 1970. Like the BC union's set-up, the NFU constitution made provision for both harvesters and plant workers as members.

Funding was a major obstacle for the newly constituted union; Cashin explains how that problem was addressed:

> George Lavers, Ralph O'Keefe, Jean Gould (all Port au Choix area men) and Des and I met with the CLC (Canadian Labour Congress) vice-president. This led to me and Des going to Toronto to meet with (CFAWU head) Fred Dowling, and subsequently to Chicago where we met with Pat Gorman, the international secretary-

treasurer. We set up a committee and were granted a charter as Local 465—Northern Fishermen's Union.

The international union also agreed to provide $50,000 in start-up money to get the new union up and running. Over the next 12 months, harvesters from various parts of the province along with the Port au Choix plant workers came into the NFU fold. But for organizing in the inshore sector to deliver meaningful results, collective bargaining legislation was a must.

By the spring of 1970, the plant workers and the harvesters were affiliated with the same international union, but in separate locals. They were residents of the same communities, lived in the same houses, dealt with the same fish companies. It was time for a conversation. A meeting in Corner Brook between Cashin, McGrath, and CFAWU representative Fred Locking, who had been transferred to Newfoundland from Saskatchewan to assist in the organizing and servicing of plant workers, led to a press conference in St. John's on October 7, 1970. The *Evening Telegram* reported the following day that Cashin, McGrath, and Locking were to form a committee to carry out a province-wide organizing drive in a combined union to be called Newfoundland Fishermen, Food and Allied Workers Union (NFFAWU).

The inshore organizing drive was hardly a conventional affair. Bill Broderick, who, like many young people at the time, had left the fishery to teach school, recalls attending Mass in Conche in White Bay, where he was teaching. "Father McGrath was filling in for the priest, who was on holidays. After Mass, he said, 'Boys, we're going to have a meeting.'" The fish harvesters who stayed behind heard a different sort of sermon.

Richard Cashin.

Organizing continued through the winter of 1970/71 and preparations were made for the NFFAWU founding convention, held in St. John's in late April 1971. Memorial University's Extension Service was active in the province at the time, particularly in encouraging and supporting social and economic development in rural areas. They provided six people from their staff to record the convention, take notes, and provide an extensive written account of the proceedings.

Just days before the convention, according to David MacDonald, FANL said in a presentation to a House of Assembly Select Committee looking into the issue of bargaining rights in the fishing industry "that contractual agreements covering inshoremen would not be in the FANL's interests and that a house committee to review fish prices would be preferable to collective bargaining being 'imposed on an industry that it was never designed to embrace.'"

Of course, the processing sector was accustomed to getting policy shaped their way, going back to the formation of the Newfoundland Salt Codfish Association in 1936. What they weren't accustomed to was the organized, democratic breakthrough that would unfold and challenge their iron grip on the industry.

FANL's views notwithstanding, the union's founding convention was attended by 46 inshore and 40 industrial delegates, 11 media, and a number of invited guests. The delegates adopted a constitution that provided for two sections of the union—inshore and industrial—and a provincial council to provide overall leadership and administration. Executive board members were to be elected at the convention by their respective sections, the top officers by the convention as a whole. Cashin was elected the union's first president, Condon secretary-treasurer.

On the evening of the convention banquet, attention focused on the guest speaker, Premier Smallwood, who was under pressure to commit clearly to collective bargaining rights for fish harvesters. Cashin introduced the premier by saying he had "an opportunity to lead the way in what many felt would be his second greatest accomplishment, to have the government enact legislation that would become a Magna Carta of the rights of all fishermen in the province."

Smallwood's speech was nothing short of bizarre. After a long-winded introduction, prattling on about his involvement with fish harvesters' organizations, Smallwood told delegates "not to put too much faith in getting the law passed," saying that it was in the hands of a select committee of the House of Assembly which would meet to "receive ideas from unions, merchants and fish buyers." The committee, he said, would recommend "a law of some kind that would give some kind of collective bargaining" and he would be in favour of it.

His comments moved from inconsistent to incomprehensible. The convention proceedings report the following comment:

> Again the Premier warned that members not put too much faith or too much confidence in getting the law passed, as the law, if it were strong enough and had enough teeth in it, could easily replace a union, that

Father Des McGrath collects ballots at an early union meeting.

> the fishermen would say that they no longer needed a union with such a law, and recommended that they not let that happen.

The comment made no sense then, or now. Collective bargaining legislation does not replace a union. It provides a framework and a set of rules and procedures that make it possible for a union to attain bargaining rights, if they follow these rules and demonstrate to the Labour Relations Board that they have the support of a majority of the members of a bargaining unit they wish to be certified to represent.

Convention delegates were so concerned (and, no doubt, confused) about the premier's performance that an emergency debate was held the following day. After considerable discussion, they passed two emergency resolutions—one calling for a delegation to seek clarification on the matter from the premier and to contact each member of the House of Assembly seeking their stand on the matter, and the other giving the new executive board the power to call a special convention to "take the necessary action" if no legislation was in place by the end of May.

The convention proceedings reported: "The possibility of a strike was considered and the need for our members to be ready to fight."

The minutes of the founding convention hadn't even been written up, and already the newly minted union was off to a fighting start. The union's official publication, *Union Forum*, later reported that the brand new union's first decisive action had paid off—the Smallwood government passed the *Fishing Industry Collective Bargaining Act* on May 21, 1971. For the first time, the right to negotiate fish prices and conditions of sale was enshrined in provincial legislation.

Starting with FANL's predecessor, the Newfoundland Salt Codfish Association, the processing sector had become accustomed to being the only industry voice to have the ear of the government. But now they had stiff competition, and despite their arguments strongly opposing collective bargaining rights in the fishery, that is exactly what the provincial government enacted.

By May 1971, the task of improving the sharing of the wealth of the fishery, reshaping the power structure in the fishery, and revitalizing the economy of coastal communities was well under way, with two crucial building blocks—the union and the collective bargaining legislation—firmly in place.

"Never Again Will We Beg"

In these isolated outports, I contend there is no place for a union. I'm not anti-union. I just think that in certain circumstances, unions are not practical. and this is one of them: isolated outports in Newfoundland. You haven't got the local leadership to run them intelligently, with all due respect to the people — I'm very fond of them.

—Spencer Lake, owner of Burgeo Fish Industries

The paint was barely dry on the upstart NFFAWU when organizers started signing union cards in Burgeo, a small community on Newfoundland's southwest coast, accessible only by small plane or coastal boat.

As Gerald MacDonald, one-time trawlerman, then fish plant worker and later mayor of Burgeo, recalls, "This was a one-man town."

That one man was Spencer Lake. At the time the union came knocking on the doors of potential members in Burgeo, Lake owned not only the fish plant and the trawler fleet that supplied it but also the town's only supermarket, beauty parlour, dairy, barber shop, and oil and gas distribution company.

The organizing drive was tough going. Eventually the union succeeded in signing 105 out of 205 plant workers and narrowly won a certification vote. That was unusual — most often, if a union signs up a bare majority in an organizing drive, they lose the subsequent certification vote. Lew Hann, a key supporter of the organizing drive, who was elected to head up the local union committee, picks up the story: "We'd have little meetings with the company. You knew you weren't getting anywhere. There was no negotiations to it. There was nothing else to do clear of go on strike."

It was obvious from the beginning that this would be a critical test of the newly minted union's strength. After negotiations broke down, Lake told the media: "I'll never agree to a closed shop union. My family owns (Burgeo Fish Industries) lock, stock, and barrel. If they go on strike, I'll close the plant down until they get better sense and come back to work. I'm prepared to shut down that plant for as long as I have to ... And I'll never agree to a closed shop union."

You couldn't accuse Spencer Lake of being wishy-washy about his position. But in his paternalism and sense of entitlement, he seriously underestimated the strength of the union leadership and the resolve of the local people.

As a crewman on the *Caribou Reefer*, which transported frozen fish from Burgeo to Massachusetts, Frank Strickland had a first-hand look at the grandeur of Lake's life in comparison to the daily struggle endured by the people who worked for him: "In Gloucester, you'd see the big mansion Lake had. We'd do free labour work on it. He had another big house here [in Burgeo]. He was paying us nothing, $197 a month."

Commenting on the solidarity of the Burgeo people throughout the strike, George Coley, a key leader of the strike, told Gordon Inglis, "If there's one man who made this union, I'd have to say it's Spencer Lake."

At a time of changing political landscape in the province, the battle lines in Burgeo caught the imagination of the public.

Picket line in Burgeo. The man in the middle is Ray Greening, union secretary-treasurer.

Cashin gave one of his trademark fiery, eloquent speeches at a Newfoundland Federation of Labour convention in the summer of 1971 and delegates supported a resolution calling for a campaign of sit-ins, demonstrations, petitions, rallies, and picketing supporting the Burgeo strikers. According to a news reporter covering the convention: "The common theme in almost every speech was that the Burgeo dispute will decide the fate of the labour movement in Newfoundland for a long time to come."

That was quite a burden on the new union and the people of Burgeo. Adding to the pressure, the strike had, in Lew Hann's words, "turned brother against brother, wife against husband, father against son."

Bumper stickers declaring "It Started in Burgeo" were in demand around the province, and Cashin recalled that the union used these bumper stickers in subsequent organizing drives. While the union itself didn't start in Burgeo, the challenge to the previously unfettered power of the fish merchant that the Burgeo strike represented, resonated throughout the province.

Meanwhile, one of the picket signs in Burgeo captured the essence of the struggle: "Never again will we beg."

Tackling the company's adamant refusal to recognize the union required special people and unorthodox tactics. Cashin and two Burgeo workers, Ron Swift and Gord Hare, flew to Gloucester, Massachusetts, to set up a picket line against the *Caribou Reefer*. Cashin recalled that they met with the stevedores' union in Gloucester, where they received a friendly reception. The stevedores respected the picket line, which made the front page of the local newspaper.

Back in Burgeo, Lake said he would operate the plant if he had the support of the people, and he had a petition circulated to solicit that support. Cashin recalled that Hann promptly circulated a

Gloucester Daily Times, June 15, 1971. When Cashin and two members of the bargaining unit in Burgeo picketed the company boat while it attempted to offload product in Gloucester, stevedores respected the picket line and refused to offload the *Caribou Reefer*.

counter-petition, which gained signatures from 85 per cent of the people in Burgeo.

As president of NFFAWU, Cashin was in the spotlight throughout the strike. One of his most important decisions was to assign Ray Greening to Burgeo. Greening was, in Hann's words, "a very likeable man," who told the Burgeo people, "I never lost a strike in my life and I'm not about to lose this one." Beneath his polite, pleasant demeanour, Greening was possessed of a steely resolve and a strong sense of fairness and trade union principles. Employers and other adversaries underestimated him at their peril.

A banner recognizing the significance of the 1971 Burgeo strike.

For the union, Greening provided critical, level-headed, hands-on leadership and support in a challenging situation.

To win the dispute, the Burgeo workers had to shut down the plant despite an earlier court injunction that limited picketing.

"The employer tried to operate the plant using a boat to bring in scab labour," Gerald MacDonald recalled nearly 50 years later. "We had to stop that, and we did." "It was a pretty dangerous place for a while," he added, referring to the day the company tried to force scabs across the picket line to break the strike. "It got to the point where they withdrew their scabs. We weren't going to give up. It was a pretty hot and tense situation—anything could have flared up."

Hann knew when he left his home that morning that the events of that coming day would probably determine the outcome of the strike. "I got out of bed, kissed my wife and my children, and said, 'I might not be coming back.' Everyone's nerves were on edge."

Hann said that when the boatload of scabs tried to land at the plant, "We were there to meet them, 110 of us, for sure. There were rocks and pans and everything flying. We went through the plant. The cops were there, and told us, 'You've gone as far as you can go.' A guy said, 'I don't give a good god damn how far you can go, we're not going back.'"

George Coley told Gordon Inglis about a pivotal meeting of union leaders the previous evening, October 17, 1971: "We had to violate the injunction. We had no other choice. It was supposed to be a mass demonstration. We were going to stop the scabs from going into plant ... We were worried. We were afraid it would turn violent."

There was property damage to some of Lake's businesses that day, and the plant never re-opened under Lake's ownership. The following day, Frank Moores, soon to become the province's second premier, announced that, if elected, he would settle the strike immediately, by whatever means necessary.

Within days, Lake announced from Massachusetts that he was closing Burgeo Fish Industries and resigning as mayor of Burgeo.

This flurry of activity coincided with the dying days of a provincial election campaign. Behind the scenes, Cashin and McGrath had been busy, McGrath meeting with Moores and Cashin with Smallwood.

"Des asked Moores for a commitment to intervene in the Burgeo dispute, and Moores said yes," Cashin recalled nearly 50 years later. "I met with Joey. He paced the room, and then said, 'Unions can get too strong.' We had a Board meeting the next day and came out publicly to support the PCs."

The PCs were narrowly elected. The new government bought the Lake holdings in Burgeo and reached a collective agreement with the union. Then they retained the services of National Sea Products to manage the plant. The Nova Scotia-based company eventually bought the Burgeo operation, operating it until 1992, when it was one of the casualties of the moratoria on northern cod and other key groundfish species that devastated the fishery in Newfoundland and Labrador (see Chapter 8).

The Burgeo strike was a test by fire for the new union. A loss there would have seriously undermined its ability to organize new members and negotiate with employers. But its success in standing up to the belligerent tactics of Spencer Lake opened those doors wide, and the union confidently moved in, to advance its goal of improving life in rural communities.

Ray Greening, an exceptional organizer, had been forced to interrupt his fish plant organizing activity to go into Burgeo, but once the strike was resolved, he resumed. Plant after plant fell into the NFFAW fold over the next few years.

The Burgeo success carried over to the bargaining table as well. Chapter 14 describes the breakthrough agreement achieved in Harbour Breton the following year. The union successfully applied the terms of the Harbour Breton agreement in other fish plants, an outcome which would have been much more difficult to achieve without the determination of the people of Burgeo when they were put to the test.

Goodbye Co-adventurer System, Hello 20th Century

Richard Cashin came along and offered us some hope—a lot of hope. Most people, myself included, couldn't believe someone was going to do anything for us, except take advantage of us. We had no say in anything.

—Guy Hackett, Fortune Bay trawlerman

Guy Hackett remembers his first trip as a crew member on the side trawler *Blue Haze* 50 years ago, as if it were yesterday: "I was 15 years old. Living conditions were bad. The skipper was God. There was no protection from being fired. Safety was obsolete."

Guy joined his father, Clayton, who was also a crew member on the Job Brothers vessel, which fished out of St. John's. Guy and Clayton hailed from English Harbour East, a beautiful outport in Fortune Bay whose population of barely 300 in 1972 included 54 trawlermen.

At the time, trawlermen fished under the so-called co-adventurer system, a name which implied a partnership or equality between trawler owners and crew members that did not exist in the real world.

"If you didn't catch anything, you didn't get anything," Marystown trawlerman Ches Cribb explained. "I remember one year, as chief engineer, on the last trip before Christmas, after 11 days at sea, the company paid me $44—less than the cash advance. I owed them $6 to start the New Year. There was no money to be made."

So in 1973, when Richard Cashin came to English Harbour East for a meeting of trawlermen, he met a receptive audience for the message that there was a way for trawlermen to have some say in their industry. That way was the union.

At the time, trawlers were sailing out of a dozen ports, primarily on the south coast. But the turning point in the status of the hardworking men in the trawler fleet that was the cornerstone of the south coast economy had its origins hundreds of miles away in Port au Choix, where the NFU had been born in 1970.

Negotiations between the union and Fishery Products for 1974 inshore fish prices on the Northern Peninsula were at a standstill. It was a difficult time to be negotiating fish prices. Groundfish export prices in the US had declined dramatically, consumption in the US was down, inventories were building up rapidly, and the companies wanted nothing to do with inshore price negotiations. But the union was determined to make progress at the bargaining table.

By the time negotiations between the union and Fishery Products came to a head, FANL had announced the prices its member companies would be paying, just as they had done in the pre-union days. Fishery Products took a hardline position that it would not pay even a fraction of a cent more than the prices FANL had unilaterally announced.

In the face of this ultimatum, the Northern Peninsula fish harvesters went on strike on July 1, 1974. As Cashin told the *Evening Telegram*, "The company refused to negotiate except on a take-it-or-leave-it basis, hence putting itself in a position as arch defenders of the traditional position of fish merchants in Newfoundland. If they can get away with that, we might as well fold up the union. We're demonstrating to the companies that they have to take the fishermen seriously."

After several weeks on strike, the union decided to take advantage of its strength as an industry-wide organization and ratchet up the pressure on Fishery Products by bringing the south coast trawlermen into the dispute.

Enter Bill Short, a colourful and outspoken union staff representative, who grew up in a fishing family on the north shore of Conception Bay. When Short started fishing in the early 1950s, unemployment insurance for fish harvesters did not exist. Like many other inshore people at the time, he fished on an inshore boat in the summer and on a side trawler in the winter. This gave him first-hand experience in the hard, dangerous, poorly paid life of the trawlerman and made him a logical union representative for Cashin to send with a small delegation of Port au Choix fish harvesters to talk to trawlermen on the Burin Peninsula.

Although they were still under contract until the end of the year, the trawlermen started tying up their boats in support of the inshore fish harvesters. The union's initial intention was to limit the tie-up to the Fishery Products fleet, but it quickly spread to trawlers owned by other companies.

"When Bill Short came to see the trawlermen," Ches Cribb recalled, "we tied up in support, and then we got into our own issues—the co-adventurer system, no rights, no pay. After we were out for six weeks, people started to take notice."

Among those who took notice was the provincial government. Premier Frank Moores and his labour minister Joe Rousseau became involved in trying to find a resolution to the dispute. A critical element of the province's involvement was a commitment to establish a

Trawlers tied up in Burin.

conciliation board that would investigate the dispute while the crews returned to sea. Crucially, Moores agreed to broaden the terms of reference for the conciliation board to consider both the ability of the companies to pay increased fish prices and what were referred to as "the social needs" of trawlermen—the requirement for an adequate level of income.

The conciliation board was chaired by Dr. Leslie Harris, who later served as president of Memorial University and chair of a task force which studied the northern cod stock in the years just prior to the moratorium. The 1974 conciliation board would forever change the relationship between trawler operators and crew members.

While Harris's name is the one primarily associated with the conciliation board's report, the other board members were significant players. Paul Russell, a senior executive with Bonavista Cold Storage, a provincial trawler company, was the FANL nominee, while the union nominated Ed Johnston, an experienced CLC official who Cashin credits with being "a key player in getting a settlement."

The appointment of the conciliation board with its broad terms of reference helped set the stage for a temporary truce. Trawlermen agreed by a vote of 74 per cent to return to sea, to allow the board to do its work, although there were hiccups along the way. Meanwhile, a settlement had been reached for inshore prices in the Port au Choix area.

Cashin had a letter dated September 6, 1974, from Moores committing the provincial government to head a delegation to Ottawa to attempt to convince the federal government to fund any difference between the income needs of trawlermen and the financial ability of the trawler companies to pay that level of income.

"Where the Federal Government does not agree to complete funding of the agreed difference," Moores wrote, "then the Provincial Government will undertake to fund the remainder of the total difference as agreed to following the Report of the Conciliation Board."

Cashin held on to this letter, and with the trawlers back at sea and inshore prices settled on the Northern Peninsula, the union turned its attention to preparing a model contract for presentation to the conciliation board.

For trawlermen, the Harris conciliation board report was well worth waiting for. Among its 13 recommendations, it proposed the elimination of the co-adventurer system, proposing instead "that trawlermen should negotiate with companies not the price of fish but rather the income level that will be available for full time work."

This was the one recommendation that company nominee Paul Russell refused to accept. The union accepted the report in its entirety, but there was no agreement with the companies as Christmas approached. On Christmas Eve 1974, FANL tabled a price offer that was significantly higher than the old collective agreement, but it did not follow the Harris board's recommendation to fundamentally change the way trawlermen were paid.

During meetings over the Christmas break, trawlermen gave the union an overwhelming strike mandate, rejecting the FANL offer by a vote of 450 to 5, and endorsing the substance of the Harris recommendations.

On January 2, 1975, the day the trawlers would normally resume sailing after Christmas, the trawlermen began what was, this time, a legal strike.

FANL, never ones to understate their case, blamed the strike on "the totally irresponsible actions of the union" and said that the adoption of a guaranteed wage for trawlermen would mean the "destruction" of the fishery.

In early January, the premier announced, contrary to established practice, that social assistance benefits would be denied to "persons who voluntarily and in concert withdraw their services from the labour market although jobs are available"—bureaucratic language to describe people who exercised their right to strike.

Government also locked the doors of Confederation Building when the union held a demonstration of trawlermen on a bitterly cold day in January. These actions convinced the trawlermen that they were battling not only the fish companies but their own government.

As the strike dragged on, Cashin recalled, "the issue became, when do we drop the letter?" It was a reference to the September 6, 1974, letter to Cashin from Moores. Cashin was heading to a meeting in February with municipal leaders and clergy on the Burin Peninsula when he was tipped off. "You're going to be sandbagged," he was told. "Alex Hickman had told the clergy about the letter before I got to Marystown."

At these meetings with municipalities and clergy, fisheries minister John Crosbie tried to walk back the significance of the provincial government's commitment in the letter. Cashin's frustration at the betrayal of Moores's commitment in the letter was compounded by being snowbound for several days on the Burin Peninsula.

Cashin returned to St. John's and called a press conference to explain the background of the Moores letter and the union's understanding of its meaning. He lambasted Moores and Crosbie for reneging on the commitment of his letter, and attacked Alex Hickman:

St. John's trawlermen maintain a picket line.

> Alex Hickman turns my guts! What he and Crosbie wanted me to do was to add my name to the long list of Newfoundlanders who sold out their own people ... If they want to drive us out of the province, let them ... If they want to fight, they'll get a fight.

Reporters agreed among themselves after the press conference that they'd never seen anything quite like it.

With conflicting versions of the intent and significance of the Moores letter being publicly expressed by the union and the government, the media turned to Harris for his interpretation. Harris confirmed that he had known about the letter at the time he was appointed to chair the conciliation board and that he had agreed to accept the appointment on the understanding that the province had committed to fund any shortfall between the required income level for trawlermen and the companies' ability to pay. Harris's interpretation of the intent of the letter materially strengthened the union's hand.

The uproar over the premier's letter and the continuing economic pressure caused by the strike put political heat on the provincial government. Moores met separately with the parties, and contacted the president of the CLC, Joe Morris, seeking his assistance in resolving the strike. This led to a resumption of negotiations in Ottawa, with Morris and provincial labour minister Ed Maynard assisting the parties.

After several days of meetings in Ottawa, the negotiating teams took a break, resumed negotiations in St. John's, then had another round of meetings in Ottawa.

These talks ultimately produced a tentative agreement that revolutionized the status of trawlermen by creating two components of a trawlerman's income: a per diem (daily pay) of $20, fish or no fish, and a schedule of prices for every pound of fish landed and numerous important improvements in benefits and contract language. No more would trawlermen run the risk of owing the company money after 10 hard days at sea. Trawlermen ratified the agreement by 92 per cent and the vessels were back to sea before the end of March.

"The co-adventurer system was gone," said Ches Cribb. "We had a $20 per diem. It was more money than we had ever seen. It was a major, major achievement."

It was an achievement that benefitted communities as well as the trawlermen and their families. As the vast majority of trawlermen lived in coastal communities, the union's success at the bargaining table meant that there was more money in circulation in these communities, to the benefit of local businesses.

Another groundbreaking and related achievement of the union in 1975 was to finally effect a meaningful change to the way the federal government intervened during times of market crisis in the fishing industry. In July 1974, Ottawa had announced a financial assistance program to help the fishing industry get through the market downturn. But as so often in the past, they implemented a fisheries version of the trickle-down theory—a program of financial assistance to the companies without any assurance that any of it would be passed on to the primary producers.

Cashin had repeatedly demanded that government financial assistance arising from market crises should include direct payments to fish harvesters. The trawler tie-up increased the union's profile and influence. As well, federal fisheries minister Romeo LeBlanc was an Acadian from New Brunswick with an empathy for inshore fish harvesters. Cashin went to Ottawa to meet with LeBlanc and made a pitch for direct assistance to inshore fish harvesters.

In April 1975, just a few weeks after the trawler strike ended, LeBlanc announced a groundbreaking "bridging program" of financial assistance, effective May 1, 1975. Crucially, for the union and its inshore members, this program included "deficiency payments" directly to groundfish harvesters of 2.5 cents per pound, as well as similar payments to crab harvesters. (Two and a half cents was deemed to be equivalent to the assistance the feds gave the trawler companies to help settle the trawlermen's strike.)

As Reg Anstey, later the union's secretary-treasurer, put it, "In the early days, [Cashin's] political connections were key. He knew how to work the system in Ottawa."

This outcome demonstrated the value of having a strong industry-wide union in the fishery.

Inshore harvesters started the strike. They received the support of the trawlermen on the south coast who subsequently achieved a revolutionary change in their status. And the government aid that was part of the trawler settlement included, for the first time, direct payments to primary producers throughout Atlantic Canada, including the Northern Peninsula fleet.

Not only that, but the union's power and public profile were greatly enhanced because of the strength it demonstrated throughout the difficult dispute. It was no coincidence that, in 1975, the union was successful in negotiating inshore fish prices on a systematic basis for the first time. These outcomes consolidated the union's earlier gains and positioned it to continue improving the quality of life for people in rural parts of the province and strengthening the rural economy.

What's not so well known is that to enable the union to withstand the serious financial squeeze created by the strike, the union staff went without pay during the strike and Cashin wrote a personal cheque to the union for $17,000 and backed a loan for $100,000. Thanks to Greening's careful stewardship of the union's precarious finances, the union eventually paid off these loans, but it was anything but guaranteed at the time that this repayment would ever be possible.

1980: United We Stand

Fishermen were going on strike. I couldn't believe it.
— George Chafe, inshore harvester, Petty Harbour

The Burgeo strike. Major improvements to plant workers' wages and benefits, accelerated by the 1973 Harbour Breton contract. Revolutionary changes to trawlermen's lives arising out of the 1974/75 strikes. A direct price subsidy to groundfish fish harvesters. Rapid progress in organizing new members. A collective agreement stipulating fish prices and conditions of sale. These were major achievements in a short period that established the union as a potent political force. Its influence was strongly felt at both the federal and provincial levels and in rural communities around Newfoundland and Labrador.

Ongoing collective bargaining in Canada was restricted in the late 1970s by the federal Anti-Inflation Board (AIB), which the Pierre Elliott Trudeau government had put in place to control inflation by limiting wage and price increases. Richard Cashin went to Ottawa to make a special case for an exemption from the limits based on the wage history in the fishing industry and the need for catch-up, and AIB made only what Cashin calls a "slight change" to the negotiated agreement. NFFAWU negotiated wage increases that exceeded the percentage guidelines mandated by the AIB.

The union's increased profile and power paid off for the inshore sector in 1977, when it negotiated an inshore collective agreement with FANL, which provided significant price increases and extended the coverage of the collective agreement to all areas of the province where FANL member companies bought fish and where the union was active, regardless of whether the union had been certified by the Labour Relations Board as bargaining agent in a particular area. It's difficult to imagine any economic outcome in the province that would distribute wealth to more families and more communities in the province than a significant increase in the price of fish.

The union made further improvements to the inshore contract in 1978, but negotiations in 1979 came perilously close to collapse. Mediation from the provincial deputy ministers of fisheries and labour helped the parties reach an 11th-hour settlement, but did not bode well for a peaceful 1980.

By June 1980, the union and the fish processors were far apart in early negotiations in both plant and inshore bargaining. Compounding the union's challenges, Ray Greening had been diagnosed with cancer, and his prognosis was bleak. The position of secretary-treasurer is critical in any union. It was a huge loss to Greening's family and to the union when Greening died early in June at the age of 43.

The union executive board had the responsibility of choosing a successor to complete the four or five months remaining in Greening's term of office. Acting on Cashin's recommendation, the board appointed me to the position. I had been with the union for barely three years as the editor of the *Union Forum* and had limited experience to draw on when I took office in early July, just days before the union plunged into three major industrial disputes.

Events had already taken an ominous turn in June 1980 when FANL unilaterally implemented fish prices, including a four-cent drop in the price of crab as well as other price reductions. The companies made it clear that their goal was to put the union out of business when, in addition to these price cuts, they stopped the deduction of union dues from inshore harvesters. The union's early success in redistributing some of the wealth of the fishery was obviously not to their liking.

FANL had identified a scapegoat for the prevailing troubles of the fishery. In a speech to a St. John's service club, FANL president Bill Wells noted that the problem in the fishery was "too many fishermen chasing too few fish." He did not mention too many fish companies doing a poor job marketing that fish.

On July 9, six days after my installation as secretary-treasurer, 2,300 plant workers at five year-round Fishery Products plants went on strike. The union's plan had been for Fishery Products workers to set the collective bargaining pattern for fish plant workers, but the situation was complicated when National Sea Products, fed up with wildcat strikes at their plant in St. John's, locked out the 450 workers at that facility on the day the Fishery Products workers went on strike.

The plant workers' strike and lockout were barely under way when the union brought regional inshore committee members from around the province together for a meeting to consider strategy options in response to FANL's provocations.

The challenge for the union was to have a decisive response that we could realistically pull off. A strategy was agreed upon during a meeting on July 13: the union would, at least initially, picket four crab plants on the Avalon Peninsula, plus the Fishery Products seasonal plants in St. Anthony and Port au Choix—plants that were not being picketed by plant workers. By closing specific plants, the union hoped to drive a wedge between the various companies.

FANL's response played into the union's hands. Within two days, FANL announced a lockout at the remaining 75 plants owned by 21 member companies. By picketing six plants, the union virtually shut down the entire industry. Only a few plants owned and operated by small inshore companies who were not members of FANL remained open. Inshore harvesters salted their catch. Many were assisted by union staff representative Kevin Carroll, who had grown up splitting fish in a fishing family on Red Island in Placentia Bay; he offered a crash course in splitting and salting fish to anyone who requested it.

The picketing of selected plants and the lockout at the others began on July 21. Two days later, then-premier Brian Peckford, without consultation with the parties involved—or at least none with the union—publicly suggested that the parties go back to work under a "30-day cooling-off period."

One thing that would certainly have cooled off was the union's bargaining power. The inshore fishery, then as now, was highly seasonal. If the union had accepted Peckford's proposal, the bulk of the inshore fishery would have been over by the time the 30 days elapsed, and any pressure on the processors to dig deep to find a settlement would have been dramatically reduced, if not eliminated.

Peckford claimed that his proposal was neutral, but as Cashin said at the time, the proposal "was tilted in its consequence toward the fish companies. It would save the bacon of the fish companies and make a fool of the fishermen."

This didn't stop the St. John's *Evening Telegram* from continuing its anti-union editorials. "Thirty days is not a long period," one editorial declared. "The fishermen won't suffer by it, not nearly as much as they will if the impasse continues."

This was a classic example of the paternalism of the St. John's elites that motivated Cashin in the first place; he wasn't going to pay any attention to an editorial in a St. John's paper.

Fishery Products, the FANL member with the largest operation in the province, was smarting from having its five trawler ports as well as its two Northern Peninsula plants targeted by the union. The company's senior operating executive, Gus Etchegary, thought he had found a way to bring matters to a head. On August 8, Fishery Products tried to break the strike in St. Anthony. After a scuffle at the plant gate, the company succeeded in getting a small amount of fish into the plant.

It was only a trickle of fish from a few harvesters who broke ranks with the union, but FANL saw in this development the potential to compromise the union. The day after the breach of the picket line in St. Anthony, FANL announced that all plants would re-open several days later. Once again, the union brought together the regional committee members to plan a response. A decision was made to escalate the action by adding picket lines in several other communities. Nearly 300 determined fish harvesters attended a meeting in Old Perlican on August 11—the day the companies re-opened their plants—and voted unanimously to strike the plants they normally supplied with fish. Similar action was taken in Bonavista, where 200 fish harvesters picketed the plant.

The companies had been banking on the fish harvesters turning on the union. Instead, the fish harvesters doubled down on their support.

A day later FANL announced they were re-imposing the lockout.

But Etchegary wasn't ready to give up in St. Anthony, where the company continued to get small amounts of fish into the plant. So the union found itself tested again, this time on the Northern Peninsula, where the NFU had been born a decade earlier. Cashin sent staff member Reg Anstey into St. Anthony to work with the area staff representative, Max Short.

"That was the only time I saw Richard think it was over," Short recalled years later. "Etchegary thought they had a clique to supply fish to the plant. I said, 'if we can't close St. Anthony we've got a problem. We've got to try it.'"

The union called on its inshore members to show up at the plant gate and, on August 14, more than 300 of them from around the Northern Peninsula answered the call. A few plant workers were inside at the time. Ren Genge, owner-operator of a fishing enterprise in Anchor Point and a union member since the early days of the NFU, was one of the members on the picket line that morning. Years later, he described a tense situation: "We were directly involved in St. Anthony. Fishery Products got some small boats to sell fish. We tipped the fish out of a pickup. There was a guy on top of the hill with a rifle, firing shots."

Anstey recalled there was also "a guy with an axe" near the wharf. The RCMP officers on hand told Short and Anstey that they couldn't control the situation. Short said the company, as a provocation, sent a cement truck down on the wharf. Short made a final call to Etchegary, having tried unsuccessfully earlier that morning to convince him to close the plant, but again Etchegary said no.

"We beat the gate down," Genge recalled. "A lot of people—a couple of hundred or more. A bunch of us went in with Max to meet the manager."

This time the manager, fearful of the consequences of doing otherwise, convinced Etchegary that the plant had to close.

It was a tremendous victory for the harvesters—the turning point of the strike. Had the company been successful in operating the St. Anthony plant, the solidarity of the picket lines around the province would have been severely compromised.

Within four days, Mr. Cooling-Off Period himself, Premier Peckford, announced the appointment of a Royal Commission of Inquiry into the fishery. The commission would start by examining the books of the processors and recommending fish prices within 60 days, to be paid retroactively.

To keep spirits up, the union held a rally at Quidi Vidi Lake in St. John's a few days later. Close to 2,000 people attended, listened to music and speeches, then went by motorcade across town to the Fishery Products and FANL offices, where they left picket signs on the lawns.

That night, price negotiations resumed. After a late-night round of meetings, a settlement was reached that included modest price increases and much stronger protection in the collective agreement for bona fide, as opposed to casual, fish harvesters. The latter issue had been a major priority for people who depended solely on the inshore fishery for a livelihood only to see it negatively affected by the participation of what they termed "moonlighters"—people with full-time employment elsewhere who dabbled in the fishery from time to time, to the detriment of the full-timers.

In the collective bargaining arena, as in life, progress sometimes comes in instalments, or what CAW organizers used to call "delayed victories." In 1981, despite a significant decline in market and currency factors, the 1980 strike was fresh enough in the minds of the processors that they agreed to modest increases in fish prices.

They didn't want another showdown. The union's inshore sector, tested to its limit in 1980 for the first time, had met the challenge head-on. It would be several years before the processors were ready for a full-fledged battle with the union over fish prices.

Once the inshore dispute was settled, the spotlight switched back to the plant workers. Workers at other plants had voluntarily been paying higher union dues to supplement strike pay, and the union locals in Harbour Breton, Marystown, Burin, Trepassey, Port Union, and St. John's had maintained disciplined, spirited picket lines, with ongoing support from staff reps Matt Murphy, John Blackmore, Reg Anstey, and John Boland. It took another month after the inshore settlement to resolve the plant dispute, starting with an agreement with Fishery Products.

The settlement was worth waiting for. The union achieved major gains: significant improvements in benefits and contract language, and wage increases of $2 an hour (a 40 per cent increase) for production workers and $2.50 an hour for skilled trades workers in a 32-month agreement. A few weeks later, a similar agreement was reached at National Sea Products in St. John's. A new benchmark had been achieved for fish plant workers in the province. These gains injected substantial amounts of money into the pockets of fish plant workers and into the economy of rural communities.

Peckford's Royal Commission was a bust. Unlike Leslie Harris's conciliation board a few years earlier, which had boldly recommended revolutionary changes in the lives of trawlermen, Peckford's commission recommended nothing of consequence to deal with the continuing financial challenges in the inshore industry; it was soon gathering dust on bookshelves in government offices.

"Some People Might Have to End Up on Welfare"

Although the industry has many problems, a shortage of fish is not one of them.

— Michael Kirby, chair, Task Force on Atlantic Fisheries

While the NFFAW was growing rapidly and establishing itself as a potent force in the province in the late 1970s and early 1980s, other developments that would play a major role in shaping the fishery and the province were unfolding.

Total catches of northern cod had peaked in 1968 at a massive, irresponsible, and totally unsustainable level of nearly 800,000 tonnes—about 85 per cent of it by foreign factory-freezer trawlers. By 1974, total landings had declined by more than half, but the decline in the inshore catch was particularly severe; inshore catches of northern cod, typically in the order of 160,000 tonnes a year in the 1950s had fallen to a record low of 35,000 tonnes in 1974, and people were leaving the inshore fishery in droves.

But the grim outlook in 1974 gave way to widespread hope and optimism after the Canadian government announced in June 1976 that, effective January 1, 1977, it would extend its fisheries jurisdiction to 200 miles from shore. Under pressure from politicians to estimate future fish populations in the wake of the extension of jurisdiction, scientists painted a rosy picture of future prospects for the northern cod stock in particular, although they made a point of saying that these estimates were "projections of what is possible, not predictions of what will happen."

Even before there was any tangible evidence of the stock rebuilding that scientists had indicated was possible, provincial governments and fish companies were putting together reckless plans for expansion.

The union advocated caution. An editorial in the May 1977 *Union Forum* stated: "We feel the 160,000 mt [metric tonnes] quota of cod in northern waters should be reduced in 1978, to allow stocks to rebuild. It has been pointed out that in the last couple of years the inshore fishery has improved, but that does not mean the cod stocks have been adequately replenished as government has suggested."

The provincial government championed no such caution. Without any consultation with the union, the Newfoundland and Labrador Moores government joined with the Government of Nova Scotia to propose to the federal government a $900 million capital investment plan for fleet development, including $135 million for the construction of nine ice-strengthened freezer trawlers to exploit the northern cod fishery. To put this in perspective, $900 million was roughly triple the annual total landed value of fish in all of Canada at the time.

The September 1977 *Union Forum* pointed out the risks and follies associated with this scheme: "The plan involved the catching offshore, in the winter months, of the northern cod stocks, which could only be done by ice-reinforced trawlers. At the present time, such trawlers exist only in Europe, so such a proposition would have to involve some form of joint venture. The provincial government opened a real can of worms when they first brought up the question of joint ventures because these schemes have the potential of seriously jeopardizing the future of the inshore fishing communities."

At a time when a committee of the federal government was looking at the future harvesting of northern cod in what it called "an Atlantic perspective," the union was concerned that the provincial government approach was opening the door to having the northern cod stock divided up among the five eastern provinces (the Atlantic provinces plus Quebec).

"In other words," said a feature article in *Union Forum*, "the problems associated with the glut in the trap fishery would be dealt with by increasing the level of the offshore fishery and reducing the inshore fishery ... The problem is that government is proceeding in totally the wrong direction. Its policy should be directed at catching, processing, and marketing fish in the way that is most beneficial to the Newfoundland society, and this means a bias toward the inshore fishery."

When Moores and his fisheries minister hosted their Nova Scotia counterparts as well as executives from the trawler companies at a meeting in Gander in October 1977, they received more than they had bargained for. The union found out about the meeting and staged a demonstration outside the hotel where it was being held.

"Bill Short called me the night before," Petty Harbour fish harvester George Chafe recalled. "I was gone to bed. Bill said you're on a flight to Gander at 5 o'clock tomorrow morning for a demonstration. Can you round up a couple of other guys?"

The union scrambled together enough demonstrators on short notice to make their opposition to the government's plan known to the union membership and the public. Interviewed at the demonstration, inshore vice-president Kevin Condon summarized the union's view of the provincial government's approach to the fishery: "It's hard to expect the federal government to have a policy for Newfoundland if we don't have one ourselves."

Fortunately, the federal minister responsible for fisheries, Romeo LeBlanc (Canada's Governor General from 1995 until 1999), rejected the Nova Scotia and Newfoundland governments' proposal for federal financing for their massive fleet development. "Do we want to double a fleet that is getting half loads?" he asked. "I hardly think so."

The fish processing companies, in the meantime, thought they had a "Plan B" that would work for them. They wanted joint ventures with European distant water fleets whose availability of fish in the northwest Atlantic had been reduced because of the extension of Canadian jurisdiction. The inshore fish processing company Ocean Harvesters in Harbour Grace proposed a joint venture with the West German giant Unilever, which would be a 51 per cent shareholder in a scheme involving the catching of northern cod by its subsidiary Nordsee for landing and processing in Harbour Grace.

Cashin was fiercely against the proposal, even though, not surprisingly, union members who worked in the Harbour Grace fish plant supported it. I went with Cashin to a public meeting in Harbour Grace, where he defended the union's position and explained why joint ventures with foreign companies went against the interests of coastal communities adjacent to the northern cod stock. The Harbour Grace people were not thrilled with Cashin's message, but at least he dared voice his opinion in a public meeting, although he was under no illusions for how his message would be received.

Had the union acquiesced, the joint venture in Harbour Grace would almost certainly have gone ahead and served as a template for more of the same. But the union's opposition resonated with LeBlanc, and the plan ran into enough roadblocks that Unilever eventually backed out of the deal.

The connection between the northern cod stock off the northeast coast of Newfoundland and Labrador and the state of redfish populations in the Gulf of St. Lawrence is not immediately obvious. But the collapse of the Gulf redfish stocks in the mid- to late 1970s upended the fishing plans of the offshore companies in Newfoundland and the Maritimes. Ignoring the caution the union had been advising, the federal government offered subsidies to the trawler companies to go north in the winter to fish northern cod.

Earlier, in December 1977, the province's federal Cabinet minister, Don Jamieson, hosted a special fisheries meeting in Marystown to discuss future planning of the fishery, particularly in light of the optimism surrounding the northern cod stocks. The union presented a comprehensive brief at this meeting, advocating, among other things, that the management of the northern cod stock "should have as its basic premise the maximum revitalization of the inshore/nearshore fishery on the northeast coast and the Labrador coast."

Notwithstanding the optimism in some quarters, LeBlanc implored the fish companies to be careful. In a speech to the 1978 annual meeting of the Fisheries Council of Canada, a powerful lobby organization representing the fisheries corporate sector, he said: "I would like to see you join with me in resisting suggestions that fleets should be vastly expanded, that plants be vastly enlarged—in other words, to resist the temptation of exaggerated expectations. I see no faster road to disaster than forgetting the very simple lesson that the biology cannot keep up with the technology; that the wealth of the ocean cannot yet match the greed of man."

Prophetic words these may have been, but they essentially fell on deaf ears. Companies rapidly expanded onshore processing capacity, notably in Newfoundland. In his comprehensive book *Managing Canada's Fisheries from the Early Days to the Year 2000*, longtime DFO communications official Joe Gough reported that the number of plants in Newfoundland and Labrador increased from 61 in 1973 to 225 by 1983. Much of this investment was financed by debt, not equity. Government financial incentives for plant construction had helped fuel the rapid expansion in capacity. When excessive debt loads were compounded by (at best) flat markets, sky-high interest rates, and adverse foreign exchange factors, the deep-sea companies found themselves in serious financial trouble.

As these ominous storm clouds gathered, the federal government met with executives of the deep-sea companies late in 1981. This led to the appointment in early 1982 of the Task Force on the Atlantic Fishery, generally referred to as the Kirby Task Force, under the chairmanship of Michael Kirby, a rising star in the Ottawa bureaucracy who would later become a senator. His task force had a dual mandate: to make recommendations generally on future policy and management of the fishery and to develop a plan to restructure the troubled deep-sea industry.

With respect to the fisheries policy aspect of its mandate, the Kirby Task Force was a serious underachiever. Its most influential member, with the possible exception of Kirby himself, was Peter John Nicholson, an executive with the Nova Scotia-based seafood processing company H.B. Nickerson & Sons. Nickerson's had expanded rapidly on a foundation of unmanageable debt, much of it tied to rampant and at times baffling expansion of its operations in Newfoundland. Nicholson's influence was reflected in the task force's final report, which tilted heavily in favour of large corporate interests, particularly with respect to proposed future allocations of northern cod.

The task force did not share LeBlanc's caution about the resource. As investigative journalist Michael Harris recounted in *Lament for an Ocean*, Kirby said, "Although the industry has many problems, a shortage of fish is not one of them. By 1987, the groundfish harvest should reach 1.1 million tonnes, an increase of about 370,000 over 1981."

Most of this increased harvest was expected to come from the northern cod stock, and Kirby proposed a drastic reduction in the inshore share of the stock that for centuries had been the lifeblood of hundreds of adjacent coastal communities. Projecting an increase in the total allowable catch (TAC) of northern cod of nearly 80 per cent by 1987, Kirby proposed that the inshore allocation increase by only about 20 per cent and the offshore by 66 per cent. He also proposed nearly a tenfold increase in what at the time was a relatively small allocation to the "resource-short plant program," a scheme to have fish caught by offshore trawlers in the winter and distributed to seasonal inshore plants in the five eastern provinces during their off-season and a 50,000-tonne allocation for a proposed fleet of so-called Scandinavian longliners, even though no such fleet existed at the time.

In December 1982, Cashin publicly warned that there was "nothing in the Kirby approach for fishermen, no major change in marketing, and nothing much coming at all, except mergers and a bailout of the big companies, plus plant closures."

The fate of communities dependent on fish plants owned by the deep-sea companies hung in the balance. A federal negotiating team headed by Kirby was considering the closure of fish plants in Grand Bank, Burin, Gaultois, Fermeuse, and St. Lawrence, which

The union rallied the troops during the 1984 fishery crisis with a campaign it called "Unity '84." Father McGrath speaks at one of the rallies.

would have been a devastating outcome for these primarily single-industry towns. While the prospects of these and other communities were still under active debate by the federal Cabinet, the union, working with affected municipal leaders and other community groups, led what became known as a people's conference on the deep-sea fishery in March 1983. The conference adopted an "all plants open" resolution which also called for public ownership of the troubled deep-sea companies.

Meanwhile, inshore fishing enterprises were experiencing serious financial distress because of many of the same factors that had plunged the deep-sea companies to the brink of bankruptcy. The task force essentially dismissed the problems of the inshore sector, concluding that inshore harvesters "are not in a significantly worse position than other groups like farmers"—a comment totally at odds with the task force's own research about fish harvester incomes.

The task force found that "distress selling" arising from the poor financial condition of the processors caused some of what it found to be "unnecessarily low prices that some processors accepted for some products from time to time," yet it had nothing of any value to offer in terms of recommendations to improve the marketing of our fish products.

Even more galling, the task force referred to the inshore fishery as a "social fishery," and the offshore sector as an "economic fishery," even though the expensive financial support it recommended to the federal government was used primarily to bail out the offshore, not the inshore, sector. And it provocatively offered a fisheries version of the generally discredited trickle-down theory of economics, commenting that "inshore fishermen ... clearly benefit from a strengthened processing sector, a fact all too often ignored by some spokesmen for fishermen's organizations."

One of the arguments the task force used in dismissing the inshore fishery was its seasonality. Yet instead of looking at what appeared to be a promising mackerel resource as an opportunity to extend the inshore season later into the fall, the task force recommended the development of a fleet of large boats to harvest this resource. It's a good thing that that recommendation went nowhere, as the mackerel stocks went into a long period of decline shortly thereafter.

By the end of 1982, four of the troubled deep-sea companies— H.B. Nickerson, Fishery Products, the Lake Group, and John Penny and Sons—had combined loans outstanding of $222 million to the

Bank of Nova Scotia and about $20 million each to the Newfoundland and Nova Scotia governments.

Ultimately, a multi-million-dollar government rescue plan devised by Kirby's restructuring group created two "super companies." The assets of Fishery Products, the Lake Group, and John Penny and Sons were combined with H.B. Nickerson's Newfoundland operations and its scallop operation in Riverport, Nova Scotia, to form Fishery Products International (FPI), based in St. John's. The Nova Scotia assets of Nickerson (minus the Riverport scallop operation) were combined with the assets of National Sea Products in both provinces to form a Nova Scotia-based company.

The new FPI was initially owned 60 per cent by Ottawa, 25 per cent by the Government of Newfoundland, and 15 per cent by the Bank of Nova Scotia. One of its first operational acts was to demand sweeping rollbacks of plant and trawler contracts in its Newfoundland operations.

In the case of trawlermen, the outrageous contract demands would roll back the clock to the pre-Harris report days, including a proposal to reduce turnaround times (the time trawlermen had with their families between 10-day fishing trips) from 48 to 36 hours, even though there was plenty of time to harvest available quotas using 48-hour turnarounds. Apparently oblivious to the union's proven track record of militancy at the bargaining table, the company also proposed a major attack on wages, benefits, and contract language for plant workers. If successfully implemented, this would have dramatically reduced incomes for FPI employees and would have undermined the economy in communities where FPI plants were situated. It would also have inevitably spilled over into collective agreements with other fish plant operators.

Union members and leaders reacted furiously. A company that was primarily owned by the two levels of government, including the provincial government led by Brian Peckford, was proposing to strip bare the collective agreements the union had fought for years to build up.

Peckford's participation was consistent with remarks he had made during the course of the restructuring exercise when he told an audience of St. John's businessmen that "sacrifices" would be needed from people who work in the fishery. Peter John Nicholson, a key architect of the restructuring plan, was even more arrogant. He casually remarked that some people "might have to end up on welfare."

The union wasn't prepared to accept this, and once again the trawlermen went to the front lines in a strike, which lasted six months. The union launched a public campaign it called Unity '84 to keep members actively engaged in the struggle, fighting to save coastal communities and protect their collective agreements. Rallies, banners, petitions, and meetings with politicians kept Unity '84 in the spotlight.

Eventually, the governments brought in a new management team, led by Vic Young, to take over the company, and the union was successful in beating the demanded concessions off the table and restoring its hard-fought wages, benefits, and contract language in both the trawler and plant collective agreements.

After a shaky beginning, FPI gradually developed into the flagship company of the Newfoundland and Labrador fishery. Buoyed by improving markets and more favourable foreign exchange rates, and building a reputation for high-quality products, the company had highly profitable years from 1986 to 1988, bought out the government's equity, and converted FPI into a publicly traded company.

"Dog Eat Dog and Vice Versa"

It was a gutsy move.

— Bob White, founding president, CAW

Mergers in the trade union movement can be a tricky proposition. Some unions have a history of militancy and social activism; others regard the union as a collective bargaining agent and not much more; still others, often referred to as business unions, have little room for democratic participation or debate and tend to work on a friendly basis with the corporations which employ their members. For a merger to work well, the values of the merging unions need to be compatible.

Chapter 1 outlined the early history of our union, when NFFAWU was formed as an affiliate of the Amalgamated Meatcutters and Butcher Workmen of North America. In 1979, the Meatcutters combined with the Retail Clerks to form the United Food and Commercial Workers International Union (UFCW). Ray Greening knew right away that this was not a positive development. He had worked briefly with the Retail Clerks several years earlier but left because he felt he didn't belong with the Retail Clerks' brand of business unionism.

As time passed, it became clear that the joining of the Meatcutters and the Retail Clerks wasn't a merger: it was a takeover. The first president of the UFCW, Bill Wynn, came from the Retail Clerks, and he quickly infused the new organization with Clerks-style business unionism. Our approach of social and political activism was a very poor fit, as Greening had realized from the start.

Because of the ill-will between some of the unions who merged into UFCW, the Canadian membership was split into two "regions": Region 18, the Meatcutter locals, and Region 19, Retail Clerks locals. Both had members across Canada.

While for the most part the international union was irrelevant to NFFAW's day-to-day operations, one significant positive aspect for the first few years was that Frank Benn, initially assistant director and later director of Region 18, was a good trade unionist and a reliable friend who helped our union in critical times—for instance, he was instrumental in helping negotiate the eventual settlement to the 1980 inshore strike. (More than 20 years after he retired, I was pleased when Benn accepted our invitation to come to St. John's to participate in the official opening of FFAW's new headquarters, which we had decided to appropriately name the "Richard Cashin Building.")

But under the UFCW constitution, the directors of the Canadian regions were elected not by Canadians but by a vote of all delegates at an international UFCW convention where Canadians were outnumbered by about 10 to 1. When a vacancy occurred between conventions, the international UFCW executive board would decide on a replacement.

There was virtually no Canadian autonomy in the UFCW. A Canadian local had to apply to Washington for strike authorization, without which there would be no strike pay. The UFCW treated Canada as just another region, with two votes on the UFCW executive board of about 50 people.

So when Benn retired between conventions, Cashin spearheaded a group of reform-minded Canadian leaders within Region 18 in a push to give the Canadian membership the right to decide on his replacement. This was rejected out of hand by the top brass of the UFCW, and Bill Wynn's hand-picked successor, Bill Hanley, replaced Benn. Cashin was incensed at this manifestation of UFCW's colonial mentality. Then one of his key allies in the reform effort, Leif Hansen, president of Local 2000 in British Columbia and a strong believer in socially progressive unionism, felt the sharp edge of UFCW's tactics.

The January 16, 1987, *Globe and Mail* picks up the story: "On Wednesday morning, about two dozen men, many from the United States, showed up unannounced at the [UFCW's] Local 2000 with orders from Washington to take over. A glass door was smashed. One woman who was working in the office told reporters that she saw the butt end of a rifle on one of the men, although police say there is no evidence of a gun."

Cashin had had enough. The democratically elected president and executive board of a sister local had been thrown out of office and the union placed under the control of a trustee appointed by Washington. The local leadership's offence appeared to be failing to blindly follow the tune dictated by Washington. If that was a crime in the UFCW, Cashin would surely be found guilty; he was no yes-man.

Would Fishermen's Union Local 1252 (as our union was called at the time) be the next local to be taken over by force? Under the

UFCW constitution, its president had virtually unfettered power to do just that.

Cashin had put too much of his heart and soul into building the union from scratch to risk that. A few weeks after the incident in British Columbia, Cashin went to Toronto to meet with Bob White, the charismatic president of the CAW. White knew all about international unions. Less than two years earlier, he had led the breakaway of Canadian locals from the United Autoworkers and the formation of a brand new, high-profile Canadian union, the CAW.

White recalled that meeting with Cashin in his autobiography, *Hard Bargains: My Life on the Line:* "[Cashin] told me the fishermen had decided to get out of the UFCW. They had two choices, going back to being an independent union of some 23,000 people (this was before the northern cod moratorium) or joining another big union. They had decided on the latter. They weren't shopping around, they had decided they wanted to be in the CAW. We spent a day talking it through at the end of which I invited Cashin and other leaders of the Fishermen's Union to attend the meeting the next week of our Executive Board."

Reg Anstey and I joined Cashin at this follow-up meeting. Cashin recounted the events that had gotten us there, and a lengthy discussion followed. White then asked us to leave the room so the board could make a decision.

"I said I knew that what the fishermen wanted to do would be controversial in the labour movement and that we would be attacked if we accepted their proposal," White recounted. "But I also said that the CAW could not and should not turn its back on the fishermen at a time when they were fighting to remain true to their principles and continue as a vibrant organization within Newfoundland and within Canada."

Bob White led the breakaway of the Canadian division of the United Auto Workers and became the founding president of CAW.

We didn't have to wait outside the board meeting for long. We were invited back in, and White advised us that the board had voted unanimously to pursue discussions with us.

There was no time for dilly-dallying. Word got around about what had happened, and we knew we had to move quickly to avoid having our assets seized by UFCW. A few weeks later, on March 10, 1987, Bob White, national secretary-treasurer Bob Nickerson, and senior CAW staff members flew to St. John's for decisive meetings. They must have wondered what they were getting themselves into; 1987 was a particularly harsh winter, and there were enormous mounds of snow on both sides of the road as we drove White and his delegation to their hotel late on a bitterly cold, windy winter's night.

The next day White and his colleagues met with the executive board of our union, and immediately after that with a group of about 130 of our top elected rank-and-file leadership from the various sectors of the union. Support for the move to the UFCW was overwhelming. As White put it: "When I met them, they were excited and happy as hell."

We immediately notified the UFCW in writing that we were leaving. Then we waited for their response.

On March 23, UFCW secretary-treasurer Jerry Menapace and Jay Foreman, a top advisor to the president, flew to St. John's in the UFCW's private jet to meet with Cashin and me. They were cordial; they said they admired Cashin, understood he was acting from principle, and did not expect that they could change our minds. But they ruled out any possibility of an amicable separation, including a suggestion from Cashin that there be a secret ballot vote of the membership to determine the future affiliation of the union. They made it unmistakably clear that UFCW would fight us with every weapon at their disposal, not because they expected to change our minds and not because they expected to succeed, but to make it painfully obvious to all other locals in North America that anyone trying a similar move would be in for a major fight with a very powerful enemy. Then they went back to their private jet and flew home to Washington.

Two days later, the UFCW made a formal request to CLC—the central labour body in Canada consisting of dozens of affiliated unions—to expel CAW for "raiding." Bob White described what came next: "A week later, the top officials of about 10 unions gathered in Toronto to figure out their strategy. Bill Wynn vowed that he would do everything in his power, 'offensively and defensively' as

UFCW lawyers prepared actions against Cashin, me and the CAW in various courts. On April 9, the UFCW sued me, the CAW, Richard Cashin and others for $43 million in damages, declaring that I was guilty of a 'flagrant, cynical and high-handed breach of duty.' $10 million of that was personal damages against me."

At around the same time, UFCW filed raiding charges under the CLC Constitution, although those were doomed to fail because the CLC constitution does not allow a union to proceed with raiding charges against another affiliate if the union making the charge has taken action in court on the same matter.

The *Globe and Mail* quoted Cliff Evans, the UFCW Region 19 director and de facto UFCW head in Canada, saying with respect to Cashin, "We're going to get that guy."

We were convinced it was only a matter of time until we were put in trusteeship, which would mean someone appointed by the UFAW president—probably someone from Ontario or the United States—running the union, with full control of the finances. Putting the issue to a democratic vote of the membership was out of the question because, under the UFCW constitution, such a vote would fail if seven members opposed it. *Seven*. Out of 23,000.

We could see only one way forward. We had to leave the UFCW and start from scratch. On April 21, 1987, Cashin and I, along with the entire executive board and staff, resigned.

"It was a gutsy move," said White. "Many staff people gave up pensions and other benefits with the UFCW. That decision, made just days before our collective bargaining convention in May 1987 caught the UFCW off guard."

Cashin was invited to speak at the CAW convention. "This is not a legal battle," he told delegates. "It's a political struggle. The workers want a union that represents a value system, and if some people have differences with that, they can go to hell."

Convention delegates responded with enthusiasm, there was a unanimous vote of support, and the National Executive Board authorized national secretary-treasurer Bob Nickerson to advance sufficient funds to get the new union started.

Two weeks after the CAW convention, we held the founding convention of the Fishermen, Food and Allied Workers/CAW (later gender-neutralized to Fish, Food and Allied Workers/CAW) at the Hotel Newfoundland. UFCW tried to interfere by telling the hotel we had no funds to pay for the convention, and the hotel was at the point of cancelling, but when we advised Nickerson of this, he phoned the hotel to assure them that CAW would pay the bill.

The convention was a major success. About 300 delegates attended and unanimously passed a resolution to merge with the CAW, once bargaining unit reorganization was complete. They also adopted a constitution that included election of the officers and executive board members by mail ballot by the rank-and-file membership.

"Delegate after delegate went to the mikes and spoke about how proud they felt that soon they would be a part of the CAW," White recalled. "It was a very emotional time for me. If men and women like this wanted to join us in the CAW, then I knew we were and will be a dynamic voice for change in Canada."

One of the key decisions that had to be made in drawing up the constitution of FFAW was how to deal with the bargaining units we had organized during the early 1980s in Nova Scotia and Prince Edward Island. Our lawyers advised us that if we included bargaining units from other provinces under the FFAW umbrella, we would risk a legal challenge from UFCW that would have had a good chance of success under the Newfoundland labour legislation. It made more sense for CAW to organize these bargaining units into separate local unions than to gamble on the outcome of a court case that could jeopardize the legal standing of our new union.

Perhaps the most flagrant example of UFCW's style of trade unionism exhibited during this battle occurred at the Cavendish Farms processing plant in Prince Edward Island. Under the punitive provisions of the UFCW constitution, it is a violation punishable by fine, loss of union office, and/or loss of membership to even advocate breaking away from the UFCW. Loss of union office is one thing, but UFCW stripped away the membership of three elected rank-and-file workers who had led the campaign to move to the CAW, thereby depriving these young men of their livelihoods. CAW enjoyed overwhelming support in the Cavendish Farms plant, but their attempt to escape the shackles of the UFCW got tied up in endless legal proceedings at the PEI Labour Relations Board and in the courts, and the workers in that facility never had an opportunity to vote on their union affiliation, despite virtually 100 per cent of them having signed CAW cards.

An episode that occurred shortly after we decided to join the CAW underlined the wisdom of our decision.

Even before we were officially part of CAW, a crew of offshore members had been working for the shrimp factory-trawler *Thor Trawl*. But the vessel's owner failed to pay the crew for a long shrimp trip. The company had fallen into financial difficulties, and it looked as if the crew members would never receive the wages owed them. Then one day a crew member called me at the office to say that he had just seen the vessel, with a new name and a fresh coat of paint, in port in St. John's, and he wondered if the union could take legal action to recover the overdue wages. I contacted our lawyer, Randy

Buzz Hargrove, national president of the CAW joins me, secretary-treasurer Reg Anstey, vice-presidents Bill Broderick and Pius Power, and the inshore council at a press conference in St. John's.

Earle of the local law firm O'Dea Earle, who advised us that it would be possible to arrest the boat but to do so would require that we post a bond in the order of $300,000. We didn't have that kind of money available to us—we were still in the process of re-signing our members—so I called Bob Nickerson. When the rights of workers were involved, we could always count on Nickerson. Although we still weren't officially part of CAW, he had the money transferred within a few hours, we had the vessel arrested, and ultimately recovered every cent the crew members were owed, thousands of dollars each, as well as recovering the money CAW had posted for the bond.

The task our new union had set for itself in starting from scratch was monumental. It involved re-signing more than 20,000 members, scattered in dozens of fish plants and other workplaces and hundreds of inshore fishing communities throughout Newfoundland and Labrador.

In some bargaining units, depending on technical details, such as the expiry date of existing contracts, it made sense for us to have members sign union cards right away. In other units, including many of our bigger plants, it was a two-step process: first the members signed petitions asking the provincial Labour Relations Board to revoke their certification order in UFCW; then, when that was completed following a membership vote, we signed those members into our new union and applied to the board for certification as bargaining agent.

It was a bitterly fought battle. The UFCW sent in business agents from Ontario and elsewhere to run Local 1252 under a trusteeship headed up by Bill Hanley, the man whose hand-picked appointment as Canadian director had set the chain of events in motion in the first place. They didn't try to defend UFCW's reputation or track record but relied instead on vicious personal attacks, particularly against Bob White and Richard Cashin. They even wrote a sarcastic song about me called "Earle the Pearl," which gave me a nickname for life. Our staff reps and in-plant committees had a major responsibility combatting these attacks at the plant level, while coordinating sign-up campaigns within the strict protocols of the Labour Relations Board.

In the plants that had to initially go through a decertification process, we explained to members who weren't familiar with legal terminology like "revoking the certification of the bargaining agent" that the simplest way to look at it was this: if you support FFAW, vote "yes" in the secret ballot vote the Labour Relations Board would eventually conduct in the workplace. This led to an amusing episode. Dan Chapman, a longtime rank-and-file leader in the FPI fish plant in Harbour Breton told me about a conversation he had with several older members, good supporters of ours, who had just finished voting.

"Well boys," said Chapman, "I guess that's a couple of yes votes in the box."

Chapman was shocked when one of them said, "I didn't vote yes, I voted no."

"Why did you vote no?"

"Well," the member replied, "there was a guy there from the Department of Labour who said vote X opposite your choice. My choice was "yes," and the opposite of yes is no, so I voted no."

Fortunately, Harbour Breton was an FFAW stronghold, and we had plenty of votes to spare. I understand that the Labour Relations Board subsequently amended its standard instruction to voters and now says, "Vote X next to your choice."

Because bargaining units remained in the UFCW until Labour Relations Board votes were completed, it was in the UFCW's interest to drag proceedings out as long as possible, and drag them out they did. This included requesting hearings before the board for each bargaining unit, then calling dozens of plant workers as witnesses for no other purpose than to prolong the proceedings.

In one of these hearings, the UFCW lawyer asked a fish plant worker to describe the atmosphere in the plant throughout the dispute between the unions. "Well sir, it was like this," the plant worker replied. "It was dog eat dog and vice versa."

Despite UFCW's delaying tactics, slowly but surely, bargaining unit by bargaining unit, the workers had their chance to decide whether they wanted to join the new FFAW under Cashin's leadership and with the affiliation to CAW, or to remain with UFCW. We didn't win every vote, but we won most of them.

A critical battle took place at the FPI plant in Port Union, the largest plant in the province, with about 1,000 workers. The union sent in Matt Murphy, an experienced and capable staff rep from Marystown, to bolster the campaign. I received a call from a supporter the morning the vote was scheduled to take place. The previous evening, UFCW had forged and delivered to the homes of plant workers a letter bearing a photocopy of the CAW letterhead with Bob White's photo and signature, saying that union dues would increase to $50 a week to cover the costs of starting up the new union. This obviously had the potential to cause serious confusion and undermine the vote. I had someone fax a copy of the letter to me and forwarded it immediately to the Labour Relations Board. The board agreed that the letter was prejudicial to the conduct of a fair vote and delayed the vote a few days to allow us time to set the record straight. We won the vote in Port Union.

The biggest and most complicated vote involved the inshore fish harvesters, of whom there were about 12,000 living in every nook and cranny of the province. The sign-up campaign presented a significant challenge, but the union's staff reps and rank-and-file leadership were up for it. Whereas it was relatively straightforward to hold a vote among workers in a particular fish plant, usually in the plant boardroom or the lunchroom, it was no small task to figure out how to conduct a vote among a widely dispersed group like the inshore fish harvesters.

What the Labour Relations Board eventually decided to do was to use the full resources of the provincial Chief Returning Office, the people who conduct provincial elections. Voting was set for one day in April 1988 at about 80 locations, staffed by the same people, mainly casual workers, who officiate at provincial elections. At our request, the board agreed to have advance polls available in about a dozen locations a week earlier, to accommodate people who might not be able to vote on the main day.

Even determining who was eligible to vote was a challenge. While most people who fished depended on it for their livelihood, some part-time or casual holders of personal fishing registrations had little or no meaningful attachment to the industry.

The Labour Relations Board decided to allow anyone who showed up to vote to do so. The ballots were then put in a "double envelope": each ballot was put in a blank envelope, which was then placed inside a second envelope containing the name and identifying information for the person. Once an individual's right to vote was determined, the outer envelope was discarded and the blank envelope put in the box, so no one would know how the individual voted.

About 13,000 people cast ballots in the inshore vote. We had membership lists of fishing people on a community-by-community basis and had to wade through the names on these lists one by one. It took several days and nights of meetings involving FFAW, UFCW, and Labour Relations Board officials to determine which ballots would be counted. Where both unions agreed on eligibility, which was most cases, the ballots were included. In the absence of agreement, the board would determine whether the individual in question was eligible to vote.

Finally, the sorting was completed, with approximately 12,000 people deemed eligible. Facilities were set up in several rooms at the Department of Labour to facilitate counting, which was done in

Founding Unifor president Jerry Dias.

batches of 100. As it happened, in the room in which I was acting as scrutineer for FFAW, the first 100 votes were split almost right down the middle—51 for us, 49 for UFCW. I swallowed hard after that tally. But as more votes were counted, it became obvious that we were well ahead, and we eventually won with 64 per cent of the votes.

A few good years in the fishery, driven by strong markets and favourable foreign exchange factors, made 1987 and 1988 good years to tackle the massive job of re-organizing our union from top to bottom. At the CAW Constitutional Convention in Ottawa in the fall of 1988, FFAW officially became affiliated with CAW under a new section of the constitution that gave us an unusual level of autonomy in light of our structure, and provided FFAW with a seat on the National Executive Board. We were warmly welcomed into the union by the delegates.

One of the first major tasks the CAW undertook on our behalf was to join us at the bargaining table with FPI, which had just enjoyed several years of significant profits. Bob White joined us for the opening of negotiations, as the national president often does with major employers. His assistant, Buzz Hargrove, stayed at the table throughout the complex negotiations and was a huge help in achieving new agreements with significant breakthroughs on behalf of both plant workers and trawlermen that would serve as a model for negotiations with other fish companies.

Hargrove succeeded White as CAW president in 1992, when White stepped down to run successfully for the position of president of the CLC. Recalling the challenges about 30 years later, Hargrove called the CAW decision to stand up to the UFAW and assume the very substantial costs involved in taking us on board "a good exercise for us as a new national union. It fit right in with our Statement of Principles."

Hargrove felt that FFAW's success in the face of bitter opposition from the UFCW was the result of "the amazing rank and file support. UFCW tried to paint it as a power grab by you and Richard. It strengthened our union beyond any amount of money we spent. We weren't going to stand by and see workers treated as chattels [property]."

It was a costly exercise, to put it mildly. Before the dust cleared, both unions had spent millions of dollars in a battle that took several years to complete.

There was an interesting byproduct of the campaign—something we used to refer to as "bycatch," which is fisheries terminology for incidental catch of a species other than the target species on a fishing trip. The battle between us and the UFCW was part of an ongoing Canadianization of the labour movement, as workers in many sectors of the economy moved away from US-based international unions in favour of independent Canadian unions, many of which were relatively small. Many of these unions started looking for a larger Canadian union that would provide services that were beyond their own resources.

"All those small independent Canadian unions wouldn't have come to us if we hadn't welcomed FFAW," Hargrove said, adding that this was also true of the much larger Canadian Brotherhood of Railway, Transport and General Workers Union (CBRT) which merged with CAW in 1994. Leaders of several Canadian unions which eventually merged with the CAW told me the unwavering support CAW had given us was a significant factor in their decision to join CAW.

One of the defining features of CAW was the continuous engagement between the top officers of the union and the rank-and-file leadership. In addition to a constitutional convention, which is held every three years and is standard practice in national and international unions, CAW had the CAW council, sometimes referred to as the "parliament of the union." Twice a year the council came together (as did a separate Quebec council, where most of the members were French-speaking) to allow members to engage with their leaders on the most pressing issues of the day. Each of these meetings was the size of a convention, with several hundred rank-and-file leaders in attendance from the various locals.

CAW Council meetings were learning experiences for those fortunate enough to attend them. There would be a comprehensive "state of the union" report from the national president and guest speakers brought in. This would be followed by a free-wheeling debate among delegates on recommendations brought forward by the national president dealing with current issues and other contents of the president's report. It was an opportunity to learn from the experiences of other union leaders dealing with challenging problems, as well as a chance to learn to speak assertively, emotionally, and concisely at the floor microphones. Speakers on the debate were limited to five minutes, which not only gave many a chance to speak but it also helped delegates develop the valuable skill of making public presentations in front of a large audience within a tight time frame.

I made some great friendships at these meetings, as well as during my 21 years on the National Executive Board, and I came away each time reinvigorated to tackle the challenges I would face at home. These inspiring meetings equipped local leaders from across Canada to better represent their membership.

Will Reid, a fish cutter in Port Union, was at various times the unit chairperson of that plant, industrial vice-president of FFAW, and eventually a full-time staff representative. Reid had the opportunity to attend CAW events over the years, including training courses. "The biggest change for industrial workers was the day we decided to join the CAW," Reid recalled. "I think it was the best thing ever we did as a union. CAW took a lot of pride in training rank and file leaders, shop stewards, health and safety reps, and so on. It really helped us deal with our membership in the plants."

Gerald MacDonald of Burgeo was active during the Burgeo strike of 1971 and later became unit chairperson in the plant, a member of the union's executive board, and ultimately worked on the FFAW staff. He also served several terms as deputy mayor and later mayor of Burgeo. He described the CAW leadership courses he took as "a great help with stuff like that. It helped you not just with your union work, but in any organization."

A huge asset of CAW (and now Unifor) was their Family Education Centre in Port Elgin, Ontario, on the shores of Lake Huron. Port Elgin is home to a variety of conferences, training courses, and National Executive Board meetings. One of the highlights of the year is the family education program which brings members and their families to Port Elgin for the vacation/learning experience of a lifetime.

The top CAW leadership was always readily accessible to union locals, and that continues with Unifor. FFAW has experienced tough challenges in the 30-plus years since the merger with the CAW, and the national president—Bob White, Buzz Hargrove, Ken Lewenza, or Unifor president, Jerry Dias—always answered the call if a problem needed support from the top of the house.

By 2012, the global economic recession and the hollowing out of the Canadian manufacturing sector had taken its toll on both the CAW and another major private sector Canadian union, the Communications, Energy and Paper Workers (CEP), prompting the leaders of the two unions to explore the possibility of combining their organizations into a single, strong, modern union. After a long process that included extensive engagement, these unions agreed that their members' interests would be best served by coming together to create a larger, stronger Canadian union. The new union, known as Unifor, came into existence in the fall of 2013. Like its predecessors, it is a militant, socially progressive union that retains the council structure, education programs, and other resources and services—and most important, the values—that had brought FFAW into the CAW fold 26 years earlier.

A footnote to the saga of our departure from the UFCW: As Bob White described, UFCW sued CAW, FFAW, White, Cashin, and me, among other defendants, for $43 million. We joked that we would be more concerned if we were being sued for $43,000—where were you ever going to come up with $43 million?

Ultimately, the Supreme Court of Newfoundland dismissed most of UFCW's allegations but ruled that we had overstepped by

Then-CAW president Ken Lewenza speaks at an FFAW-CAW convention in Gander.

removing a membership list from the UFCW offices when we vacated the premises. The judge awarded UFCW $60,000 in damages. UFCW immediately proclaimed a glorious "victory," then announced a few weeks later that they would be appealing the decision.

I had fun with that one, telling CAW Council delegates, to their amusement: "We have a firm policy in FFAW. We don't appeal our victories."

CHAPTER 8

"How Are We Going to Feed Our Children?"

If we continue to insist upon walking the very edge of the precipice, the laws of chance ordain that we daily walk in greater peril of falling over.

— Harris Northern Cod Review Panel

The future of individuals, families, and communities who make a living in the fishery is highly dependent on the ability of the authorities to accurately evaluate the condition of fish stocks and the level of annual catch they can sustain. I have long felt that it is as much an art as a science. Measurements can be taken, data time series can be developed, and mathematical models can be used, all of which are important. But there is more to it than a mathematical calculation. When the models and theories blind you to what is happening on the water, the result can be disastrous.

The classic case in point is the once-great northern cod stock which covers a huge expanse of ocean from northern Labrador to Cape St. Mary's, including the nose and tail of the Grand Banks, more than 200 miles from shore. For centuries, it was our biggest fishery. Dr. Leslie Harris called our province "the great ship moored near the fishing banks."

Dr. George Rose, a well-known Newfoundland cod scientist, described developments in the theory of fish science in his book *Cod: The Ecological History of the North Atlantic Fisheries:*

> There were several developments in scientific theory in the 1950s that would have profound influence on the Newfoundland and Labrador fisheries ... Fisheries science, as practiced in the North Atlantic, took on a much more mathematical persuasion and focused on abstract dynamics of the fished stocks ... Many new fisheries scientists were trained as statisticians rather than as biologists or marine scientists. They knew numbers—not fish.

Glenn Blackwood, who became head of Memorial University's Fisheries and Marine Institute, noted in his study of the northern cod stock that from 1850 to 1950 the northern cod fishery, prosecuted by inshore boats and schooners, was "a model of stability and sustainability." But the development of European distant-water factory-freezer trawler fleets changed that. These fleets fished 12 months a year, and their appetites were never satisfied.

"According to all scientific evidence," said Rose, "overfishing and stock collapses ... did not exist to any serious extent in Newfoundland and Labrador until the arrival of the foreign fleets. The 'too many fishermen' notion should have been applied to the foreign fleets when it mattered, not to Newfoundland fishing communities after the fact. The northern cod stock never recovered from this onslaught."

Inshore catches plummeted in the mid-1970s, but concerns about the state of the stock were displaced by optimism in the wake of the extension of Canadian jurisdiction to 200 miles.

Compounding the shortcomings of the abstract models used to estimate stock abundance and sustainable harvest levels, scientists "tuned" their calculations using the catch rates from the offshore trawler fishery. The resulting forecasts of increasing abundance of northern cod in the 1980s were at odds with the fishing experience of inshore harvesters, who found that each year they needed more gear to catch less fish, and the fish they did catch were getting smaller.

"In hindsight," said Blackwood, "the consistent failure of the inshore sector ... should have been sufficient evidence to seriously question the health of the northern cod stock."

But to the frustration of inshore harvesters, their catch rates and observations of the stock that had sustained their families and communities for generations were not factored into the stock assessment process. While their experience pointed to a stock in decline, the mathematical models said something entirely different.

"Finally," said Joe Gough, "in the January 1989 assessment, CAFSAC (Canadian Atlantic Fisheries Scientific Advisory Committee) scientists concluded that they had made a grave overestimate. The high catch rates by increasingly efficient trawlers, whose captains were learning more about the stock, had helped to mask the reality. Fishing mortality rates were about double the earlier estimates."

Shock waves rippled through the fishing industry when, essentially overnight, DFO scientists changed their TAC advice for northern cod from 266,000 to 125,000 tonnes.

The federal government reduced the quota modestly, but to nowhere near the recommended level. Government also appointed the Harris Northern Cod Review Panel, which studied the situation in depth and made 29 recommendations. The DFO minister at the time,

Repairing gillnets. In the years leading up to the moratorium on northern cod, gillnets had become the most widely used gear. As years went by, harvesters needed more nets with smaller mesh to respond to the dwindling stocks.

Bernard Valcourt, said he shared the view of the Harris Panel that the stock was in decline, but he did not accept its recommendation to reduce the already-announced quota of just below 190,000 tonnes for the 1990 fishery.

The situation was not much better in other important cod stocks. The south coast stock 3Ps was showing signs of significant decline, and in the northern Gulf of St. Lawrence, the 4RS3Pn stock that was so important to southwestern and western Newfoundland, southern Labrador, and the Quebec north shore was in such abysmal shape that the fixed-gear sector landed only about 10 per cent of their allocation in 1990. Cashin highlighted this disastrous situation in the Gulf in a brief to the Atlantic Groundfish Advisory Committee in October of 1990 in which he suggested the federal, Newfoundland, and Quebec governments "come together for a tri-governmental approach to examine what would be involved in a moratorium."

That same year, northern cod landings improved significantly, an outcome Rose attributed to "hyper-aggregation" of the stock into a few very dense schools. Catch rates on these concentrations were the highest ever recorded, and the cod trap fishery in 1990 was the best it had been in decades, despite the seriously declining state of the resource.

But any hopes that the stock might be recovering were dashed in 1991, when the inshore landings declined sharply to 35,000 tonnes.

Yet, according to Michael Harris, in *Lament for an Ocean*, when John Crosbie took over the politically charged position of minister of fisheries and oceans in April 1991, his briefing book said: "Scientific advice is that lower inshore catch rates and smaller fish in the inshore fishery in recent years do not indicate stock decline."

In his autobiography *No Holds Barred: My Life in Politics*, Crosbie recounts an installment of the CBC Fisheries Broadcast in which Harris stated that the stock was at a "dangerously low level, so low, in fact, that he worried whether the species would survive," only to be followed a few minutes later by DFO's assistant deputy minister for science who, according to Crosbie, said "the stocks appeared to have increased since the Harris panel did its study and, in his view, the situation was not as alarming as Harris found it."

Scientists and managers had been willing to explain away long periods of declining catch rates in the inshore fishery, but the real shocker came in the winter of 1992, when Canadian offshore trawler companies, which had maintained excellent catch rates up to that point, suddenly found themselves confronting a desert. Cod were nowhere to be found. In his book *Management of Marine Fisheries in Canada*, Dr. Scott Parsons, a scientist from Lumsden, Newfoundland and Labrador, who had risen to the position of DFO assistant deputy minister for science, described the scientific community's reaction to this shocking development: "In June and July, 1992, NAFO Scientific Council and CAFSAC concluded that there had been a sudden, drastic and unexpected decline in the abundance of northern cod during 1991. The total biomass had been reduced by half and the spawning stock by three quarters ... While no single factor was identified as the cause of the sudden drastic decline, the primary factors suggested were ecological."

This theory of a sudden collapse of the resource may have helped explain the inadequacies of the stock surveys, but I find that explanation to be out of synch with the inshore experience in the mid- to late 1980s and unsupported by empirical evidence. Where did all those dead fish go? It's much more plausible that the stock assessment findings had been seriously flawed for some time, that for many years the actual abundance was much less than the scientists thought, and that the stock had been fished to the brink of oblivion, helped along, no doubt, by what were clearly very adverse environmental conditions, including exceptionally cold water. For 15 years, we had been living in a fool's paradise. I don't say that for the purpose of blaming anyone; I'm just trying to make sense of it.

Whatever the cause, by June 1992 it was obvious we were facing a catastrophe.

In the St. Anthony area, there was not a fish to be caught, and people were getting increasingly desperate, without a cent coming into their households. Staff representative David Decker and union leadership in the area organized a rally, which had a remarkable turnout of more than 1,000 people. The dread these people were experiencing was reflected in homemade placards: "How are we going to feed our children?"

To the frustration of our members in the region and despite considerable effort, the union was unsuccessful in getting television stations to send news crews to St. Anthony to cover the event.

In an attempt at levity in a grim situation, I said at the rally that while the television stations didn't bother to go to the Northern Peninsula to cover this significant event, "if a cat had kittens on the steps of Confederation Building, they'd have a full report."

I watched the news that night, and while there was no mention of a cat having kittens, there was detailed coverage of a doghouse getting struck by lightning just outside St. John's. But the event in St. Anthony, important as it was to so many people, was not mentioned.

Ten days after the rally in St. Anthony, there was still no sign of cod. On June 26, Richard Cashin and I attended a meeting in the premier's boardroom with Premier Clyde Wells, John Crosbie, and several senior government officials and industry representatives.

Crosbie told the meeting: "We're contemplating a moratorium (on northern cod) for several years."

It was only a matter of when the axe would fall.

July 2, 1992 was the worst day of our lives. That announcement tore the guts out of everything in Newfoundland.
— Will Reid, retired plant worker, FFAW vice-president and staff representative

If we didn't have the union when they closed the fishery, we'd have starved to death.
— Eric Miller, fish harvester, Grand Bank

The moratorium did a lot of damage to outport Newfoundland. A lot of dying communities, a lot of plants gone, a wicked amount of talent gone from the province.
— Andy Careen, fish harvester, Point Lance

Communities just closed down. It was terrible, terrible, terrible. What the union did getting through that, getting money for people, that was a tremendous help.
— Loomis Way, FFAW inshore executive board member, Green Island Cove

The moratorium—I still have trouble talking about it. A lot of people went through an awful hard time. A lot of people left the community—a lot of young people. Off the fire department, off the recreation committee—a big loss to the community.
— Tony Doyle, FFAW inshore vice-president

"A Famine of Biblical Scale: A Great Destruction"

*The moratorium, the devastation—there's no way
to explain it—the impact on families, trying to feed your kids ...*
— Karen Caines, plant worker, OCI Fortune

As the magnitude of the catastrophe in the northern cod stocks became clear, it was equally obvious that those who lost their jobs would need a source of income. In his autobiography, John Crosbie, the fisheries and oceans minister, explained the box in which he found himself: "Given the overall financial position of the government and the frightening dimensions of the deficit, I was unable to convince my colleagues that the amount of assistance they were prepared to approve was woefully inadequate from a political or human point of view. With a meagre assistance package in hand, I set off for Newfoundland for the 1992 Canada Day weekend."

When Crosbie showed up for what would normally be a routine appearance at the Canada Day ceremonies in Bay Bulls, hundreds of people were on the wharf and surrounding area, instead of the few dozen normally expected.

"The CBC vehicles were a sure sign I was in for a rough time,"

Crosbie said. A rough time he certainly got. He and other scheduled speakers addressed the crowd from the deck of a Coast Guard vessel. The assembled crowd—mostly inshore harvesters from the Southern Shore—were in no mood to listen to the local mayor and others talk about Canada Day, and they became increasingly restless as the speakers gave their remarks.

"Shut up," one man shouted during one of the speeches. "We want to hear Crosbie."

Eventually Crosbie came to the microphone and got a going-over from the crowd when he made his remarks. Harvesters yelled at him, and I had a go at him with the help of a bullhorn provided by union staff rep Kevin Carroll. On his way up the hill at the end of this set-to, Crosbie, surrounded by protestors, got into a heated exchange that included his famous retort: "I didn't take the fish out of the goddamn water."

"It was clear from the scene in Bay Bulls that I could expect the worst when I made my announcement in St. John's the next day," Crosbie recalled. "And that's what I got. A huge crowd waited in the lobby of the Radisson Hotel."

The Radisson Hotel was the setting for Crosbie's press conference on the evening of July 2, 1992, when he announced the unthinkable: the great northern cod stock would be closed for a minimum of two years.

Someone in a position of authority had decided that it would be a good idea to have Crosbie deliver the bad news in a room that was closed to the public, while TV monitors were set up in a large adjacent ballroom for public viewing of the announcement.

As then-FFAW communications director Lana Payne—now national secretary-treasurer of Unifor—recalled, "Complete quiet came over the room." It didn't stay quiet for long.

When Crosbie announced that $225 a week compensation would be paid to those who lost their jobs, all hell broke loose. Harvesters charged the doors of the room where the press conference was taking place, while TV monitors showed security staff frantically jamming chairs into the crash bars inside the doors to keep the protestors at bay.

To his credit, Crosbie refused a suggestion from security staff to escape the crowd through the adjacent kitchen, insisting he was going to leave by the same door he had entered. But he needed a sizable escort of police officers, who had their hands full with the angry crowd. Crosbie was jeered mercilessly as he walked through the hotel lobby.

I've been through some wild situations over the years, but I don't think I've seen anything quite as dramatic as the scene at that hotel. Or as effective.

"The pandemonium in St. John's was broadcast across the country," Crosbie recalled. "The televised outrage of Newfoundland fishermen had a profound effect on my colleagues in Ottawa. Within two weeks I was authorized to return to Newfoundland and announced the NCARP program."

It was the dramatic visual image of a powerful federal Cabinet minister requiring a heavy police escort to walk through an angry, shouting, potentially violent crowd that moved the dial in Ottawa. But Crosbie needed someone with whom to work to quickly design a workable support program, and that's where the union came in.

Richard Cashin and I, along with other union staff and officers, were at the hotel for the momentous announcement, and we knew our members expected the union to step up. At a press conference

Richard Cashin speaks to reporters in St. John's prior to joining a protest at sea which brought international attention to the issue of foreign overfishing.

the following day, Cashin announced: "The union has rejected out of hand the government's compensation package. They have no right to set arbitrary figures. If they want to make this moratorium work, they have to have an adequate compensation package."

As usual in times of emergency, we brought our elected leadership together on short notice to debate what was needed. The prevailing view was that weekly compensation should at least match the level people received from UI. There was also a requirement for support for boat owners whose investment in their enterprises had been jeopardized by the closure of the fishery.

On July 8, less than a week after Crosbie's announcement, the union bought half an hour of prime time on local television station NTV so that Cashin could give a comprehensive response to the announcement directly to union members, as well as to the general public.

"If we lie down and take what is given to us with cap in hand," Cashin said, "we will have done a disservice not only to ourselves but to the society of which the fishery is such a critical part. Therefore we have advised both levels of government that if we are unable to negotiate a better arrangement both as to the principles of the moratorium, as well as the financial part, we will have to take measures to thwart what has been imposed on us."

The political stakes were high, and Crosbie knew it. He also knew that the union would be a powerful opponent if he couldn't work something out, so he instructed his top officials to meet with the union leadership to hear our views on what would be needed and to try to negotiate an acceptable program.

Cashin and I were in meetings in Ottawa almost continuously over the next several days. The powder keg that was on national display at the Radisson Hotel on July 2 had not been defused, and the feds knew they needed answers fast.

On July 16—an exceptionally short time frame for an Ottawa bureaucracy that routinely took forever to design programs of far less cost, significance, and complexity than this one—Crosbie advised us in a meeting that he had received Cabinet approval to raise the weekly compensation to 95 per cent of each eligible individual's average UI benefits over the past several years, with a minimum rate of $225 and a maximum of $406 a week. On the matter of eligibility rules, he told us: "We just want to be sensible." The changes to the program would dramatically increase the amount of money in people's pockets and in circulation in the rural economy.

On behalf of the federal government, Crosbie made a public announcement of the Northern Cod Adjustment and Recovery Program (NCARP) the following day. The pressure-cooker atmosphere of the Radisson Hotel and the immediate follow-up from the union had produced in record time a program estimated to cost $920 million over two years. In addition to income replacement, program elements included an early retirement program as well as retraining opportunities and a bare-bones licence-buyback scheme.

The announcement eased the pressure considerably, but many details still had to be resolved, and a massive communications challenge had to be met. We also had to contend with a provincial government with a tendency to make policy pronouncements that were detrimental to the people affected without consulting their union.

A program known as Program for Older Worker Adjustment (POWA) was triggered from time to time by a provincial government and Ottawa when a particular industry experienced major job loss. The program was traditionally cost-shared 70 per cent by Ottawa and 30 per cent by the affected province, and applied to workers aged 55 to 65. Because of the magnitude of the fisheries crisis, the union had pushed to have the age eligibility expanded to also include workers aged 50 to 54. The federal government had indicated a willingness to examine the idea, but the provincial government adamantly refused to consider anyone below 55. The outcome was that those aged 50 to 54 were eligible for only the federal share, which was such a meagre amount that for most it was not a viable option.

There was also the matter of clawback from NCARP benefits of any fishing income earned from fishing species other than cod. Even though the weekly cheques were being funded entirely by the federal government, Premier Clyde Wells adamantly refused to support the exclusion of fishing income from clawback provisions. Since he didn't talk to the union about these matters, he missed the point that most alternative fishing possibilities were marginal propositions at best, and a clawback of gross earnings from income support payments meant that harvesters would lose money by fishing these species, leaving them with no choice in many cases but to stay ashore when they might have engaged in productive work.

Another issue involved clawback from early retirement income for anyone who could find work here and there. The union favoured a policy of no clawback, and DFO was open to this, but the so-called central agencies in Ottawa (Treasury Board, Department of Finance, Privy Council, etc.) wanted clawback, and when the provincial government supported that position, it became inevitable.

It didn't escape our attention that a provincial government which was regularly demanding a greater share of jurisdiction over the fishery was falling well short of the standard set by the national government in terms of engaging and paying attention to the organization representing the people whose lives had been thrown into disarray. We were trying to make the best of an unbelievably challenging situation; unfortunately, the Wells government did not consult with the union before announcing its position on the clawback issues.

Dealing with Ottawa was no bargain. Fortunately for us, DFO was the lead department on NCARP, and Crosbie saw to it that we had a reasonably positive working relationship with top DFO officials, who were smart enough to realize that it was in their interest to work out mutually acceptable solutions where possible.

More difficult to resolve were those aspects of the program which fell under the authority of Treasury Board, Human Resources Development, or other federal departments which lacked even a basic understanding of the fishery or the province. To illustrate this point, I need look no further than a meeting we held with Human Resources Development officials at which a private consultant engaged by the department explained their approach to a six-week course for displaced fishery workers by saying that they would be using "the same approach we used in Brazil working with peasants."

Whether their approach was of any value to Brazilian peasants, I can't really say, although I have my doubts. But we knew that with the level of turmoil the moratorium had caused, it would make matters worse to have someone with that mindset in charge of explaining the program to moratorium victims. We prepared a detailed proposal which we presented in Ottawa to representatives of several government departments.

I was fascinated at how these meetings took place. No one shook hands, no one introduced themselves. People just came in, apparently from various departments and agencies, sat down and listened to our presentation. Few asked any questions. Then they got up and left.

Fundamentally, our message was that to undertake the massive communication program that was required, we needed people who knew and understood the province, the fishery, and the people. Those who had lost their livelihoods because of the moratorium had tough choices, and they needed answers from someone they could trust to make informed decisions. The last thing they needed was people acting as if they were talking to Brazilian peasants.

We argued that normal federal adjustment programs and services were not suited to a situation of the scale and complexity of the catastrophe we faced. As it happened, we had about 60 union members who had already received three weeks' training under the CAW "local union discussion leader" (LUDL) program, an effective leadership dynamics course which equips rank-and-file union members with public speaking skills and the confidence to make presentations and facilitate discussions. We made the case that these members, supplemented by others who would receive similar training, would be best suited to travel to the affected communities to conduct information workshops, including individual needs assessment surveys, and explain moratorium programs and options.

The federal government eventually bought our idea and agreed to fund the project. The union deployed 115 trained discussion leaders to conduct 1,300 meetings involving 20,000 NCARP recipients within a seven-week time frame. It was a massive undertaking.

The drastic decline in fish stocks was not limited to northern cod. In November 1992, DFO scientists recommended severe cuts in several groundfish quotas, including cod in the Gulf of St. Lawrence and in 3Ps off the south coast of Newfoundland. These stocks were not as large as northern cod but were as important to the fish harvesters and plant workers who lived in adjacent communities.

The union proposed that these fisheries be closed as well and that affected people be covered by a package equivalent to NCARP. Ottawa opted for drastic quota reductions, not a moratorium, and announced a temporary assistance program that provided little for anyone.

By this time, there had been significant changes in critical government positions. An election was due in the fall of 1993, and Kim Campbell had replaced Brian Mulroney as Canadian prime minister. A number of prominent Cabinet ministers—John Crosbie among them—had signalled that they would not be running in the upcoming election. To prepare for the election, Campbell replaced some of these political warhorses. Crosbie was succeeded as fisheries minister by Ross Reid, the MP for St. John's East.

It was not only at the federal Cabinet level that a changing of the guard took place. After 22 pressure-packed years as president of FFAW, Cashin announced in May 1993 that he would be stepping down. A special mini-convention involving the union's executive board and what were then three councils—inshore, deep-sea, and industrial/retail—was convened to elect a replacement for the 18 months or so remaining in Cashin's term of office. I was elected to replace Cashin, and Reg Anstey, who had been serving as director of the industrial/retail division, moved up to my former position of secretary-treasurer. Not quite a year into the moratorium was, to say the least, an extremely challenging time for Anstey and me to take on these positions.

In the spring of 1994, the NCARP income support was about to expire, but the condition of fish stocks had worsened. Not only did the northern cod moratorium turn out to last far longer than the initial two-year NCARP program, but the resource collapse had also spread to other areas and other groundfish species. The federal government eventually closed directed fishing for 25 groundfish stocks throughout Atlantic Canada.

At the time NCARP was due to expire, Jean Chrétien and the Liberals had taken power in Ottawa. They were overwhelmed—obsessed might be a better word—by the size of the federal deficit and debt, and had no appetite for new spending initiatives. But the Atlantic fishery was in shambles, and they would have had even less appetite for a repeat of what Crosbie had endured two years earlier. The new DFO minister was Newfoundland MP Brian Tobin who was astute enough to realize that his political standing in the province depended on his ability to secure funding for ongoing fisheries income support and adjustment. He eventually succeeded in squeezing $1.9 billion out of Treasury Board to fund The Atlantic Groundfish Strategy (TAGS), the successor program to NCARP which also covered those affected by the closure of fisheries in other areas, including the south coast of Newfoundland, the Scotia Shelf, and the Gulf of St. Lawrence. This included eligible fishery workers from all five eastern provinces.

When TAGS was announced, government emphasized adjustment out of the fishery rather than income support to allow people to remain in the fishery. As a result, there was a significant change in the administration of the new program. Human Resources Development replaced DFO as the department in charge, which was a setback in that the people who ran the program had no basic understanding of the fishery or its significance to the communities and regions that had been devastated by the resource collapse.

Co-operation at the regional level of Human Resources Development was reasonable (with some exceptions), but those in charge of the program in Ottawa were obsessed with numbers, as in how many people they could persuade or browbeat into leaving the fishery.

"The moratorium was the most difficult period in my time with the union," Anstey recounted years later. "It was demoralizing. You could see people slipping into poverty. We went from making progress to trying to find a way for people to survive."

One of the toughest challenges was dealing with the patronizing attitude of some charged with implementing government adjustment programs. Nowhere did this attitude manifest itself more than in a six-week course called "Improving Our Odds." This course may have improved the odds of profitability for the private colleges that delivered it but it did precious little to help those who'd lost their livelihood to the moratorium and were trying to figure out how they were going to rebuild their lives.

Trudy Byrne, a plant worker from St. Anthony who suddenly found herself with no job to help raise her newborn child, recalled an Improving Our Odds instructor "pretending to wash an elephant. It was an embarrassment." A handbook prepared for the course included a cartoon of a codfish driving a tractor and a suggestion that students "pretend you're a sea urchin." How this program would help anyone deal effectively with their devastating circumstances was a mystery to most.

What was clear was that the TAGS program was running seriously over budget. The program was designed to support 26,000 affected people, but 40,000 qualified for support. As a *Globe and Mail* columnist quipped, "Not only couldn't the feds count the fish, they couldn't count the fishermen."

Compounding the problem were steep increases in fishing licence fees and a major attack by the federal government on what was then called the Unemployment Insurance program (since changed to Employment Insurance, although you would have thought that it was unemployment from which people sought protection, not employment). August 1995 brought widespread rumours that TAGS income support payments would be significantly reduced. The union organized simultaneous demonstrations in Harbour Grace, Bonavista, Marystown, Burgeo, Englee, St. Anthony, and Baie Verte to send a clear message to Ottawa that there was no room to cut weekly benefits. About 1,500 people attended the Harbour Grace rally alone. This gave me lots of ammunition when I met in Ottawa the following week with fisheries minister Brian Tobin and human resources minister Lloyd Axworthy, who eventually thought better of their intentions and left the weekly benefit rates untouched. Once again, the union's powerful intervention, strongly supported by the membership, was critical to maintaining the flow of money to members' pockets and into the rural economy.

I've touched on some of the perverse aspects of the NCARP and TAGS program, but I would be remiss not to mention some of the program elements that had a more positive impact. A few months before he left office, Crosbie had asked Cashin to head up the Task Force on Incomes and Adjustment in the Atlantic Fishery to advise the federal government on a strategy to deal with the devastating impact of the collapse in groundfish stocks.

The final report of the task force didn't mince words. "We are dealing here with a famine of biblical scale—a great destruction," it stated. "The social and economic consequences of this great destruction are a challenge to be met and a burden to be borne by the nation, not just those who are its victims."

In addition to its powerful description of the circumstances created by the crisis, the task force made practical recommendations. Its extremely helpful recommendations on improvements to the UI program are detailed in Chapter 12. It also proposed the setting up of regional boards to administer a more effective licence buyout program than the inadequate offerings of the NCARP program. This new program accounted for an individual applicant's historic income in the fishery, rather than the lowest-common-denominator approach offered by NCARP. The Liberal government, which inherited the task force report, accepted this advice, and significantly higher payments were possible under the TAGS (and later post-TAGS) programs than had been available under NCARP.

The union also succeeded in building on an earlier pilot project to fund 15 adult education centres in various locations around the province, enabling people to upgrade their education to high school equivalent in familiar, non-threatening surroundings—community halls and the like. I was particularly struck by the observation of a former fish plant worker in St. John's who said this program allowed him to read a newspaper for the first time in his life.

These centres were among the initiatives funded through Fishermen's Training Incorporated, an entity established by the union in conjunction with Human Resources Development and various provincial agencies for the purpose of providing training and upgrading opportunities for fish harvesters and fish plant workers. Among these opportunities was the creation of a group that became known as Folk of the Sea, an idea brought forward by a group of harvesters. Overseen by a small committee of harvesters and with the help of union support staff, more than 90 fishery workers from around the province came together, as the group's director, Ged Blackmore, put it, "to sing, play, dance, recite, and tell the story of their proud heritage. Perhaps at no time in their recent history had it been more important for the choir members to share the precious bounty of our music and narrative with the people of the province and country."

Choir members learned their songs from tapes and practiced in small groups on a regional basis. The full group assembled for the first time at the St. John's Arts and Culture Centre the day before their first public performance. What followed was a succession of sold-out performances around the province, as well as at the National Arts Centre in Ottawa and the Roy Thomson Hall in Toronto. In 1997, Folk of the Sea played for Her Majesty, Queen Elizabeth II, at the Cabot 500 Celebration in Bonavista.

Blackmore described the Folk of the Sea phenomenon as "a

moment in time," but it was an important moment of pride and hope amidst the gloom and doom of the moratorium years.

Meanwhile, work continued on programs to assist those dislocated by the moratorium. An early retirement option remained in place under the TAGS program for those who qualified. A retraining program also enabled former fishery workers to train for other sectors, although in smaller communities there was no obvious answer to the question, "Retraining for what?" The outcome in some areas was an increase in the number of qualified hairdressers, while the population was shrinking significantly, which presumably meant that a lot less hair needed to be dressed. The program also trained people in health care and long-distance trucking, to name several areas, which enabled people to move on productively with their lives.

A new entity created under the auspices of the union was Deepsea Training Inc. (DTI), a coordinating body with a mandate to provide training opportunities and seek employment options for the hundreds of trawlermen who lost their jobs because of the moratorium. Offshore oil tankers proved to be an attractive destination for a large number of these men, and DTI coordinated the required training with the offshore oil industry and the training institutions.

A common element of these programs—FTI, DTI, the education centres, and other initiatives—was the union's fundamental belief that the affected people and their union should be involved in the coordination and delivery of adjustment programming.

TAGS was initially scheduled to be a five-year program, from 1994 to 1999, but by 1997 there were strong rumblings out of Ottawa that funds would run out after the fourth year and the program would end a year earlier than promised.

Part of the boisterous crowd of union members that protested at the Canada Revenue Agency's regional headquarters in St. John's on April 29–30, 1997. Like the Bull Arm protest, this was a fightback against Ottawa's planned elimination of the final year of the TAGS program.

During the federal election campaign in 1997, Prime Minister Chrétien was scheduled to visit the province for an event at the Bull Arm offshore fabrication site. For us—to the great (and understandable) consternation of our union colleagues in the building trades—this presented an opportunity to make a high-profile pitch to the feds to honour their original five-year commitment.

I contacted CAW national president Buzz Hargrove to ask him to join us in a demonstration we planned to coincide with Chrétien's visit. I didn't have to ask twice. As we were driving from St. John's to Bull Arm on a miserable morning, I said, "Buzz, there's no instruction manual available to tell us how to deal with what we'll be facing today." Hargrove, no stranger to controversy or militant trade unionism, agreed. When we arrived, more than 500 union members were waiting in a heavy downpour.

When a media bus arrived on the scene, our members blocked access to the road to the Bull Arm site. We found out that buses containing dignitaries—including the prime minister and the premier—had pulled into a parking lot a few miles back to await developments. In response to a request from the RCMP to allow the buses to pass, I said that for this to happen, the prime minister needed to take a few minutes to speak to the crowd and to listen to our demands. We had a bullhorn on hand for just that purpose. Who knows? Maybe it was the same one I had used to holler at John Crosbie five years earlier on the wharf in Bay Bulls.

I'm not sure who made the decision, but the premier and prime minister eventually decided not to speak to the protestors or to try to get past the crowd. A national news media report later described this as the only significant protest in an otherwise uneventful election campaign that returned the Chrétien government for another four-year term.

We later obtained an internal Human Resources Development memo which showed that the department had tried to bury the report "Incremental Net Cost of TAGS" and had instructed staff to destroy any copies because "the department does not agree with all the findings." The report, which had been prepared by consultants for the department, reported that "the true costs to government are substantially lower (than the reported costs)" when all factors—including federal and provincial taxes paid out of TAGS support payments, reduced dependence on other programs such as UI and social assistance—were taken into account.

But in late 1997, the prime minister's office circulated a memo to aides and Liberal MPs advising that there would be no replacement for TAGS after its new expiry date of May 1998. The five eastern premiers called for a post-TAGS program, and an All-Party Committee of the House of Commons recommended reinstating the fifth year of the program. A consultant hired by Human Resources Development to examine the situation warned that "many individuals will be in dire circumstances unless financial support is continued."

But as the May 15, 1998, termination date drew closer, we knew we needed more than committee reports and press releases. Once again, it was time for the union to step up.

Following a meeting with our executive board, I issued a press release on April 23, 1998, asking members and supporters to gather at a shopping mall parking lot in the early morning of April 29. "We urge people to bring campers and sleeping bags because this might take a while," I told the media.

It was widely assumed we would be holding our protest at the DFO regional headquarters in White Hills, in the east end of St. John's. That was reinforced when two of our staff reps, Ben Baker and John Boland, went to the DFO building the evening before the scheduled protest and asked the security guard about the best spot to locate a few portable toilets. The decoy was a success. The focus of the authorities was on the DFO building, to the point that staff were told not to report for work.

Bearing in mind the April 30 deadline (the following day) for income tax returns, we targeted the regional Revenue Canada office for our protest. The media lapped it up. People brought their sleeping bags and many stayed overnight at a local Lions club, where they were dry, warm, and fed by hard-working union staff members and volunteers. Comfort was at a premium, but the Revenue Canada office was shut down for two days right at the tax return deadline, and the event received national media attention. News reports estimated that 1,000 union members participated. When the FFAW holds a rally or demonstration, it's all hands on deck. On this occasion, that included Hemi Mitic, an assistant to Hargrove, who came down to help us out.

Fred Mifflin, a Newfoundland MP who by then was minister of fisheries and oceans, said of the Revenue Canada protest: "The demonstration has been very helpful to me. It's been helpful in that it's been a peaceful demonstration and it has focused a need for attention."

Like John Crosbie six years earlier, Mifflin had been struggling to get an adequate response from his Cabinet colleagues, and the political pressure strengthened his hand.

It was clear that the fightbacks over the years—from the original potent backlash on the night of Crosbie's moratorium announcement to the Bull Arm demonstration to the shutdown of the Revenue Canada headquarters—had put us on the political radar in Ottawa as a force to be reckoned with.

Notwithstanding the memo at the end of 1997 indicating that there would be no replacement or successor program for TAGS, it was clear that the fightback had had an impact and that the federal government was ready to fund some form of post-TAGS program. But our information was that they were working on a budget in the range of $500 million, which would not have been enough to achieve what needed to be done.

Shortly after the Revenue Canada protest—with no fanfare or media attention—I joined Premier Tobin along with Mifflin's senior political advisor Max Short (the union's former inshore director) in a conference call with Eddie Goldenberg, the prime minister's closest and most trusted political advisor, to press the case for post-TAGS funding at a higher level than the $500 million figure.

Mifflin was scheduled to make an announcement of the post-TAGS program on June 19, 1998. The night before the announcement, Anstey and I, along with a few provincial officials, were briefed on the proposed program by federal officials who had come from Ottawa for the unveiling. Anstey and I lambasted the officials about some of the details of the announcement which to our mind did not use the available money wisely. "We drilled them," Anstey understated. We found out later that federal officials worked late into the night rewriting some of the details of the plan to make it more acceptable.

What Mifflin announced the following day was a $760 million program for Atlantic Canada, including Quebec. This included $30 million that remained in the TAGS budget, plus $730 million in new funding. About $200 million was spent on "final cash payments," amounting to up to $9,000 apiece paid in two installments to about 22,000 people still on the TAGS rolls. The program also included funding for early retirement for older workers, a licence-buyout program and short-term job creation.

It wasn't perfect, but it helped many people. The licence retirement component funded the buyout of more than 1,600 groundfish licences—three times the number that had been bought out under the TAGS program. Most of these licences were retired in Newfoundland and Labrador—an important development in our struggle to find new fishing opportunities for our members.

Once again, events bore out the union's unofficial motto: Fighting back makes a difference.

Ken Carew was a DFO economist and policy analyst who worked extensively on these programs. "The union was vital to it all," he said. "We couldn't have done it without the union. We didn't always agree by any means, but it was important to have their input on what might fly. The union was certainly more important to getting through it than the provincial government or any of the other federal departments."

The NCARP, TAGS, and post-TAGS years were extremely challenging. Families experienced hardship and communities declined. But the changes in the oceans weren't all negative, by any means. As discussed in a later chapter, by the time these adjustment programs had run their course, new fishing opportunities were bringing hope back to coastal communities.

Troubled Waters: The Onslaught of the Foreign Fleets

Canada will pay!

— EU Head of Delegation as he stormed out of special NAFO meeting in 1995

Nature endowed Newfoundland and Labrador with phenomenal fish and shellfish resources off our coast, but our majestic natural environment includes a fundamental weakness that has bedeviled responsible fisheries management for decades. Of all the significant fishing regions of the world, our continental shelf is one of the few that extends beyond 200 miles from shore. Because the continental shelf of most fishing countries lies entirely within 200 miles from land, 200 miles became the internationally accepted yardstick for the extension of national fisheries jurisdiction, adopted by many countries—including Canada—in the 1970s and 1980s in particular.

International factory-freezer trawler fleets began assaulting our fish stocks in the mid-20th century. An international regional fisheries management organization, the International Commission for the Northwest Atlantic Fishery (ICNAF) was established in 1949, supposedly to manage fish stocks in a sustainable way.

But as Dr. Leslie Harris pointed out in his study of the northern cod stock, "As an agency of conservation, ICNAF was a total failure." The unregulated harvest of northern cod peaked at an unsustainable 810,000 tonnes in 1968. The traditional inshore catch in Newfoundland and Labrador collapsed, from a range of 200,000 to 250,000 tonnes annually in the early 1900s to about 35,000 tonnes by 1974.

"The social and economic impact of this decline was enormous as tens of thousands of people abandoned the fishery as a means of livelihood and many communities were deserted," Harris reported.

So it was understandable that optimism accompanied the declaration by the Government of Canada in 1976 that, effective the following year, the Canadian Exclusive Economic Zone for fishing would extend to 200 miles from shore, giving Canada jurisdiction over a vast fishing zone.

Unfortunately, the hope was not tempered, as it should have been, by a sober appraisal of the strengths and weaknesses of the new regime and a recognition of the enormous vulnerability created by the Achilles heel of Canada's extended jurisdiction—the transboundary nature of so many important fish stocks.

The Grand Banks of Newfoundland are historically among the richest fishing grounds in the world. Most of the area which makes up the Grand Banks lies within Canada's 200-mile limit, but two areas known as the nose and tail of the Grand Banks jut out beyond 200 miles. Cod, flatfish, and other groundfish, oblivious to the finer points of international law, migrate back and forth across the imaginary line delineating the outer limit of Canada's area of authority. It is in these two areas that the bulk of the damage was done to some of our most important fish stocks. A separate fishing area known as the Flemish Cap lies entirely outside the Canadian zone. Scientists believe most Flemish Cap stocks are separate from stocks on the Grand Banks and northeast coast of Newfoundland and Labrador, and they are managed accordingly.

With extension of jurisdiction came the termination of ICNAF—to the grief of nobody—and its replacement by a new organization, the Northwest Atlantic Fisheries Organization (NAFO), which started its life in an atmosphere of hope, but which later became just as reviled, and ineffective, as ICNAF had been. A particularly glaring flaw in the new NAFO Constitution was the "objection procedure"—"objectionable procedure" would have been a more fitting description—whereby any NAFO member could object to a particular decision, and by so doing would not be bound by the terms of that decision. It was equivalent to allowing motorists to object to posted highway speed limits and set their own individual limits.

Until 1986, the European Economic Community (EEC, later European Union) was a reasonably responsible NAFO citizen. They participated in the decision-making processes of the organization and fished within the quotas that NAFO had assigned them.

But in 1986, Spain and Portugal became part of the EEC. A condition of their joining the EEC was that they were excluded from fishing in European waters for the first 10 years. Their huge factory trawler fleets were a driving force of the economy of coastal regions of both countries. Both had a history of fishing off the coast of Newfoundland and Labrador dating back centuries. The vulnerable stocks on the nose and tail of the Grand Banks presented massive fishing opportunities for them and solved a political headache for the EEC. The consequences for our members would prove devastating.

The 1986 NAFO annual meeting in Havana, Cuba, marked a major turning point which showed just how serious a threat the new political configuration in Europe posed to the people and communities on the Newfoundland and Labrador coast.

As scientific advice was presented stock by stock at that meeting, the EEC—through their obnoxious head of delegation, a bureaucrat from Brussels—objected to the scientific advice and pressed for higher TAC. When they were outvoted by the majority of NAFO member countries, the Europeans simply objected to each TAC and to their quota share, and unilaterally set much higher quotas for themselves.

By the fall of 1986, it was clear that it was only a matter of time until we would feel the shocking consequences that were described in the previous chapter.

As cod and various flatfish stocks took a relentless pounding, and Newfoundland and Labrador plant closures followed, political pressure mounted on the federal government, which under the Terms of Union between Newfoundland and Canada was responsible for management of the fishery.

For FFAW members, the future was grim unless the foreign fleets could be brought under control, so we seized all opportunities to highlight the issue. In 1990, NAFO's annual meeting was being held in Dartmouth, Nova Scotia, while the Canadian Autoworkers Union's constitutional convention was taking place across the bridge in Halifax. At our request, the CAW arranged buses to transport hundreds of delegates to stage a rambunctious protest outside the NAFO meeting site.

CAW also funded the creation of a video entitled "Troubled Waters," which depicted the plight of the people, families, and communities that were in serious jeopardy from the unrestrained foreign overfishing. I presented the video to delegates attending the 1993 NAFO annual meeting, as well as at public meetings in several major Canadian cities. We met with foreign government representatives, environmental groups, and unions representing Spanish and Portuguese fish harvesters. We attended meetings sponsored by the United Nations in New York to deal with protection of straddling and highly migratory fish stocks. A union delegation picketed European embassies and the EEC headquarters in Ottawa.

And the assault on the fish stocks continued.

In March 1992, FFAW executive board members met with Prime Minister Brian Mulroney and Fisheries Minister John Crosbie to highlight the magnitude of the problem. They made sympathetic comments, but as Michael Harris points out in *Lament for an Ocean*, "Mulroney was not inclined to use force."

We had to find a way to ramp up the pressure. At meetings with Newfoundland fish company representatives, we proposed a protest at sea to bring as much national and international media attention to the crisis as possible.

National president Bob White and other CAW leaders joined us in St. John's as we bused in thousands of our members from around the province. People came from as far away as Labrador. The crowd jammed the large ballroom of the Delta Hotel and spilled over into the lobby and the adjacent streets. The media estimated the turnout at 15,000.

After a brief round of speeches in the hotel ballroom, thousands of people marched to the site on the waterfront where seven deep-sea fishing vessels of various sizes were ready to head to sea. Spectators lined both sides of the road along the waterfront, while hundreds looked on from each floor of an adjacent seven-storey parking garage, as well as from various other vantage points around and overlooking the harbour.

Lana Payne, who had become the union's communications officer only a few months earlier, was our chief contact with the news media. Not only did national and international media along with local news agencies cover the event in St. John's, many boarded the fishing vessels for the voyage beyond the 200-mile limit.

At the time, there were no cellphones or electronic hookups. Journalists used ship-to-shore radio—as did Newfoundland comedian Rick Mercer, who was on board one of the vessels and did one of his earliest rants from the edge of the Grand Banks.

"The protest at sea was a huge task," Payne recalled years later. "The TV reporters threw their film in a basket, which was picked up by helicopter (donated for the purpose by local helicopter proprietor Craig Dobbin) and brought to St. John's."

The union office on the St. John's waterfront was open all week for national and international journalists. For the first time, the international press was given the Canadian side of the story from those whose livelihoods were directly at stake—the fish harvesters and fish plant workers who made their living from the stocks that were being decimated by foreign fleets.

The event generated a massive amount of publicity, locally, nationally, and internationally. The British Broadcasting Corporation's reporter assigned to St. John's for the event did a five-minute report that was broadcast to a worldwide audience of 27 million people, just one of the countless media reports sent around the world. It put the pending disaster in our fishery on the national and international stage. But even as a dory attached to a buoy bearing the national and provincial flags was launched outside the 200-mile limit, symbolically claiming jurisdiction over the nose and tail of the Grand Banks for the people of Newfoundland and Labrador, 99 foreign factory ships were fishing nearby. It would be barely three months later that John Crosbie announced the closure of the northern cod fishery.

The magnitude of the European overfishing was staggering. From 1988 to 1994, the EU had NAFO quotas totalling 164,000 tonnes of various species of groundfish. The catch reported by European captains in that time frame—mainly cod, turbot, and species of flounder—was 851,600 tonnes. Canadian enforcement officials were convinced the landings were being under-reported. Applying typical daily catch rates to the number of vessel-days at sea observed by Canadian patrol vessels, they estimated total EU landings in this period at 1,362,600 tonnes.

In other words, Europeans admitted catching five times as much fish as their quotas, while the Canadian fisheries officers calculated that it was more like eight times as much. Either way, it was an onslaught of epic proportions against which no fish stock had a chance.

After the moratorium was announced, even the Europeans agreed to discontinue directed fishing for northern cod, but they quickly found a substitute in Greenland halibut, known to local fish harvesters as turbot, a flatfish historically fished primarily inshore in gillnets. Changing environmental conditions in the early 1990s pushed more turbot than normal out on the nose and tail of the Grand Banks, where the stocks were pounded mercilessly by the Spanish and Portuguese fleets in particular.

Because turbot did not come under NAFO quota management until 1994, foreign fleets were free to fish as much of the species as they liked outside the 200-mile limit. In February 1994, Canadian scientists reported that the turbot stock off the east coast of Newfoundland and Labrador had dropped by two-thirds from the biomass just three years earlier.

A crowd waits in St. John's harbour in April 1995 for the arrival under arrest by Canadian authorities of the Spanish factory-freezer trawler *Estai*.

This set the stage for a dramatic confrontation at a special NAFO meeting early in 1995. Decisions in NAFO are made by a majority vote among NAFO member countries. When a stock comes under NAFO quota management and is allocated to member countries for the first time, historical fishing has traditionally been a significant consideration. Europeans, who had the highest turbot catches in the immediately preceding years, proposed a quota-sharing arrangement that gave them the lion's share of the TAC. Arguing the principle of adjacency and its primary interest as the coastal state, Canada scrambled to get the support of enough NAFO member countries for an alternative sharing arrangement which included significantly more for Canada, much less for the Europeans than they had been demanding, and sweeteners for Russia and Japan to lever their votes.

After much arm-twisting by both Canadian and European negotiators, the NAFO Fisheries Commission accepted the Canadian proposal by a one-vote margin, with several countries abstaining.

When the result of the vote was announced, the head of delegation for the EU, a Spaniard, leaped out of his chair, pointed his finger dramatically at DFO deputy minister Bill Rowat, the head of the Canadian delegation, shouted "Canada will pay," and stormed out of the meeting.

The EU's official response was no surprise. They formally objected to the decision and unilaterally announced that they would be fishing a much higher amount than the quota that had been voted on.

The union, along with others in Newfoundland and Labrador in the fishing industry, the general public, and the provincial government, demanded that Ottawa take whatever action was necessary to challenge the European fleets. By this time, Max Short, who had worked for the union for 15 years, first as a staff representative and later as inshore director, was a trusted advisor on fisheries and oceans minister Brian Tobin's political staff. Years later, he recalled the pressure-packed political environment: "I told Tobin turbot had to be fixed. Tobin said, 'Crosbie had a go at it, and couldn't get it done—what am I going to do with it?' But after a while Tobin got pissed off. Andre Ouellette [Canada's minister of foreign affairs] was opposed to doing anything. Tobin wrote a letter of resignation. He told me, 'I'm going to see the Prime Minister. When I come back, you and I may not have a job.'"

But Prime Minister Chrétien overruled his foreign affairs minister and sided with Tobin. Short said he was called into the boardroom for a meeting with Tobin, deputy ministers of the respective departments, and other officials. Enforcement officers were given instructions to use force, if necessary, to stop the Spanish and Portuguese vessels.

On March 3, 1995, Foreign Affairs advised the EU that Canada's Governor General had given royal assent to amendments to Canadian fisheries protection legislation making it illegal for Spanish and Portuguese vessels to fish straddling stocks contrary to NAFO conservation rules. Spain dispatched warships.

Canadian fisheries patrol ships stepped up their presence on the nose and tail of the Grand Banks, with the support of Canadian naval vessels. On March 9, they confronted the Spanish trawler *Estai*. The captain disregarded orders to stop fishing, prevented the enforcement officers from boarding the *Estai*, and took off, with three Canadian patrol ships in hot pursuit. Eventually one of the Canadian vessels fired several machine-gun bursts over the bow of the vessel as a warning. Chrétien told the news media that he had personally given the fisheries officers the authority for this action.

The warning shots apparently convinced the *Estai* captain that the game was becoming too dangerous, and he gave up the effort to escape. A Canadian boarding party placed the *Estai* under arrest and escorted her to St. John's to face charge in court. Meanwhile, other Spanish vessels ceased fishing on the nose and tail, steaming out to the Flemish Cap to wait out the situation.

After years of inaction from the federal government against blatant foreign overfishing, the FFAW felt it was important to demonstrate public support for this decisive action. Working with the labour movement and various church and community groups, we organized a rally on the St. John's waterfront to coincide with the *Estai*'s arrival in port.

Not everyone agreed with the action. Premier Clyde Wells told the *Globe and Mail* that he was opposed to the rally and was concerned that an unruly crowd could send the wrong message to members of the international media who would be covering the event. I received several calls from officials in Ottawa fretting about whether the crowd would turn violent.

I didn't have time to worry about any of that. To me, the wrong message would have been sent if a large crowd *hadn't* showed up when the *Estai* arrived. I was willing to take the chance of what would happen when the pirate vessel arrived with thousands of people on the waterfront.

As usual, the union staff, rank-and-file leaders, and activists worked diligently to organize busloads of fisheries workers from around the province. The yellow school buses were lined off near the waterfront, as a crowd estimated at 6,000 hooted and hollered when the *Estai* was escorted to port. A few people pelted the captain and European officials with eggs.

DFO inspectors found evidence of serious fisheries violations aboard the *Estai*, including 25 tonnes of American plaice, a species under moratorium, hidden behind a false bulkhead; two sets of logbooks, the captain's personal log and a fake one for the NAFO authorities; double the proportion of turbot in the catch compared to what the captain had reported to NAFO; and a catch of turbot that was far too small to have spawned even once.

There was no way that catch could have been landed with nets of legal mesh size, but unmistakable evidence of the use of illegal fishing gear was needed. Because the captain had discarded the *Estai*'s net at sea before being arrested, DFO chartered the FPI trawler *Zandvoort*, which located and retrieved the *Estai* net from the ocean floor.

The net was the smoking gun. In a fishery with a minimum mesh size of 130 millimetres, the *Estai* had been fishing with an 87-millimetre liner inside a 118-centimetre net. The combined effect of the two nets, especially when wet and stretched tight, was a barrier from which juvenile fish could not possibly escape. It was a reprehensible piece of fishing gear designed to scoop up everything that came in its path.

"There's nothing getting through that thing besides water," said Overton James, an FFAW member and crew member aboard the *Zandvoort*.

Eventually the *Estai* was released and returned to Spain, and the stage shifted weeks later to a conference on straddling and highly migratory fish stocks at the United Nations in New York City, which I attended as part of the Canadian delegation.

What EU fisheries minister Emma Bonino did not know when she addressed the conference was that Canadian authorities had taken the net to Manhattan, where it sat aboard a barge in the East River, immediately adjacent to the UN headquarters.

"Where is the net?" she said in front of conference delegates. "Who has seen the net?"

Soon the whole world had seen the net. In a brilliant public relations manoeuvre, Brian Tobin held a press conference aboard the barge during a break at the conference. In front of a large gathering of international news media, with the UN headquarters in the background, the sheer size and destructive power of the net was on display for the world to see. Tobin brandished a tiny turbot that fit in the palm of his hand to illustrate the irresponsible nature of the *Estai*'s catch. The pictures and videos of the press conferences made the front pages of newspapers and were highlighted in televised news reports worldwide.

But within a few weeks, the Spanish fleet was back on the Grand Banks fishing turbot. As Michael Harris reports in *Lament for an Ocean*, "On April 16, Easter Sunday, fisheries officers got the order to board and seize other Spanish vessels fishing in the Canadian zone. Although it was never reported, Canada came within 20 minutes of a shooting war with Spain ... The best peace-maker turned out to be the weather."

Eventually there was a negotiated settlement between Canada and the EU which gave the Europeans less turbot than they had been demanding but significantly more than their allocation under the earlier NAFO decision. On the face of it, the agreement gave greater rights to Canadian inspectors, providing for on-board observers on foreign vessels, as well as increased satellite surveillance of vessels fishing in the NAFO regulatory area, but this aspect of the agreement contained significant shortcomings as well—the EU would designate the observers aboard European vessels, and fishing violations would be prosecuted by the flag state of the vessel, not by Canada.

The number of foreign vessels fishing in NAFO waters dropped dramatically thereafter, but this may have had as much to do with poor catch rates as it did with stepped-up enforcement rules. While the events of the "turbot war" are now 25 years old, the vulnerability caused by the straddling nature of fish stocks, along with the objection clause, remains, and NAFO continues to be a source of uncertainty and aggravation for people who depend on our fishery for a living.

In the 2006 federal election campaign, Stephen Harper's Conservatives promised, if elected, to extend Canadian jurisdiction to the edge of the Continental Shelf. Of course, once they won the election, they did no such thing. Over a period of several years, a NAFO working group eventually put together a modified NAFO constitution with rules that, in the estimation of virtually the entire Canadian delegation, me included, was, at best, a modest improvement over the old set of rules. It was certainly no game changer. It was ridiculous for DFO minister Loyola Hearn to claim that the new set of rules was equivalent to extension of jurisdiction and that the Harper government had "fixed NAFO."

The federal minister responsible for fisheries has the ultimate sign-off on Canada's position on controversial issues within NAFO, although the heavy lifting during NAFO meetings is done by government officials. Some federal fisheries ministers have been aggressive and helpful in dealing with this issue, and some have not. I was appalled to hear in the spring of 2019 that Canada's minister of fisheries and oceans had allowed the Canadian offshore fishing industry to negotiate a deal to catch Japanese turbot quota within the Canadian 200-mile limit. This decision set a dangerous precedent by allowing NAFO quota trades to be conducted by the corporate sector instead of by DFO as they had for the first 40 years of NAFO's existence. It also made the Japanese turbot allocation available to offshore corporate interests only, with no consideration for the inshore fleet, which has continually had turbot fishing rights and opportunities reduced and even removed over the years. And it allowed the fishing to be conducted within the Canadian zone, whereas other non-Canadian NAFO allocations had to be fished beyond 200 miles.

NAFO had made poor decisions over the years, but this one could not be blamed on NAFO. The responsibility fell squarely on the shoulders of the minister of fisheries and oceans.

Northern shrimp was a saviour for us. Only for that, there wouldn't be a northern shrimp fleet, or only a very small one

— Ren Genge, shrimp harvester from Anchor Point

I remember the grand re-opening of the shrimp plant in Port Union. The shrimp license was a godsend to us. I didn't think the plant would operate any more

— Bernice Duffett, unit chairperson, Port Union plant

Restoring Hope to Coastal Communities

Access to crab saved enterprises, families and communities. Those first crab permits gave everyone hope

— Tony Doyle, inshore harvester, Bay de Verde

Coastal communities are an essential ingredient of Newfoundland and Labrador's character and identity. The fishery led to the settlement of most of these communities, and the link to that industry is vital to the ongoing vibrancy of these special places. The very survival of these communities has been jeopardized from time to time, never more so than during the demoralizing years of the moratorium on northern cod and other key groundfish stocks.

I described earlier how income support from the NCARP and TAGS programs helped people affected by the fishery closures survive. But a cheque in the mail every few weeks is no substitute for the productivity the people of coastal communities were accustomed to, whether they fished or worked in fish plants. There was also an underlying unease about what would happen when the money ran out, as reports circulated about major overruns on the TAGS budget.

Alternatives to the cod fishery were desperately needed if the link between coastal communities and adjacent fishing grounds was to be maintained. Nature, fortunately, abhors a vacuum, and as the moratorium dragged on, exciting economic opportunities presented themselves. When cod stocks collapsed, one of the consequences was a significant decline in predation of young crab and shrimp, a development that was reinforced by a cold-water regime in the ocean off our coast. Crab and shrimp stocks blossomed. The sharing of that endowment would shape our post-moratorium fishery and province.

To the FFAW and its members, the explosion of these valuable shellfish stocks presented both an opportunity and a challenge. To us it seemed obvious that the primary beneficiaries of this development should be those who lost their livelihoods in the groundfish collapse—or at least as many of them as could reasonably be accommodated. The devil, as they say, was in the details.

Up until 1995, the snow crab fishery in Atlantic Canada had been the preserve of the so-called longliner fleet—decked vessels, mostly between 35 and 65 feet in length, which fished in midshore waters where areas of commercial concentration had been identified. Very little crab had been fished in waters immediately adjacent to shore, and none by small boats. But the changing ecosystem of the mid-1990s opened new doors. Crab was not only being found in much greater abundance than in the past; it was also distributed over a much broader area, including the bays along our coastline.

The crab fishery had started on a very small scale in the late 1960s. Prior to the mid-1980s, only 67 crab fishing vessels were licenced in the province. But as the groundfish stocks declined, pressure mounted to have access to the crab stocks expanded to what became known as the "supplementary" fleet.

Cashin recalled attending a meeting in Twillingate where this was a hot issue: "Jack Troake tore a strip off me, making the case for supplementary crab licenses. Jack had quite an impression on me. I set up a meeting with Eric Dunne [regional head of DFO at the time] which I attended along with a group of fishermen to make the case for supplementary crab licenses."

Their message got through to DFO, and by 1991, the crab fleet had expanded nearly tenfold, with a total of 659 enterprises issued licences. Most of these were in the 35–65-foot range, although a few were just less than 35 feet.

Crab saved many midshore enterprises in Newfoundland and Labrador, and the small-boat fleet understandably wanted to participate in that fishery.

With crab now in reasonable abundance within the fishing range of the less than 35-foot fleet, small boat owner/operators demanded access. There had already been a breakthrough on the west coast, starting in 1992 when union staff representative David Decker worked out an arrangement with the Corner Brook area office of DFO, which for some reason had more autonomy than other area offices, to issue temporary permits to the less than 35-foot enterprises in Bay of Islands, Bay St. George, and later in Bonne Bay.

But the number of small-boat enterprises from the coast of Labrador to Fortune Bay meant that any decision to accommodate these fleets in the crab fishery could not simply be made in area offices. In October 1994, a key meeting took place in St. John's between the full FFAW executive board and fisheries and oceans minister Brian Tobin. Various issues were discussed, including the TAGS program and foreign overfishing. When I introduced the subject of access to crab for small boats, and we had a discussion

A pot full of crab is a welcome sight, especially after the despair of the moratorium years.

around the table, Tobin asked me point-blank what I recommended. With the support of the board, which included two supplementary crab licence holders, I responded that the small-boat sector should have access to crab in their traditional inshore fishing areas.

Additional meetings took place between DFO officials and committees representing the small-boat fleets in various bays in the months leading up to the 1995 fishing season. Jim Baird, one of DFO's senior fisheries management officials in Newfoundland Region at the time, and later the regional director-general, recalled that there was opposition to the idea within DFO, particularly in Ottawa, but we did have a crucial ally in Max Short, who ran Tobin's political office in St. John's and whose influence with Tobin went far beyond the normal clout of a regional political advisor. Max was also well regarded by Pat Chamut, assistant deputy minister of DFO responsible for fisheries management.

"You and Max and [then DFO director of Fisheries Management Wayne] Follett and I worked together on the plan for small boat crab, and Chamut pushed it through," Baird recalled. He noted that the significant number of small-boat licences that were bought out during NCARP, TAGS, and the post-TAGS program was helpful. "It was difficult enough to get the small boat permits approved with 3,000 permits. It would have been a much more difficult row to hoe without the buyout. The bigger the number, the harder it would have been."

The plan that was ultimately adopted in 1995 was a pilot project in which DFO designated inshore areas (bays for the most part) to be assigned 25 one-year permits each for small-boat crab operators. Core licence holders in the respective areas were entitled to apply, with successful bidders determined by means of a draw. Each permit would entitle the holder to land 10,000 pounds of crab, which in that particular year was priced at a record $2.47 a pound. Crab-processing companies had resisted the move, claiming that the small boats would not be able to land acceptable quality crab, but these concerns turned out to be unfounded.

A new draw was held in the same areas for the 1996 fishery. Stock status reports showed the crab resource to be in healthy condition on the coast of Labrador, the northeast coast of Newfoundland, as well as in Placentia Bay (fishing areas 2J3KL and 3Ps). This increased the pressure for access to the crab fishery for all small boats.

In Quebec and the Maritime provinces, where inshore and midshore harvesters belonged to separate organizations, violent confrontations marred the similar efforts of small-boat harvesters to gain access to crab. In New Brunswick, what was described in the media as "an angry mob of over 500 crab fishermen" threw rocks and smashed windows in the home of the provincial fisheries minister to protest having a portion of the crab quota shared with small-boat operators who had been shut out of the cod fishery. The situation in Quebec communities was tense as well.

But in Newfoundland and Labrador, both the pre-existing crab fleets and key regional officials with DFO were more accommodating of the entry of the small-boat sector. It was extremely helpful to have committees who were members of the same union sit down with DFO to work out a sharing of the resource that everyone could live with. The key to making it work was the creation of separate inshore fishing zones for the small-boat fleets. Another DFO minister from Newfoundland, Fred Mifflin, approved a breakthrough in 1997, authorizing temporary crab permits for all core enterprises in the less than 35-foot fleet in areas ranging from coastal Labrador to Fortune Bay. Future minister Herb Dhaliwal from British Columbia later agreed to convert the permits to licences, following representations on the matter from the union.

"The union did a lot of work getting the small boat fleet in the crab fishery, setting up zones, getting a licence," recalled Tony Doyle, who became inshore vice-president of the union. "We would never have accomplished it without having the union there to fight the battle with us. Crab access saved enterprises, families, and communities. In Bay de Verde at the time there were one fulltime and two supplementary licences. We would have been sitting on the hill looking at guys land a million dollars' worth of stuff and us with nothing. Those first crab permits gave everyone hope."

Mifflin was also the minister of fisheries and oceans who had to deal with controversy over access to the northern shrimp resource off the northeast coast of Newfoundland and Labrador. Fishing started on that stock in the late 1970s in the Davis Strait, far to the north, initially with foreign boats. A separate shrimp stock in the Gulf of St. Lawrence off the Northern Peninsula had been fished by 45- to 65-foot vessels mainly from Port au Choix and Anchor Point since the early 1970s, but the northern shrimp fishery had been fished exclusively by large factory-freezer trawlers until an explosion in the shrimp population occurred in the mid- and late 1990s. I have never read such positive stock status reports as the ones DFO scientists prepared on the northern shrimp stocks during those years.

This time the union, the Newfoundland and Labrador processing sector, and the provincial government all realized that the shrimp population explosion had resulted at least in part from the collapse of the predatory cod populations and demanded that those who had lost their cod fishery should be entited to the shrimp stocks that exploded in the wake of the cod's disappearance. But the existing offshore shrimp licence holders fought to keep any newcomers out of the fishery, and they had powerful allies within DFO headquarters in Ottawa.

Once again Max Short played a key role and the union and its members enjoyed the support of the DFO regional officials in St. John's. Meetings with Mifflin were productive, and it appeared he would allocate some northern shrimp to our midshore fleet, which in turn would create onshore jobs by landing the shrimp at processing plants in the province. It is a yardstick of the cozy relationship between the offshore shrimp industry and key DFO officials in Ottawa at the time that on the night before the new management plan was to be announced, DFO deputy minister pulled his officials out of the meetings at which press announcements were to be prepared. It was left to several people in Mifflin's political staff to write up the press material. I spent the night back and forth on the phone with these political officials doing what I could to shape the following day's announcement in a way that would be most beneficial to our members.

The new shrimp management plan in 1997 gave shrimp fishing opportunities along the northeast coast for the first time to owner/operators in the 35–65-foot sector in Labrador as well as in NAFO areas 3K and 3L on the northeast coast of Newfoundland and the Avalon Peninsula, and the 4R fleet on the northwest coast. The allocation for these fleets started at about 20 million pounds in 1997, increasing to about 65 million the following year. Not only did this create meaningful fishing opportunities for enterprises that desperately needed them but it also paved the way for several thousand jobs in shrimp-processing plants. At the peak of the inshore shrimp fishery, quotas totaling 130 million pounds provided raw material to feed 13 processing plants, including one in Labrador and four on the Northern Peninsula, with the remainder scattered around the coast.

In the initial stages, core enterprise holders in the respective areas had to demonstrate to DFO officers that they had invested in shrimp fishing gear before being issued a permit. But some of the shrimp-processing companies were creative, making the same shrimp gear available to one enterprise owner after another, passing it on once the DFO inspection was complete. The ensuing number of paper permit holders who had made no real investment in the shrimp fishery compounded a tough choice in how the fishery would be managed. One option was a competitive fishery, but this

Access to northern shrimp was a boost to the midshore fleet and the plants and plant workers they supplied with raw material.

had safety implications: it was likely to create a glut at the plants, and it was unclear how well the timing would work with other fisheries, such as crab. An individual quota (IQ) scheme was another option, but this had at least two significant disadvantages—the fees were high (three cents a pound compared to a flat $100 fee under a competitive fishery), and the number of paper licence holders who hadn't invested in the shrimp fishery would undoubtedly have created a processor-driven demand for quota-peddling.

To deal with this problem, David Decker met with regional shrimp-fleet committees to propose an alternative in the form of a ceiling (a "cap") on the amount of shrimp each licence holder could catch. This system had some of the advantages of an IQ regime, while avoiding the downside. The initial idea was to have a cap system enforced under the DFO shrimp management plan, but DFO refused to administer that type of program.

Since neither a competitive fishery nor an IQ system was a desirable approach, the union presented the concept of a cap regime to FANL at the bargaining table, and FANL eventually agreed. The cap was the maximum amount an individual fishing enterprise could catch. As far as DFO was concerned, it was a competitive fishery, so the fees were set at $100 a year per licence. Elected fleet committees from the various areas would establish, and from time to time adjust, the harvesting cap for their fleet. Any violation of the cap was administered through the collective agreement to ensure that nobody gained at the expense of other fishing enterprises by exceeding the cap. Whereas violations of an IQ system were enforced by DFO through the courts, the cap system was administered through the collective agreement. It was simple—an enterprise didn't get paid for landings that exceeded its cap. An added benefit was that the enterprise didn't end up in court over relatively minor violations.

"The cap system worked really well when the shrimp was there," Port au Choix shrimper Dwight Spence recalled. "We saved in the tens of thousands of dollars with a cap system compared to IQ fees."

Glen Winslow of St. John's also had a positive view of the cap

Here I'm talking to reporters at a demonstration at the DFO office in the White Hills, advocating a place in the crab fishery for small-boat harvesters.

system: "There were millions of dollars in fees saved by fish harvesters under the shrimp caps compared to an IQ system. Under a competitive quota, you had to be prepared to go in all kinds of weather. Caps put safety back in the picture."

Retired FFAW inshore director Bill Broderick estimated that "since 1997, the harvesters have saved close to $100 million because of the cap system."

In addition to the new lease on life for harvesters, access to shrimp allowed some plants to re-open after years of inactivity following the cod moratorium. This created jobs for plant workers and boosted the local economy of these communities, providing hope to families who had lived on a steady diet of despair in the years following the closure of the cod fishery.

The increased access to shrimp and crab underlines the importance of the FFAW to the broader rural economy over the years. It was also vital that there was someone who understood the Newfoundland and Labrador fishery in a position of political influence. When Brian Tobin asked Max Short to join his political staff in 1993, Short made it clear he would do so only if he had the union's blessing. Short was a valuable member of the union's staff whose departure from his position as inshore director would be a significant loss, but we felt it was essential to have someone who understood the fishery, the union, and our members working in a key position inside the federal system to help us navigate the treacherous political shoals in Ottawa.

It was the right call. Short played a critical role in getting access to crab for small boats and to northern shrimp for the longliner fleet and the plant workers. The union couldn't have done it without Max Short, and Max Short couldn't have done it without the union.

CHAPTER 12

LFUSCo—A Lifeline for the Labrador Coast

If it weren't for the Shrimp Company, a lot of communities on the coast would be closed, a lot of people would be gone.

— Frank Flynn, president, LFUSCo board of directors

I described in the previous chapter how the northern shrimp fishery provided a much-needed boost in the 1990s to inshore fish harvesters and work for plant workers in several communities. But it was foreign fleets who first fished the northern shrimp stock in the 1970s, when it was found in commercial abundance only in the Davis Strait, which separates northern Labrador from Greenland. Eventually, the federal government announced its intention to Canadianize the fishery and made it known that licences would be issued to Canadians. Because of the great distance involved to get to the Davis Strait, large vessels would be needed.

Max Short, who had just joined the staff of the union, was married to a Labradorian and knew well the hardships associated with the fishery in Labrador. He and Richard Cashin talked about the potential for the up-and-coming shrimp fishery to help the people on the coast.

"We in the union were very concerned about how these resources would be developed and who would own them," Cashin said years later.

When the federal government indicated its intentions to expand the Canadian northern shrimp fishery, Cashin went to DFO minister Romeo LeBlanc to make the case for Labrador to benefit from the growth of this resource on its doorstep. Licences were issued to private companies who were otherwise involved in the deep-sea fishery, including entities from other provinces. But in a decision that would prove to have a long-lasting positive impact, LeBlanc set aside three licences for the people of coastal Labrador—one for the Strait of Belle Isle, one for the south coast, and one for the north coast.

Once he had this commitment from LeBlanc, Cashin, along with Short, called a meeting in Labrador to discuss the issue of the shrimp licences with harvesters, who had only recently been organized into the union.

One solution proposed from the floor at the meeting was to put everyone's name in a bag and have a draw, which would have meant that only a few would benefit. Cashin recalled, "Frank Flynn got up and said it should be used for all the people."

Flynn, an inshore harvester from Forteau, recalled that moment years later: "It struck me that it would be a great thing for the fishermen in Labrador. So I got up and spoke. We always had people from the island come in and set up in Labrador and take out our product."

The initial plan was to set up a co-operative, but eventually the Labrador Fishermen's Union Shrimp Company (LFUSCo) was set up as a private company run on co-operative principles. Each fish harvester in the affected area—from Cartwright to L'Anse au Clair—would be given one share, and a board of directors elected,

LFUSCo has been the lifeblood of the Labrador coast. This photo shows General Manager Gilbert Linstead and his right-hand man, Ken Fowler, take a break from a meeting with union secretary-treasurer Dave Decker and inshore director Bill Broderick.

consisting of four fish harvesters from the south coast and four from the Straits to run the organization.

I don't know if LeBlanc realized it at the time, but his decision to award two licences to LFUSCo laid the foundation for stability and prosperity on the Labrador coast for the next 40 years and counting. (A third licence was issued to the Labrador Inuit Association to cover communities north of Cartwright, but the union was not involved in that area.) LeBlanc's faith in the people was well-founded. The founding constitution of the company stipulated clearly that it would be based on one person-one vote, that the value of shares would never exceed $1, and that any company profit would be re-invested in infrastructure along the coast, not paid out in dividends.

"It's the unselfishness of the shareholders that makes this

company successful," said Mary's Harbour owner/operator Dwight Russell, vice-president of the company's board of directors. "We invested in our communities and we invested in our people. Many times we considered not opening a plant because of the economics, but our social conscience gave us reason to think we could do it. The company is not driven by profit."

The company initially engaged Danish foreign freezer-trawlers to catch their offshore quotas on a royalty arrangement, then used the royalty revenue to sustain activities which were intended to benefit the people of the coast but were not sustainable on their own. One of their first momentous decisions was to buy the fish plant in L'Anse au Loup when the private operator went out of business. From time to time, the company also subsidized the price of salmon and other species to make fishing a feasible proposition.

In 1981, the company hired Gilbert Linstead to manage the L'Anse au Loup plant. At the time, the overall operations of the company were being run out of St. John's and it wasn't a satisfactory arrangement. As Linstead said, "We had many struggles from the time I started. There came a point when it was almost bankrupt."

But the company managed to find its footing at a critical time for the people of the Labrador coast when the only bank on the coast ceased operations.

"BMO pulled out in '84," Linstead recalled. "We started talking about starting a fishermen's credit union. We started Eagle River Credit Union. The shrimp company put in a deposit of $100,000 and paid half the manager's salary. Eagle River is very successful today."

With branches in L'Anse au Loup (the head office), Mary's Harbour, Happy Valley-Goose Bay, St. Anthony, and Deer Lake, as of 2021 Eagle River has more than 40 employees and assets in excess of $40 million.

"FFAW spawned the shrimp company, and the shrimp company spawned the credit union," said Linstead. "All of it is a godsend for the coast."

Five years later, in 1989, the board of directors made two decisions that proved to be major turning points in the development of the organization: the head office was moved from St. John's to L'Anse au Loup, and Linstead was promoted to general manager. Ken Fowler, hired as his assistant, played an important role, dealing first-hand with plant managers, plant union committees, and harvesters.

"Gilbert has been a very strong and steady person at the wheel," said Dwight Russell, a longtime board member. "He's been there through thick and thin, and we've been through a lot."

"The shrimp company is the lifeline for our coast," said Cartwright mayor Dwight Lethbridge, in a video marking the company's 40th anniversary in 2018. "I tip my hat to the shrimp company for saving our coast."

Alton Rumbolt, mayor of Mary's Harbour, called the company "the economic backbone on the south coast of Labrador." He said the company's plan for a new plant in the community "means that we will be able to keep our workers—and the community—going into the future."

The tiny community of Pinsent's Arm, with a population of about 50, was an unlikely location for a fish plant. But the shrimp company has been operating a small whelk and scallop operation there since 1994. Harrison Campbell, a member of the company's board, has been fishing out of Pinsent's Arm for the past 50 years. "We think the world of our company," he said. "Without the shrimp company, there would be nothing on the coast, not a thing."

Vicki Morris, a plant worker in Charlottetown and member of the FFAW IRO Council, spoke of the importance of the company to

Dwight Russell, vice-president of the LFUSCo board of directors, speaks at the campaign called "Rural Works," launched by the union.

plant workers at the various locations where the company operates. "Everyone is pretty pleased with the shrimp company. They treat people fairly, and you can make a good living. If not for the company, people would have to leave the communities.

Phil Quinlan, a chartered accountant based in St. John's, a trusted advisor to the company since its early days, noted: "The fundamental principles when the company was founded are still there today. The fishermen control the company and the fishermen believe they have to contribute to the communities."

Despite the ups and downs of the fishery, the company as recently as 2018 employed more than 500 people and bought fish from about 750 fish harvesters, said Linstead. "I think the future bodes well for people who want to stay on the coast of Labrador"—people like Harrison Campbell, who said, "I couldn't think of a better life."

Aubrey Russell, a harvester from Mary's Harbour, noted that private companies who operated plants for a while in the Labrador coast communities of Black Tickle and St. Lewis "never lasted long. The shrimp company is still around."

Cashin looks back with pride at the role the company he was instrumental in bringing to life has played in the economy and the life of the people of coastal Labrador. "Aside from the founding of the union itself, the most significant thing I ever did was the Labrador Fishermen's Union Shrimp Company," he stated.

The Yellow School Bus

When you fight back, you create a moment when anything can happen. When you don't fight back, you have no chance.

— Lana Payne, Unifor national secretary-treasurer

As a humble icon of working-class solidarity and the fighting spirit of the FFAW, the yellow school bus can't be beaten. To most people, it's a conveyance for transporting children to and from school. But for politicians and senior fisheries bureaucrats, nothing sends a shiver up their spines as surely as the sight of a cluster of yellow school buses on their parking lot.

They're a sure sign that trouble is close at hand.

When protestors travel from around the province to Confederation Building, to DFO headquarters in the White Hills, to the Revenue Canada Centre, or to Bull Arm, or wherever, they're making a statement by their very presence. These buses are designed to carry school children short distances. They're not built to accommodate adults, and they're not designed to carry anyone very far. The buses are generally old, they're slow, they're noisy, and they're extremely uncomfortable for extended travel.

Protestors don't board these buses in Bonavista or Marystown or Valleyfield or Twillingate or Triton or La Scie—much less Burgeo or Port au Choix or St. Anthony—unless they feel strongly about something. Depending on the starting point, the return trip to St. John's can be 10 or 15 or 20 hours, or longer. A meal is usually a pre-arranged stop at a fast-food outlet on the way home. It's a long, tedious, uncomfortable day. Notwithstanding camaraderie aboard the bus, you're not likely to be in a great mood by the time you reach your destination. Politicians know all this—or at least they should.

From the early days of the union to the fightback against unilateral cuts proposed to 2019 crab quotas, the yellow school bus as the conveyance of protest has been a staple of the FFAW fightback toolbox.

Jim Baird, a longtime DFO official, rose through the ranks to eventually become the regional director-general for Newfoundland and Labrador—the top official in the region, with a direct line to the key movers and shakers in the department's Ottawa headquarters. "The yellow school bus factor was something we always talked about," Baird recalled after his retirement from DFO.

It wasn't the buses themselves the bureaucrats and politicians were concerned about but what they represented—the mass mobilization of the people who work in the fishery to advocate a particular point of view or, as was often the case, fight back against a policy decision to which they were opposed.

By no means did all participants in the many FFAW rallies, demonstrations, and protests over the years travel by bus. Those who could do so travelled by private vehicle, and pickups dominated the landscape at demonstrations involving the inshore sector. But for many, cost and the availability (or not) of alternate means of transport made the buses arranged and paid for by the union the best option.

Over the years, membership mobilization events can be divided into three broad categories: those in which we joined with other organizations and the broader public in a common cause; those in which the union or a sector within the union was advocating for a particular policy goal; and, probably the most common, a fightback campaign against an unpopular or unfair government decision or policy. We weren't overly concerned about jurisdictional fine points. Federal and provincial governments alike, Liberal and Conservative, had their turns in the line of fire.

Many of our mobilization campaigns have already been dealt with in earlier chapters, so I won't go into them in any detail here, and it would be impractical, if not impossible, to list all the protests and rallies over the years. But a few examples illustrate the nature of events that fall into the three broad categories outlined above.

Mass events in which we joined with other groups and organizations tended for the most part to be organized by the broader labour movement, usually by the Newfoundland and Labrador Federation of Labour or the Canadian Labour Congress. We also joined with women's organizations and various social justice groups to make our voices heard on issues that affected the broader community. A recurring issue that brought out busloads of FFAW members—often in coordination with other labour organizations—was the UI (now EI) program (see Chapter 12).

Other times the FFAW reached out to the community seeking support on an issue of significance to the province. This included actions protesting foreign overfishing, as well as the campaign to terminate the insidious LIFO policy in the shrimp fishery. In the case

Union members at a meeting in Plum Point campaign against a federal decision to close the Gulf cod fishery instead of continuing the modest quotas.

of LIFO, the union organized regional meetings with community leaders in major shrimp fishing/processing areas to provide information and enlist their support for the ongoing campaign against LIFO, which became critical as shrimp quotas bottomed out. This was followed by a public rally in Gander; speakers included municipal leaders, representatives of the three main provincial political parties, MPs, shrimp harvesters, and plant workers. On another occasion the union organized a rally in St. John's, then had hundreds of members walk through the Northern Shrimp Advisory Committee meeting to put human faces on vital decisions made in remote boardrooms.

Ultimately, DFO minister Dominic LeBlanc eliminated the LIFO policy, and the inshore fishery in Shrimp Fishing Area 6 off the northeast coast survived, although with greatly reduced allocations as the stock continued to steadily decline. As longtime shrimp harvester Ren Genge from Anchor Point put it: "For us, LIFO was as important as anything the union done for us. The biggest part of the province was behind us."

Sometimes membership mobilization was proactive. In the early days of the union, a protest by trawlermen at Confederation Building brought attention to the low pay and grim working conditions aboard the trawler fleet. The campaign to get workers' compensation coverage for inshore fish harvesters (see Chapter 20) is another proactive union campaign that produced concrete results.

Generally speaking, the membership mobilizations that have been the most controversial, rambunctious, and widely supported by union members have been those held in reaction to government decisions perceived as unfair and unreasonable. A classic example of this type of fightback action occurred in 2019. To understand the context of this dust-up, it is necessary to go back more than 20 years. When the crab fishery emerged in the 1990s as the biggest money-maker in the Newfoundland and Labrador fishery, it was crucial to those who depended on that fishery that it be managed in a sustainable manner. As I described earlier, DFO and crab committees elected through the union collaborated on a management structure in which, for the most part, each fleet had its own separate fishing zone and was told in clear terms by DFO that it would have to survive on the resource in that defined area.

It's important to bear in mind that crab management is quite different from that of groundfish species. It takes about nine years for a male crab to reach fishable size, and if not captured in the fishery, that crab will normally live for another five years or so before dying of natural causes. The minimum carapace (shell) size in the crab fishery and the minimum mesh size for crab pots are conservation measures designed to allow female crab to escape.

Jim Baird describes the management of crab stocks as "inventory control." The fishery is basically an exploitation of the population of males between roughly nine and 15 years of age.

For the first 20 or so years of the dramatically increased crab biomass, the lead-up to the announcement of DFO's annual snow crab management plan for Newfoundland included meetings involving DFO scientists and managers, as well as elected crab committees from the various fleets. When the scientists shared information about the diminished state of thee resource in a particular area, rank-and-file fleet committee members not only took the bad news back to fleet meetings but in many cases supported the recommendations of DFO scientists. As Albert Wells, an owner-operator from Wild Cove, White Bay, who had fished at different times in the inshore and offshore crab fleets, put it: "All you're doing is shooting yourself in the foot if you go too heavy."

While some fleets were more successful than others in adjusting their fishing effort to a sustainable level, a collaborative approach to the management of the crab fishery brought a reasonable degree of stability to the difficult job of managing the resource that was crucial to so many fishing enterprises, plant workers, and communities. This made it especially infuriating when DFO arbitrarily discarded this model in 2019 and proposed dramatic reductions in crab quotas and allocations that had not been hinted at during the meetings a few weeks earlier.

The unilateral dismantling by DFO of this long-standing collaboration left the union committee members feeling double-crossed. Nowhere was this feeling stronger than in area 3K on the northeast coast of Newfoundland. The various crab fleets in

Union members gather outside the hotel where the Northern Shrimp Advisory Committee was meeting in St. John's. They paraded through the meeting to highlight the importance of the inshore shrimp fishery for coastal communities and to object to the LIFO policy.

3K had suffered through several years of severe quota cuts, but by 2018 they were finally seeing improved catch rates. Following preliminary meetings with scientists that for the most part pointed to stable quotas, they had passed on this information to the people they represented, only to have DFO come back with a plan suggesting cuts ranging from 25 to 35 per cent for most fleets. The union responded quickly with a meeting in Grand Falls-Windsor attended, despite the short notice, by about 300 members from 3K. This was followed by a province-wide rally in St. John's, attended by 600 to 800 people. Harvesters and plant workers spoke of the hardship these cuts would impose on them, their colleagues, and their communities. Media coverage was extensive.

"In fisheries science and in management, DFO has treated fish harvesters as an afterthought. As an inconvenience. As a box they have to check," Keith Sullivan told the rally.

DFO's approach changed quickly, at least in terms of the 2019 crab fishery. In short order, they came out with a crab management plan that was much closer to what the fleet committees had been led to expect at earlier meetings with DFO scientists—that is, not much change from the 2018 quotas. Ivan Lear of Port de Grave summed up the opinion of most FFAW members who participated in the rallies when he said, "The demonstrations definitely helped." The impact of the campaign also appeared to carry forward into 2020, when quotas were resolved without incident.

Important as they were, the demonstrations alone did not turn the tide. The union was dealing from a position of strength. Its challenge to the DFO plan was informed by the 16-year-old post-season crab-pot survey, a collaborative effort between the union and DFO which provides an index of the relative abundance of crab at the conclusion of each fishing season. The solidarity of the harvesters and plant workers under the union was crucial, and it was reinforced by the union's significant investment over the years in fisheries science.

The rallies and demonstrations held by the FFAW over 50 years on a wide range of issues didn't always achieve the desired result, but they usually moved the needle at least to some extent. And they demonstrated clearly to union members that their union leadership was on their side. For their part, the membership could be relied on to answer the bell when union leaders put out the call for action.

Over the years, there have been protests related to plant closures, minimum processing regulations, collective bargaining issues, fisheries management plans, plant licencing policies, the owner-operator and fleet separation policies, and more. On occasion, the protests involved occupation of ministerial or government offices, blockades of plant premises, or barricades on highways.

As an example of the latter point, in 2003 harvesters in the 4Rs3Pn cod stock area were shocked to hear that the fishery, which had been putt-putting along with a modest TAC for several years, was going to be abruptly subject to a long-term closure. Secretary-treasurer David Decker, inshore director Bill Broderick, and staff rep Guy Perry joined about 200 harvesters for an impromptu protest on the Trans-Canada Highway near the entrance to the Gulf ferry.

"We built a shack in the middle of the highway," Broderick recalled. "Before long, there was a two-or-three-mile backlog of traffic trying to get on the ferry. We did allow some vehicles through that evening, in cases where we identified people with medical conditions or with infants on board. We didn't open the highway until midnight and the ferry had sailed."

Hundreds of union members march through the streets of St. John's as part of the 2019 crab campaign.

There was no impediment to traffic on the ferry the following morning. Broderick picks up the story: "The next evening, we regrouped in Port aux Basques and prevented passengers and vehicles from boarding that night's crossing. The police were lined up with their backs to us, facing the people who were trying to board the ferry. The next day, our members slowed down traffic coming off the inbound ferry, distributing leaflets outlining the issue."

At various times over a three-day period, union members blocked the Trans-Canada Highway and the Marine Atlantic parking lot; they also blocked the harbour by means of a cable that ran from boat to boat.

The union later succeeded in getting Premier Roger Grimes, provincial fisheries minister Yvonne Jones, and national CAW president Buzz Hargrove to join me and others from the union in a series of well-attended public meetings throughout the affected area. The fishery remained closed for the 2003 season, but DFO abandoned the idea of a long-term closure, and that fishery has remained open with a modest quota every year since.

Our demonstrations were frequently, but not always, directed at one or both levels of government, but the fish processing companies were occasionally targets as well. A classic case involved Ocean Choice International (OCI) and its factory-freezer trawler, the *Newfoundland Lynx*. OCI went to the bargaining table with representatives of the *Lynx* crew in 2012, demanding massive rollbacks in the *Lynx* contract. The union might as well have gone out of business as agree to those demands.

When OCI brass realized that the union wasn't going to cave, they scheduled the vessel to sail from Bay Roberts, called in scabs to replace the regular crew, and demanded an RCMP escort through the picket line. The RCMP brought in enough officers to escort the scabs through the picket line. When the pickets refused to step aside, the RCMP detained them at the local detachment. It was a demoralizing moment for the men and a pivotal moment for the union. Secretary-treasurer Dave Decker knew the men felt defeated and needed a boost, so he arranged for them to shift the focus of their protest to the OCI head office in St. John's. That office is on Topsail Road, a main drag in St. John's. The response the trawlermen received from the passing public was heartening. Drivers honked their horns and waved, some dropped off coffee and doughnuts, and the spirits of the men, so low a few hours earlier, were revived.

Meanwhile, the *Lynx* was at sea, but the company was in for a nasty surprise. The people they had hired didn't know what they were doing, and the catch rates were extremely low. Some scabs demanded to be brought ashore, and the company was probably happy to get rid of them, but they had a problem—the same one the trawler companies had run into in the past: with a militant, province-wide union as their opponent, where were they going to land the boat? Undoubtedly anticipating trouble at any Newfoundland port, they chose to land in Nova Scotia.

When the union got word of her destination, Decker and a few crew members flew to Nova Scotia, went on board the vessel, and talked to the crew. Many walked off the boat when they heard the union's case, and the *Lynx* went from having an incompetent crew to having insufficient crew to sail. The attempt to break the trawlermen's union had failed. Within a few weeks, the company and the union were back at the bargaining table and worked out a new collective agreement. The company had seriously damaged its long-term relationship with valuable employees and come out empty-handed.

These are just a few examples of the union's fightback campaigns over the years. Others are dealt with in other chapters. A constant theme runs throughout: fighting back makes all the difference.

The Endless Attack on Employment Insurance

With the union, we were always fighting for our rights. That's how we got the extra five weeks on EI.

— Irene Ploughman, retired fish plant worker, Bay Bulls

My introduction to the perverse rules of what was then known as the Unemployment Insurance program came in my early days with the union at a plant workers' meeting in Witless Bay. After we had dealt with the business at hand and opened up the floor for questions, a woman asked, "If I go to work tomorrow, do I have to get paid?"

Well, I wasn't exactly expecting that, so I had to ask her to explain. It turned out that if she went to work the following day, she would be worse off for it, because at that time, a "small week" (i.e., a week with only a few hours worked) would reduce her average weekly earnings and thereby reduce her weekly UI benefit in the off-season. It would cost her money to go to work.

From that day (around 1980) to this, few issues have taken up as much of the union's time and energy as UI (now known as EI, or Employment Insurance). From campaigning for more sensible rules so that people are rewarded instead of being punished for going to work, to making seemingly endless presentations to parliamentary committees, royal commissions, and the like that always seemed to have seasonal workers and fishing EI in their sights, to representing individual members trying to resolve problems with their claims, the union was always in the thick of it.

That's not to mention frequent rallies and demonstrations, either campaigning in favour of improvements to the program or fighting against cutbacks. Any time the federation of labour called a provincial demonstration on EI, FFAW always turned out the biggest numbers.

Before I detail the union's EI-related efforts over the years, a brief history of unemployment insurance is in order. The first UI program was implemented in Canada in 1935 but thrown out by the Supreme Court over a jurisdictional question. In July 1940, an amendment was passed to the *British North America Act* which specified that unemployment insurance was a matter of federal jurisdiction. A month later, the first lasting UI program was enacted. Employers, employees, and the federal government all contributed financially to the program, but there were no fishing, seasonal worker, or maternity benefits. A major overhaul in 1955 extended the program to seasonal workers, and fishing benefits took effect in 1957. The program was further improved in 1971 when the government of the day improved benefit rates, relaxed eligibility criteria, and added benefits to cover maternity, sickness, and involuntary job loss.

Despite these improvements, the maximum benefit period for fishing claims was just 12 weeks. This was one of the many issues the new NFFAWU tackled in its representations to Ottawa in the early years of the union. Richard Cashin recalls raising the inadequacy of fishing benefits with Cabinet ministers Don Jamieson, Newfoundland's representative in Cabinet at the time, and Romeo LeBlanc.

A major step forward came in 1976, when Romeo LeBlanc was the minister of state (fisheries). Joe Gough wrote in *Managing Canada's Fisheries: From Early Days to the Year 2000*: "LeBlanc won government approval and announced in August 1976 that fishing benefits would henceforth last longer in areas of high unemployment. That could mean, in most areas, up to 27 weeks of benefits." By any measure, this was an extraordinary breakthrough.

From the beginning, wives of fishing enterprise owners were deemed ineligible for fishing EI, but an inshore harvester from Witless Bay, Rosanne Doyle, won a major victory for fishing women when she successfully appealed this policy in the 1980s.

But fishing benefits were frequently under attack in Ottawa. The first major challenge came in 1985 when the Mulroney government appointed a commission chaired by Claude Forget, an economist and former provincial politician from Montreal, to hold hearings across Canada and make recommendations on how to "improve" the UI program (i.e., reduce benefits). It was an indication of what we were up against that a CBC report about the Forget Commission started by saying, "By 1986, everyone agrees Canada's employment insurance system is broken." I guess CBC's definition of "everyone" didn't include fish harvesters or seasonal workers.

The Forget Commission eventually recommended cutting $2.5 billion from the program, most of it from Quebec and the Atlantic provinces. Forget recommended that an individual's weekly benefits be calculated by dividing their insurable earnings by 52, regardless of the number of weeks actually worked, and that fish harvesters' EI be phased out over five years, to be replaced by some kind of

One of several simultaneous demonstrations, this one in Harbour Grace, that the union held against proposed federal cuts to the Unemployment Insurance program.

A Match to a Blasty Bough

income support program that was not defined. This would have been disastrous for people in seasonal industries in the province, notably the fishery. Naturally, the union came out swinging against the report. It was disappointing that the only Newfoundlander on the commission, Moses Morgan, a former president of Memorial University, signed the report. Fortunately, the two labour nominees refused to do so. The minority report from labour nominees Jack Munro of the International Woodworkers of America (IWA) and Jean-Claude Parrot of the Canadian Union of Postal Workers (CUPW) was widely supported by the labour movement, which was helpful in convincing the Mulroney government to shelve Forget's recommendations. But it proved to be a stay of execution, not the end of the attack on the program.

Around the same time that Forget & Co. were doing their work, Newfoundland premier Brian Peckford appointed a Royal Commission on Employment and Unemployment, chaired by Doug House from Memorial University. Among other things, the Commission recommended: "The Government of Newfoundland and Labrador should enter into negotiations with the government of Canada for the implementation of a new income security system along the line suggested in this report, possibly using Newfoundland and Labrador as a pilot project for Canada as a whole." What quickly became clear to me was that seasonal workers—which included most members of our union—would be expected to pick up the tab for this pilot project. Once again, the union had to come out strongly against the proposal.

Probably because of the strong backlash to the proposal, and the inertia that Peckford later admitted had set in during his last years in power, his government never acted on this recommendation. But by 1992, Clyde Wells was premier, and Doug House, the man who had chaired Peckford's Royal Commission, was head of the province's Economic Recovery Commission. In June of that disastrous year, the month prior to John Crosbie's devastating announcement of the closure of the northern cod fishery, Wells unveiled his "Strategic Economic Plan," which resurrected the idea of working with Ottawa to design "an alternative income security system that both protects the income needs of Newfoundland households and provides strong incentives for work, education and self-employment." In his new position, House had the ear of the premier, and shortly after the Chrétien government took office in Ottawa, Wells and House met with Lloyd Axworthy, the federal minister responsible for the UI program, to push the province's proposal, which it called the ISP (Income Security Plan).

Plant worker Irene Ploughman from Witless Bay could barely keep the scorn out of her voice more than a quarter of a century later when she recalled, "Doug House's solution was for women to do some knitting and crafts."

The program included a "basic income supplement" (a family tax credit similar to the child tax credit) and a "work supplement." The proposal included some positive ideas, but once again, the rub came in the source of the money to pay for the scheme: it would come from drastically reduced (if not eliminated) EI benefits for fish harvesters and other seasonal workers. As House acknowledged in his 1999 book *Against the Tide: Battling for Economic Renewal in Newfoundland and Labrador*, the scheme "would have meant lower incomes in the short term for many families dependent on seasonal employment in fisheries, forestry and construction. Not surprisingly, as we shall see, this struck a nerve with workers and their unions.

One fisheries union leader dubbed the ISP the 'Incredibly Stupid Program.'"

Full disclosure here: that unnamed union leader was me. I was incensed that at a time when the fishery was in trouble, people struggling to make a go of it in the fishery and other seasonal industries would be footing the bill for the scheme. I took no comfort from the recommendation that the changes be phased in over a transition period—it was obvious that our members, along with other seasonal workers, would be the big losers, short and long-term.

As House described it, "All hell broke loose" in the province when the details of the proposal were leaked to the media.

"The report, which was originally intended only for cabinet, included several statements that the ERC had meant to be tentative, but that cabinet had accepted without further thought," House wrote. "For example, the report had stated: *'Fish harvesters would no longer be eligible for UI.'* (Emphasis added.) Our reasons for suggesting this were that we believe self-employed fish harvesters should be treated equally with all other self-employed people, but only on condition that the ISP be put in place first, and that it be available to all low-income self-employed people."

Once the report had been leaked, government scrambled to backpedal, changing the wording to say the fisheries UI program "*could* also be eliminated," but as House acknowledged, "Despite such attempts at softening the message, the damage had been done. The Fish, Food and Allied Workers Union was furious, and other strong unions of seasonal workers in construction and forestry quickly added their objections."

The ISP then became mired in the quicksand of federal/provincial negotiations. It lost a champion when Clyde Wells abruptly stepped down as premier in December 1995, to be succeeded by Brian Tobin. As House put it, "Brian Tobin's perspective on the Income Security Plan was very different from that of Clyde Wells. As the federal minister of Fisheries and Oceans, he was exposed to the ISP first through his connections with the fishing industry, especially the fisheries union, which was so adamant in its opposition."

Tobin put the ISP on the back burner. The union, obviously, played a significant role in this outcome. But that didn't mean seasonal wasn't the end of the story. The federal government had been pushing what it called "UI Reform," with seasonal workers again the main targets. The changes the Chrétien government implemented in 1996 included the so-called intensity rule, which reduced the percentage of average weekly earned income used to calculate a repeat claimant's benefit rate (from 55 per cent to as low as 50 per cent), and the "divisor rule," which used a minimum divisor of 14, even for those who worked fewer than 14 weeks. The two measures combined had the effect of significantly reducing EI benefits for frequent claimants, especially those whose work was condensed into fewer than 14 weeks.

Instead of constantly targeting seasonal workers, both levels of government would have been well advised to pay attention to the recommendations related to EI that had been brought forward a few years earlier by the Task Force on Incomes and Adjustments in the Atlantic Fishery, chaired by Richard Cashin. With the support of the union's executive board, Cashin had accepted John Crosbie's invitation to chair this task force because it was obvious tough times were coming, and our members needed someone who understood our industry to push from the inside for sensible programs to help them survive the crisis.

Irene Ploughman, long-time union activist, at an FFAW convention.

The provincial government's position on the UI system seemed rooted in righteous indignation. As House put it, some senior provincial bureaucrats "were morally upset at the way in which, as they saw it, rural Newfoundlanders were 'milking the UI system,' enjoying a good quality of life while working only 10 weeks each year."

Cashin took a much different approach. Bill Broderick, then a union executive board member, recalls a meeting involving Cashin, task force staff, and inshore executive board members from the union to get their views on what was needed to make the UI system work from a fish harvester's perspective.

Cashin's final report, informed by a lifetime of working in the fishery and by the input of the inshore board members, was much less judgmental and a lot more helpful. Given a broad mandate to review the income support system available to people who work in the fishery, Cashin and his team concluded:

> We reviewed a wide range of policy and program options. Our conclusion is that the best way to reform the income support system for the fishery is through improvements to the current unemployment insurance system ... Improvements to UI should include a more precisely targeted system, (and) better incentives both to encourage productive activity and to discourage distortions and misuse ... Unfortunately the uniqueness of the fishermen's situation is not reflected in Fishermen's UI ... This is based on the peculiar notion that fishermen work a regular work week.

This report was a potential game changer for fish harvesters.

Fundamentally, the task force recommendations were rooted in an understanding of how the fishing economy works. The task force resisted what Cashin called "constant agitation" against fishing industry EI from the Ottawa bureaucracy, and it did so while spending only $3 million out of a $55 million budget for the project. The key recommendation on the fishing side was a change from the concept of insurable weeks to using fishing income as the basis for qualifying and calculating benefit rates for UI, and a change from fixed to flexible dates for both the qualifying and the benefit period.

"The best thing the union ever did was change from insurable weeks to dollars," said Joan Doucette, a harvester from St. George's. It was the task force report that led to the changes, but the union played a pivotal role in two ways—Cashin's overall direction as chair of the task force, and the crucial input from the union's inshore board members. Once the task force put the concept of basing fishing EI on income instead of insurable weeks into play, the union pushed it hard.

With respect to plant workers, the task force noted the erratic hours, especially in seasonal plants. "The major problem with UI for fish plant workers is that the insurable week system creates disincentives for employees to work the full season and accept all work offered to them," the report stated, drawing attention to the problem I had run into years earlier in Witless Bay.

Instead of moralizing about it, as the provincial bureaucrats did, the task force offered a simple remedy: use hours worked instead of insurable weeks as the basis for qualifying for EI, so that there would be an incentive to work every available hour. This was a new idea at the time. It took three years, but this eventually became part of the EI program, as did the change for calculating an individual's fishing EI on fishing income instead of insurable weeks, and the move to more flexible qualifying and benefit periods.

Always at the forefront of fightback campaigns when governments looked to attack benefits for fish harvesters and seasonal workers, the union also campaigned hard for an extra five weeks of benefits in areas of high unemployment. Helen Evans worked at the plant in Hant's Harbour until the company closed the doors. As she put it: "The campaign for the extra five weeks was a big campaign. We had it, then it was taken away, now it's back again. It's very important. A lot of people ran out of income before the season started—ice delays, for example. The 14 best weeks has also been instrumental for plant workers. Before that, you'd have weeks of 10 or 12 or 14 hours, and that would knock down your benefit rate."

Jack Greenham, a harvester from Comfort Cove, put it this way: "I'd hate to think where we'd be without the union. Preserving the EI system was a fundamental accomplishment of the union. Without the EI system, we wouldn't have a fishery."

The EI system is critical to the economy in areas with a high incidence of seasonal employment. FFAW was not alone in pushing hard for a strong EI program, but along with the seasonal fish plant workers on the northeast coast of New Brunswick, probably the most consistently militant over an extended period.

I was always baffled by the seasonal fish plant owners. While the union was in the forefront of fighting to protect and strengthen the EI system, the plant operators didn't seem to grasp that they wouldn't be able to retain a workforce without that off-season supplement of fish plant wages, yet they never spoke out when the program was under attack—except occasionally to join in the attack. It was always clear to the union: the EI system was and remains a very important element in the overall incomes of plant workers and harvesters alike, and the union spared no effort in fighting to keep it as robust as possible.

The last word in this chapter goes to Irene Ploughman, longtime unit chair of the crab plant in Witless Bay, where Diane Finley, at the time the minister in the Harper government responsible for the EI program, went for a visit in 2012. "I was Diane Finley's worst enemy. We were up to our ears in crab. She visited the plant for a photo op. I wanted to talk to her about EI. She didn't want to talk to me. She went to the bathroom. I went with her."

This may not have been the only time a federal minister was ever chased into the bathroom by someone wanting to get their two cents worth in about the EI program, but it's the only one I know of. Going to Witless Bay for a photo op gave the minister much more than she bargained for.

At the next union convention, when Irene got up to the microphone to speak, I introduced her as "Diane Finley's worst nightmare."

CHAPTER 15
"We're the Women of the Union"

People still have the mindset that women can't do what men can do, that women are only fishing to get their stamps. They don't see the blood, sweat, and tears that go into it. We can do it. I love the challenge—prove to yourself that you can do it.

— Stephanie Lights, inshore harvester, Port de Grave

Irene Ploughman's challenge to federal Cabinet minister Diane Finley during a photo op was not an isolated event. In a way, it had been close to 30 years in the making. Almost from the day she walked into the plant in Witless Bay, Ploughman was a union activist. Her priority was helping her fellow workers. But to do that effectively, support is needed, and that's where union outreach and training programs come into play.

"If I hadn't had the training I got from the union, I wouldn't have had the nerve [to confront the minister]," Ploughman said years later.

But the opportunity to take training delivered by CAW (later Unifor), training for organizing and for delivering moratorium-related information sessions, gave Ploughman the confidence to seize the moment when the minister who was trying to undermine the UI system showed up at her workplace.

The training Ploughman was referring to was part of the outreach efforts of FFAW over the years to provide a comfortable setting for women members and give them the confidence to assume a more important role in the union.

A significant challenge in male-dominated industries is to make space for women in their leadership structures. Women and men do not necessarily share the same priorities, the same perspectives. The voices of both are needed at the decision-making tables of the organization they belong to.

The first executive board of the former NFFAWU consisted of 11 men and one woman—plant worker Margaret Cornick from Port au Choix. At the time, relatively few women were engaged in inshore fishing and none on the trawler fleets. As the big south coast plants had a history of electing men to the top positions, the only place where women emerged in leadership roles was in seasonal plants.

Before the merger with the CAW, little in the way of training was available for rank-and-file leaders, and there was no equivalent to today's Industrial-Retail-Offshore (IRO) Council and Inshore Council. Despite these shortcomings, women like Barb Parsons of Bareneed, Jeanette Fennell in Charleston, Emma Tilley in La Scie, Beryl Ricketts in Jackson's Arm, Bev Butler in St. Mary's, Margaret Rose in St. Anthony, and Edith Pardy in Burin, to name a few, took on prominent roles. Parsons took on the leading role, serving for several years as chair of the women's committee as well as three terms on the union's executive board.

Women's participation in the leadership of the union took a major step forward when women were elected to head the union committees in two major year-round plants—Bernice Duffett in Port Union and Linda Hyde in St. John's.

Lana Payne, waiting to speak at an FFAW Convention, became president of the Newfoundland and Labrador Federation of Labour, and Atlantic director, then national secretary-treasurer of Unifor. CAW president Ken Lewenza is in the foreground.

The merger with the CAW opened opportunities, including access to the resources of the CAW women's department. Another major development was the 1991 hiring of Lana Payne to the position of communications officer with FFAW.

"Lana was a force and pushed for women's voices to be included and heard in a male-dominated industry and union hierarchy," said Tina Pretty, a member of the union office staff who worked closely with the FFAW women's committee until her retirement. Irene Ploughman added: "When Lana joined the union, things got better for women. She was a leader for women, encouraged us, said you can do it."

Under Payne's leadership and with the support of the CAW women's department, FFAW set up a women's committee and began to offer periodic women's conferences.

The women's committee came to me while I was president and told me politely but bluntly that the union had to do more to reach out to woman members. That led to commitments, spelled out in the union constitution, for women's conferences at least once every three years, and to "affirmative action" positions for women on the executive board—positions that would be open to women members only, one in the plant section, one in the harvesting sector—as well as one, and later two, seats on the inshore council.

"That worked," said Mildred Skinner of Harbour Breton, the first woman elected to the inshore council, who went on to fill the affirmative action seat on the executive board. "That put me on the board and I was replaced on the council."

As Vicki Morris from Charlottetown, Labrador, said: "Affirmative action gives people opportunity."

The union's IRO Council did not have the same requirement for

A group of activists attending a woman's advocate program.

affirmative action because many of the local leaders in the bargaining units that make up the council are women. As of 2020, 10 of the council's 24 members were women, and 13 fish plants have had a woman as unit chairperson, the top elected position in the bargaining unit. Several of these local leaders have had the opportunity to attend women's conferences that gave them more confidence to take on the responsibilities of leadership at the local level.

"I find women's conferences good," said Doretta Strickland of Triton. "Listening to all the women speaking from the heart gives you perspective and more nerve. At women's conferences we get to speak our minds. We're more confident now."

Helen Evans, longtime union activist from Hant's Harbour, had this take: "When we first set up the women's committee, it gave you improvement. The union helped me survive a lot of things. The women's conference in 1995 involved working with families dealing with abuse. They gave me the courage to move on. Lana was a big help—a hard fighter."

Union conventions were another forum for women (men too, for that matter) to learn about the union and develop a desire to become involved.

"I attended my first convention in 2006," said Trudy Byrne, who became vice-chair and later chair of the plant workers' bargaining unit at the shrimp plant in St. Anthony. "That's where I got my passion for the union—I saw what people were doing to help other people."

That passion came to the forefront in the summer of 2009 when the shrimp fishery was shut down because of a price dispute. Byrne was one of a several plant workers who drove from the Northern Peninsula to St. John's to protest at the provincial fisheries office in support of the shrimp harvesters. She participated in an occupation of the government office that lasted several days and nights, and did media interviews speaking out in support of the shrimp fleet.

Nancy Bowers, an inshore harvester from Beachside in Green Bay, attended her first convention in 2015: "I was amazed. What a great bunch of people! They believe in you. It's unbelievable."

Bowers is one of a growing number of young women who grew up in fishing families, tried their hand at other kinds of work, then decided inshore fishing was the career for them. From 2000 to 2017, the percentage of females among those reporting fishing income in the province increased from 15 to 30 per cent.

An article in the Fall 2018 *Union Forum* featured four young women from Port de Grave who moved from other occupations to fishing. Stacey Petten worked on the mainland for a few years, fishing with her father when she came home in the summer, before

Doretta Strickland, a plant worker from Triton, became the first woman to be an officer in the union when she was elected IRO vice-president.

eventually moving back home to fish full-time, "something I always did as a child, and being able to be here now, working with family—it's good."

Chelsea Porter worked for four years as a pipefitter before joining her father in the fishing boat: "I went out and I absolutely loved it. Fishing is in my blood."

Melissa Norris summed it up this way: "I was always dressed to the tee going to work. I traded all that for the oil gear and the big rubber boots."

Training, conferences, conventions, and opportunities for leadership positions are all about building a strong team of union leaders. But none of this is done in a vacuum or as a goal in itself. It's all about giving elected leaders in the various bargaining units the tools and the confidence to provide strong representation to the membership. In a progressive union like FFAW, that means both in the workplace and in the broader community.

Bernice Duffett was like many people in rural Newfoundland and Labrador when she left school to work in the local fish plant in Port Union: "Going straight from school into the plant was a little intimidating at first. After a while I saw a lot wrong in the treatment of women. We were always put in packing—the lowest paid job. When I started work, I wanted to go trimming. The company said no, they didn't want women handling knives, they thought we'd cut ourselves. Eventually they found women to be better trimmers."

The Port Union plant was the largest in the province, with about 1,000 workers. After starting as shop steward, Duffett took on the important position of chief shop steward, where she wasn't shy about using the grievance procedure to address the problems she'd seen in the treatment of women. She was constantly trying her hand at jobs that were traditionally done by men, including operating a forklift on the wharf.

One position that interested Duffett was that of "watchman"; it had only ever been filled by a man. Duffett applied for a relief position in the watchhouse, and when the company gave the job instead to a man with less seniority, she used the grievance procedure to get her seniority recognized and to get the job. Part of the job involved filling in a form at the end of each shift and sending it up to the manager.

"I always wrote 'watchwoman' on my sheet," Duffett recalled with a chuckle—making sure that with every report, management was reminded that it wasn't only men who could do the job.

In addition to workplace-related issues that local committee members tackle on behalf of their memberships, union members also have lives outside the workplace. Unfortunately, for all too many women in our society, those lives include having to live with the scourge of domestic violence.

Once again, the expertise of the CAW came to the forefront. Starting in the auto sector in 1993, CAW negotiated joint union/employer programs to provide women's advocates in workplaces. A woman's advocate is trained to help women who are struggling in their personal lives. They are not counsellors but are trained to help women who may have been sexually assaulted or harassed, are in a violent relationship, or may be suicidal, and to refer them to community services. Women's advocates receive training in intimate violence and risk assessment, sexual harassment, suicide prevention, and addictions.

The program was designed for conventional workplaces, such as car factories or fish plants, where a clear employer/employee relationship exists. But because of some of the non-traditional workplaces in which FFAW members work—especially in the inshore fishery—a modified approach was needed.

After some brainstorming, the women's committee devised two categories of women's advocate—the traditional workplace-based format for conventional workplaces, and community-level services for inshore members. The challenges these advocates are addressing can affect the individual member's health and safety in the workplace, as well as their productivity. It's a social problem facing many union members. The first advocates were trained in 2009. Remarkably, by 2020, 30 FFAW women had taken on the challenge of providing this critical service.

"There have been women I've spoken to who have cried when they knew that this was available," said Joan Doucette, an inshore harvester from Bay St. George.

Vicki Morris from Charlottetown, who is a trained advocate, added: "That's a really good program, especially in the rural areas. People don't know where to go. There's no shelters. It gives you someone you can confide in."

Or as Doretta Strickland put it, "You learn how to handle a situation. Sometimes it's better to sit and listen."

The challenge to make sure that women are fairly represented in the leadership of the union and that their voices are heard continues. There has unmistakably been progress. Strickland became the first woman elected to one of the top executive positions in the FFAW when she was elected IRO vice-president in 2018.

In the past 15 years, Lana Payne has served as president of the Newfoundland and Labrador Federation of Labour, and as Atlantic director and more recently national secretary-treasurer of Unifor,

Melisa Norris, Stephanie Lights, Chelsea Porter, and Stacey Petten from Port de Grave took up fishing after trying other occupations.

so she has plenty of experience in dealing with male-dominated unions. "Our people [FFAW] are much more reasonable about accommodating women than a lot of male-dominated industries I've dealt with," she commented.

Joan Doucette echoes that view: "I don't think anything I've said at the table has gone unheard. They want to broaden their understanding of what woman are thinking."

Trudy Byrne from St. Anthony summed up the impact of the "learning experience" her union involvement has provided: "I went from being a shy little girl to what I am today. I'd face the devil if I had to. I have a passion for anyone I can do anything for."

CHAPTER 16

Working in the Plants: "Some Good Times and Some Hard Times"

When we talk about the history of the union, I grew up with it. My mother, Lucy Caines, went to work when the plant was built in 1952. She was on the union committee until she retired. She always said you wouldn't believe the difference from what it was like before and what it is like now with the union. I'm proud to say I'm part of FFAW.

— Karen Caines, unit chairperson, OCI plant in Fortune, and FFAW executive board member

According to the Cohen Royal Commission on Labour Legislation in Newfoundland and Labrador, before the formation of the NFFAWU about 100 fish plants operated in the province. Of these, 11 were unionized, most of them directly chartered by the Canadian Labour Congress. One was the Bonavista Cold Storage plant in Bonavista, where Murray Paul went to work in the 1950s and later became head of the Bonavista plant workers' local. Paul, 81 at the time he was interviewed, remembers it well: "Frank Chafe from the CLC came to Bonavista to help. I started working before we got the union. We were getting nothing. I worked for 55 cents an hour before we got the union. Then wages went up right away. Workers were definitely better off for getting the union."

In Harbour Breton, Allan Day also remembers the early days of unionization, which again pre-date the NFFAWU. Day started working at the plant in 1963, "the first year it opened." He was part of the group that worked with CLC representative Cyril Strong in the fall of 1966 signing people up to form a union. Day said the first contract provided only a three-cent-an-hour wage increase, but an important benefit came with it: "With the union came seniority. Without seniority, if you were a friend of the foreman, you got lots of work. They could do what they liked. Back then, if you were involved in the union, the manager would follow you around the plants."

Bonavista and Harbour Breton were among those plants that became part of NFFAWU at the founding convention in 1971. Because some of these plants were already under contract, it was difficult for the union to make significant progress in their wages and benefits until 1973, when some contracts at the larger plants expired.

A fish plant is a major economic driver in a community. As Will Reid—fish cutter, in-plant union rep, IRO vice-president, and eventually FFAW staff representative—pointed out, "The benefits always go right back into the community. The people are paid well, and they spend their money locally. It's not just the community where the plant is located that benefits. Most plants employ people from a number of communities in the surrounding area."

For plant workers, the 1970s were a period of successful organizing, as plant after plant joined the union fold. Reid said when union organizers approached non-unionized workers, they found that "a lot of plant workers were not doing very well. Organizing showed you the difference between unionized and non-unionized plants."

In the 1970s and 1980s, hours of work were long, but unionized plants provided reasonable incomes, especially in two-income families. In many households, the husband fished and the wife worked in the plant, or both of them worked in the plant. As former secretary-treasurer Reg Anstey put it, "People came out of school and went to work in the plant." After decades of outport Newfoundlanders and Labradorians leaving the province to work in factories in mainland Canada and the US, people now had the option of what Anstey called "a real good factory job" right in their home community.

One of the major challenges for plant workers, especially in the early years, was getting reasonable restrictions on the amount of work the company could compel them to do. "When I started," said Allan Moulton from Marystown, "you'd work 70–75 hours a week." But gradually the union was successful in getting time and a half after eight hours a day and 40 hours a week, with the ninth hour each day mandatory at time and a half. Any hours beyond that were voluntary. Moulton, who started work at Atlantic Fish in Marystown in the early 1970s at $1.27 an hour, recalls the union having to make it a strike issue to get every second Saturday off in the summer. At the time, work was mandatory on Saturday if scheduled by the company, which in the case of the trawler plants, it inevitably was.

In the years leading up to the moratorium, fish plants fell into two distinct categories. There were a dozen year-round ports supplied by company-owned deep-sea trawlers in a vertically integrated operation. The remaining plants depended on inshore fish and tended to operate seasonally subject to the availability of raw material in their area.

Like many industrial unions, FFAW used the approach of "pattern bargaining." The union leadership would pick a "target" company, work with the membership to develop a list of bargaining demands, then take a strike vote in support of the bargaining position. Once an agreement was reached with the target company—with or without a strike—the pattern was set and the union would then take it to other

Staff representative Will Reid with the 2015 OCI plant worker bargaining committee getting ready for negotiations.

employers with the intent of matching it with their workforce. The pattern was normally set with the year-round plant workers, who had the greatest bargaining power. Seasonal plant owners would sometimes resist some of the contract language, which they felt was not suited to an operation of their size and operating season, but the workers in seasonal plants clearly benefitted from the bargaining power of the year-round plants.

Depending on the economic circumstances at the time—market conditions and foreign exchange rates among the most significant—some rounds of collective bargaining produced major gains while others were more about holding on to hard-fought wages and benefits from prior negotiations and trying to make as much progress as possible.

Three landmark agreements reflect the progress made in plant workers' lives. In 1973, the union picked BC Packers in Harbour

Breton as the target and succeeded in increasing the wage rate from $1.75 to $3 over the life of the contract, a remarkable increase which quickly spread to other operators. The new agreement also included improvements in the seniority clause and grievance procedure, overtime pay for the sixth consecutive day of work, eight paid statutory holidays, and a health insurance plan. By any standard, this was a landmark collective agreement that greatly improved the quality of life for union members working in the plants.

Chapter 4 discussed the 1980 strike, which produced a 40 per cent increase in the hourly rate for production workers—from $5 to $7 an hour in the case of cutters—along with a host of other benefits and improvements in contract language. Then in 1988, when FPI was the obvious target, FFAW members were joined for the opening of bargaining by national CAW president Bob White, and his assistant, Buzz Hargrove. Hargrove participated in the bargaining throughout. Once again, plant worker wages and benefits improved considerably, and the first steps toward a pension plan were made, although it was eventually a casualty of the devastation caused by the moratorium.

By 1988/89, Statistics Canada reported 20,000 fish plant workers in the province, but, as we saw earlier, the industry turned out to be built on an unsustainable foundation. Over the next five years, quota cuts in fish stocks stripped these plants of their lifeblood, and plant after plant shut its doors, many of them for the last time.

The collapse of groundfish stocks took a particularly heavy toll on the trawler fleets and the plants they supplied, primarily on the south coast. At peak, there were about 80 offshore groundfish trawlers in the province. Only a few of these remain in operation in 2021, although the licences have never been cancelled. Of the

12 plants these vessels once supplied, which included four on the Burin Peninsula and four farther west along the south coast, eight are now closed completely, while four have a much reduced operation from their heyday, all but one of the four relying on species other than groundfish.

In the years following the closure of the main groundfish stocks, new operators occasionally tried to cash in on the desperation of the local people and communities, in some cases with outrageous demands for resource access that were at total odds with scientific advice and DFO allocation and access policies.

One effort that showed real promise for a period was the importation of frozen-at-sea, primarily Russian-caught cod from the Barents Sea, where the cod population had exploded. Melvin Lockyer, unit chair of what was then a High Liner Foods plant (now Icewater Seafoods) in Arnold's Cove, recalled that frozen-at-sea cod procured on world markets sustained the plant for several years, along with inshore fresh fish from 3Ps, providing up to 50 weeks of work per year. But, as happened with many sectors of the economy, this promising endeavour fell victim to extremely cheap labour that was part of the industrialization of China. Eventually, Newfoundland and Labrador plants could not compete with the prices Chinese companies could afford to pay for raw material.

FPI was also heavily involved in the production of frozen-at-sea cod. A Newfoundland and Labrador-based company, FPI had the challenging task of trying to re-invent itself after its raw material base had been virtually wiped out. Its biggest plant, in Port Union, was closed indefinitely. Many local people felt it would never operate again, although it did eventually re-emerge as a shrimp plant with a much smaller workforce, only to be destroyed several years later

Production of crab meat at the Beothic Fish plant in Valleyfield (now New-Wes-Valley).

by Hurricane Igor. Several FPI plants were in limbo during the moratorium, the workers surviving with the help of income support from NCARP and TAGS. Of the other biggest operations, the Trepassey plant was torn down and sold for scrap, while Marystown hobbled along on ever-dwindling supplies, primarily of flatfish. A company that had been groundfish-driven had to fundamentally change its operation, expanding its shellfish and value-added business in the face of ever-declining groundfish quotas.

When FPI was established with a significant infusion of federal and provincial funding, it was seen as an unofficial "flagship" company for the province, with a mandate to market on behalf of any smaller companies who might want to enter that type of arrangement. At the Boston Seafood Show and other seafood trade shows, FPI put on an impressive display, with a degree of visibility that was beyond the reach of other producers from the province.

This was particularly valuable the year cooked and peeled northern shrimp burst onto the scene.

An act of the provincial legislature called the FPI Act was intended to protect the company's status as an Newfoundland and Labrador-based company after the company bought out the federal and provincial government shares and listed the company on the stock exchange. The Act was sufficient to foil a bid in 1999 from an entity called NEOS—a partnership involving John Risley of the Nova Scotia-based Clearwater Seafoods; Bill Barry, a fish processor from Curling on the west coast; and an Icelandic partner. But two years later, Risley was back with a different approach as the lead figure in what became a shareholder revolt to get rid of the management group headed by Vic Young, who by this time had been chief executive officer for about 16 years. Risley and his supporters painted Young's group as overly cautious, accusing them of failing to provide adequate returns to shareholders. Risley and his supporters promised to "unlock the value" in the company and provide a more entrepreneurial approach that would deliver better returns to shareholders.

The union and its members had enjoyed a positive relationship with Young and his group over the years. The union leadership, along with municipal leaders in communities in which FPI operated plants, strongly supported the incumbent group. One person who bought Risley's sales pitch was private citizen John Crosbie, now retired from politics, who agreed to be part of the slate of directors Risley presented to the annual meeting of shareholders. Because of the level of public interest in the matter, the provincial government established an all-party committee of the legislature to investigate the matter. This included holding public meetings around the province.

Allan Moulton vividly recalls the public meeting in Marystown: "The hall was full. Crosbie had said he'd go to all the meetings. The room was full of boos when he arrived. Whenever he tried to speak, the people shouted him down. It was a rough night for Crosbie—he couldn't get a word in. He didn't go to the other meetings. I still think if not for the fact Crosbie supported Risley, Vic Young may have survived."

Most of the shares in FPI at the time were held by "institutional shareholders"—corporate investors who held substantial blocks of shares but were individually limited by the *FPI Act* to a maximum of 15 per cent of the total number of shares. Risley is persuasive, and he convinced most, if not all, of these institutional shareholders to back his bid. The annual meeting was almost an anti-climax; Risley had most of the votes committed before the doors opened. When the dust cleared, Young and his team, including the previous board of directors, were out the door, and Risley's group took over with Derrick Rowe, a Newfoundlander whose background was in the telecommunications business, at the helm as CEO.

The Risley group had promised an aggressive approach, with investment in the plants and an all-plants-open policy. But the company's actual performance was a different matter, and by 2004, the company had closed plants in Harbour Breton, Fortune, and a smaller operation in Baine Harbour, and Rowe was out as CEO.

The relationship between the union and the new management group was testy at best. By 2006, Risley's interest in the whole venture appeared to be waning. Complicating the matter were continuing demands from the company for exemptions from provincial minimum processing requirements (MPRs) that were designed to protect employment in the province, with a particular impact on the groundfish operation in Marystown.

The company then shocked plant workers by proposing a rollback of $2.66 in the hourly rate in the plants, from $13.66 to $11 an hour. The workers, of course, wanted no part of that, and a stalemate ensued. On September 11, 2006—the fifth anniversary of 9/11—Buzz Hargrove and I flew to New York City to meet with Risley in his hotel suite to see if we could find a way to get him off his position. While he hinted at having some flexibility, he was very clear that if the company couldn't keep wages at or below $12 an hour, the Newfoundland operations would not be viable. This was a non-starter with the bargaining unit.

With no resolution on the horizon, FPI brass began talking to other fish companies about the possibility of breaking up and selling off the company's assets in the province. Two bidders expressed interest in the trawler fleet and primary processing operations— the Barry Group and OCI—with OCI eventually emerging as the successful bidder. High Liner, the Nova Scotia-based firm, was the only serious bidder for the value-added plant in Burin and the marketing division of the company.

Before the marketing division of the company was sold, I received a call from Premier Danny Williams's office asking me to attend a meeting in his boardroom. Senior executives from the processing sector were also present. The premier started the meeting by saying, "My gut tells me the FPI marketing arm is too important an asset for our industry to be sold to someone from outside the province." He made a rather extraordinary offer to invest significantly in the company if the Newfoundland and Labrador industry would put together a plan to operate it. He said government wasn't interested in operating the business: "We're not in the business of marketing fish." He didn't go so far as to say government would foot the entire

Workers at the fish processing plant on Fogo Island.

A Match to a Blasty Bough | 221

bill to keep the operation in the province, but my sense was that if industry had responded positively, he would have been willing to do so. Instead, one by one the processing sector representatives shot down the idea, starting with Martin Sullivan from OCI. I felt the idea had the potential to increase the value of our seafood exports and give us a more coordinated presence in global markets, so I spoke strongly in favour of the idea, but I didn't have much company at that meeting.

Williams seemed taken aback by the overall reaction and suggested that everyone think about it for a week, and then have a further discussion at a follow-up meeting. The follow-up meeting produced an identical outcome, and the plan died. I was halfway back to my office following the meeting when my cellphone rang. It was an exasperated Williams saying, "You can lead a horse to water but you can't make him drink." I'm not sure why he called me—we weren't exactly pals. I think he just needed someone to vent to.

In my estimation, his gut instinct was correct. One of the fundamental weaknesses of our fishing industry has been the number of under-financed sellers who rely on brokers to move their product. Market analyst John Sackton used the term "Friday night frenzy" to describe the scramble by processors to sell off crab at the end of each week so they could have cash flow to finance the following week's raw material purchases. In a market report in June 2005, he described the marketing of Newfoundland and Labrador crab as "an almost textbook example of how to destroy a market."

Processor Bill Barry had a similar message four years later, in an interview with CBC's Fisheries Broadcast: "Seventy per cent of this industry sells to brokers and don't sell to the final market, and these brokers are a bunch of vultures out there ... They're the bankers for the industry ... They really have no ultimate concern for the amount of money that comes back to the province. So unless we eliminate the irresponsible selling of Newfoundland fish, we're never going to bring back more money home." Barry said the province needed "some creative financing instrument so we don't have distress selling. You've got 50 per cent of this industry that can't hold onto their inventory for any longer than two weeks because they'll have no money to pay their fishermen."

The outcome of Williams's intervention was typical of any attempt to coordinate the marketing of seafood products from our province: the processors stonewalled it. A few years later, the province offered to put up $5 million to kick-start a seafood marketing council similar to those many of our competitors—including Alaska and Norway—have in place, but the processors voted against the idea. Essentially their idea of a marketing strategy is to put themselves at the mercy of brokers and middlemen and adjust the raw material price accordingly. In that regard, little had changed from what Sir William Coaker and the FPU confronted more than a century ago.

Once the processors rejected Danny Willliams's offer to finance FPI's marketing arm, deals were signed to carve up what had once been seen as the province's flagship company. The provincial government agreed to revoke the *FPI Act* in return for written commitments from the successor companies to keep all plants open for at least the next five years. The agreement with OCI also gave the province a 49 per cent share for the first nine years in a holding company that would hold the enterprise allocations (company quotas) that were relinquished by FPI. There were penalties for non-compliance with the work content and other rules spelled out in the agreements, but in the case of High Liner, it became clear that they would rather pay the fines than meet the work requirements of the contract. When the five-year agreement was up, so was High Liner's interest in the Burin plant, which was soon closed.

The province had lost the company's marketing arm, while problems continued in the groundfish operation, with OCI continuing to demand more and more exemptions from MPRs. In 2011, they made a proposal to the Marystown workforce for a three-year, 18-week operation, but the workers in return would have to agree to even further exemptions, giving the company the right to export, unprocessed, up to 75 per cent of the yellowtail flounder and 100 per cent of the redfish caught by company vessels. The company and the government pointed to the results of an audit which showed the yellowtail business as a money loser, but it failed to factor into that accounting the financial benefit to the company from having the right to ship out unprocessed 100 per cent of its redfish landings.

I attended the meeting in Marystown at which a hall full of workers were virtually unanimous in rejecting the company's proposal. I vividly recall a worker coming to the microphone and saying something along these lines: "My wife and I are 63 years old, so this proposal works fine for us. But I'm going to vote against it, because it's not good for younger workers and it's not good for the province."

Once the workers rejected the proposal, instead of looking for a compromise, OCI abruptly announced the permanent closure of the largest remaining fish plant in the province. Allan Moulton still feels that the workers were let down by the provincial government: "I still think there would have been a different outcome if the provincial government had said no."

For union officers, staff representatives, and local committees, one of the toughest things they must deal with is the permanent closure of a plant. As a staff representative who serviced several seasonal fish plants, Will Reid had to deal with more than his fair share of closures over the years. He recalls one occasion when he was contacted by top management of P. Janes & Sons, a long-standing medium-sized inshore operator, who said they were shutting three plants—their entire operation. "It's not very nice to walk into three different halls and tell people their jobs were gone. The company never does it. It's always up to the union to deliver the devastating news."

Once the plant in Marystown closed, Moulton said, "Most people say it's not the plant I miss, it's the people."

What's That Got to Do with the Price of Fish?

When the union got started, we were getting nothing for our product—a cent and a half a pound for cod. When the union got going, things changed for the better.

— Albert Johnson, inshore harvester, Little Catalina

One of the biggest challenges involved in unionizing the fishing industry is collective bargaining, particularly in the inshore fishery. The plant, trawler, and non-fish bargaining units are constructed along conventional employer-employee lines. The work being undertaken at the workplace is different, but in terms of the relationship between union members and their employer, a fish plant isn't all that different from a mine or a car factory or a supermarket. The boss calls the shots, subject to the labour standards laws in effect and the provisions of the collective agreement. As we have seen earlier, in the 1970s the trawler companies tried to depict trawlermen as co-adventurers, but the 1975 strike eliminated that idea.

In a typical employer-employee arrangement, collective bargaining follows a standard pattern, regardless of the type of workplace. Company officials—sometimes with the support of outside resource people such as a lawyer or a labour relations consultant—negotiate with a committee of elected representatives from the bargaining unit, with a union officer or staff representative as the chief spokesperson for the union. This spokesperson provides advice, but committee members from the workplace decide the bargaining position of the union.

The inshore sector is different. I touched earlier on the accomplishments of the FPU. The fact that such a remarkable organization did not engage at all in negotiating fish prices speaks to the challenges that are involved.

While the traditional collective bargaining model is designed with a clear employer-employee relationship in mind, owner-operators of fishing enterprises are considered self-employed. Notionally it's up to them which plant they sell their catch to, although as a practical matter, many have entered into arrangements with processors whereby the latter provide financing—for the acquisition of boats, equipment, licences, quotas, and the like—in return for a commitment that all the harvester's catch will be sold to that particular buyer. Other owner-operators get their financing elsewhere but enter what are sometimes referred to as "supply agreements" whereby they agree to sell all their catch to a particular buyer, sometimes in return for "bonus" payments (money above and beyond the floor price that emerges from the collective bargaining process).

There is also the matter of the relationship between the captain and crew of the vessel. Many FFAW members' fishing enterprises are family affairs, in that the skipper and all members of the crew are members of a single family. Others employ crew members from outside the family; some are a hybrid of these two. Crew members are generally paid a percentage share of the proceeds of the catch.

From day one, most fish companies were bitterly opposed to collective bargaining in the inshore sector. It's not hard to see why. As long-time inshore harvester George Chafe from Petty Harbour put it, "When the union came in, the biggest thing was the price of fish."

The processors' resistance to collective bargaining goes back to the early days of the NFU when Fishery Products was willing to negotiate wages and working conditions with plant workers, but adamantly refused to negotiate fish prices with the union on behalf of harvesters. Fortunately, not all buyers took that approach. The union's first inshore certification was in the area in Bonavista North where Beothic Fish Processors was the main buyer. That put Beothic in a delicate position. They were legally obligated to negotiate with the union, while at the same time they were members of FANL, which was in the habit of unilaterally announcing prices. A key species at the time was flounder. During negotiations in Valleyfield, Beothic and the union committee had reached agreement on other species, including a modest price increase on cod. The union was looking for six cents a pound for flounder; the company offered five.

The company wanted time to think about its position, so there was an adjournment in negotiations for a week or so. During that adjournment, FANL attempted to bypass the union by announcing the same price schedule for species that were already agreed upon between the union and Beothic, and they announced a price of five cents for flounder.

"Boyd Way was livid with FANL," Richard Cashin recalled years later. "So were the fishermen. We said it was unacceptable and the boys would tie up. Boyd came back and improved the price to five and a half cents, and everybody left to go fishing."

Chapter 4 outlined the trawlermen's battle to get rid of the co-adventurer system and pointed out that this major achievement had its origins in an inshore strike by the Port au Choix fleet, a tie-up that Fishery Products executive Gus Etchegary called "almost unbelievable," considering market conditions. Unbelievable or not, the *Evening Telegram* reported that after a 10-week strike, a settlement was reached which saw the price of small cod increase by 1.25 cents to 9.25 cents a pound, and the price of shrimp increase by 1.5 cents—half a cent higher than an earlier offer.

"The fishermen had not achieved a great financial victory," Peter Sinclair states in his book *From Trappers to Draggers*. "Nor had they been squashed under corporate pressure. What they had done was to demonstrate that the union would have to be treated as a serious force in the inshore fishery as well as in other sectors of the industry. Once again, Port au Choix fishermen had moved Newfoundland fishermen as one step further along the path to effective participation in the economic decision-making of the industry."

In Newfoundland and Labrador, inshore collective bargaining takes place under the provisions of its own separate act, the *Fishing Industry Collective Bargaining Act* (FICBA), which has been amended several times. Prior to the implementation of FICBA by the Smallwood government in 1971, under heavy pressure from the union, there was considerable debate around what sort of mechanism should be put in place to determine the price of fish. Before the union arrived, fish processors would get together and decide what they would pay for fish, then publicly announce the prices. At the time (or even today, for that matter), there were very few places in the world where fish prices and conditions of sale were settled under a traditional collective bargaining model. In some parts of the world—notably in Europe—fish is sold at auctions, a system which only really works if there is genuine competition for fish. In a few areas, there is some form of intervention in the form of a price-setting board or panel.

Cashin was part of a small delegation headed by then provincial fisheries minister Captain Earl Windsor that travelled to Iceland and Norway in 1970 to look at the systems in use there. "I liked the Norwegian system," he recalled. Under that system, fish price was based on presentations to a pricing authority from representatives of both harvesters and processors. Any surplus went into a kitty to fund shortages in future years. The Norwegian government backstopped the entire system in the event of a shortfall that exceeded these reserves. Cashin made a presentation to the provincial government, advocating a Norwegian-type system, but the union lacked the resources for a detailed follow-up.

As we saw earlier, the legislation eventually implemented by the Newfoundland government was a slightly revamped version of the *Labour Relations Act*, with strike or lockout as the way to resolve a dispute. Subject to a few, mainly procedural, rules, the harvesters could strike or the processors could implement a lockout if the price and related conditions were not resolved satisfactorily. This was a significantly different approach than what the union had proposed, but at least it provided a legal framework for collective bargaining for people who fished for a living.

The threat of a strike (or lockout) is often a greater pressure point than the actual event itself. We saw that in 1979 when under imminent threat of a strike, FANL dug a little deeper into their pockets than they had intended, and the union likewise reached to find a solution. But after moving from a threat to an actual event,

Joan Doucette with a halibut. The union's approach to halibut management and pricing has dramatically improved the value of this important species.

as happened in 1980, it can drag on—five weeks in that case, which was a large chunk of the peak fishing season.

Chapter 5 details the high-profile, province-wide inshore strike/lockout that took place in 1980. Following that standoff, for the most part, the union and FANL managed to successfully resolve fish prices through the 1980s, although there were occasional localized disputes, and several close calls in the capelin fishery in particular. The capelin fishery highlights some of the challenges in trying to resolve the price when the parties are unable to reach a negotiated settlement. Nature dictates that the capelin fishery starts at different times in different areas. Because of demanding market specifications, capelin can be suitable for harvesting in a particular bay or region for as little as a few days, and how much can be landed in a single day is limited by processing capacity. A strike or lockout wouldn't have to last long to wipe out an entire year's capelin fishery.

Other fisheries have challenges as well. Opening dates for the fishery can vary widely from region to region. Some fisheries are dispersed over a wide coastline, with participants living in hundreds of communities. In some fisheries, participating vessels range from small open boats to 65-foot-plus longliners. Some bays can be closed to fishing because of heavy ice cover at the same time that harvesters in other bays are ready to go. Even the process of conducting a ratification vote is challenging in the case of late-starting fisheries, when many participants are already on the water fishing other species, and those who are ashore are scattered.

The market in some fisheries is highly influenced by supplies from other fishing countries, which can make raw material pricing in advance of the season highly problematic. In the lump fishery, the union addressed this problem in the 1990s by negotiating a starting price, then a final settlement based on actual market returns, tied to an agreed price-to-market formula. In some years, the year-end adjustment exceeded the starting price, and this approach, with occasional minor adjustments, has remained in place ever since.

Another creative approach was used more recently in the Gulf of St. Lawrence halibut fishery, where the small quota had been managed based on a "derby fishery"—a competitive fishery that lasted barely 24 hours. This resulted in the market being flooded and the return to harvesters significantly diminished. It also posed potential safety risks. The union worked with its members in that fishery to develop an alternative system whereby individual licence holders could choose from among several options as to when they fished. This spread out the landings and avoided the flooding of the market. The union then worked out an agreement with halibut buyers that tied the raw material price to the actual return of the processors, according to a pre-agreed sharing formula, with independent third-party verification of market returns. The harvester's share under this formula amounts to approximately 75 per cent of the market return.

The new approach kept the market hungry instead of force-feeding it. Blaine Crocker of Trout River said that under the new arrangement, he ended up getting about $7.50 a pound, compared to $3 or less in the days of the derby fishery.

An innovative system was also implemented in the lobster fishery to ensure a fair return to harvesters. Details of this approach are outlined in Chapter 22.

Crab proved more challenging. Differences between the union and the processors first emerged in the 1990s in the crab fishery which had by then become the lifeblood of many fishing operations. The crab fishery normally starts in more southerly areas in April, then gradually expands northward as ice conditions permit. In 1993, finding a mutually acceptable price proved extremely difficult and a price agreement was not reached until June, after several earlier offers had been rejected and strike action endorsed at membership meetings. This jammed the fishery into a more concentrated period than was normally the case. The ensuing quality problems would normally have caused trouble in the markets, but a major decline in snow crab and king crab quotas in Alaska, along with extremely favourable currency exchange conditions, provided dramatically increased prices in 1994 and 1995 without the parties having to fight to reach a settlement.

After three years of rapidly increasing snow crab prices, the market took a downturn in 1996. This triggered a strike, which wasn't settled until the middle of June. The market slide continued in 1997. Crab harvesters armed the union with a strong strike mandate and the ensuing strike dragged into July.

The entire 1997 crab fishery was at risk of being lost, which would have been a major blow to the incomes of harvesters and crab plant workers as well as to cash flow for processors. It would also have added to our growing reputation in the market as unreliable suppliers. The more frequent our tie-ups and the more uncertain our starting dates, the less reliable we'd be regarded in the market and the more likely our customers would be to look for other suppliers or to substitute other products for snow crab.

By this time, Brian Tobin had left federal politics and become Newfoundland and Labrador's premier. Max Short remained a federal employee, but he and Tobin stayed in touch. So it was on behalf of Tobin that Short called me in early July to ask me and others from the union to attend an under-the-radar meeting in a hotel suite that night with the premier, his fisheries minister, and several processors. The gathering didn't include the president of FANL, the bargaining agent for the processors, which was extremely unusual. Pat Quinlan and Terry Daley—two prominent crab buyers—attended, along with Percy McDonald from the processing side. I was accompanied by union secretary-treasurer Reg Anstey and inshore vice-president Bill Broderick.

The conversation was blunt, tense, and at times acrimonious. Tobin said that the province couldn't afford to lose the crab season and that for the longer term we needed to find some other way to resolve disputes that didn't jeopardize the economy of coastal communities and the people who lived in them. He committed that if the parties could reach agreement on a price schedule for 1997, he would appoint a task force to look at best practices in other fishing nations and recommend a new approach to resolving disputes in the Newfoundland and Labrador fishery. Tobin then tried his hand as a price mediator. By the time several hours had passed, we had a new proposed price schedule that everyone disliked, but the two parties committed to take it to their respective bargaining committees as a last-ditch attempt to salvage the season.

I heard later that there was hell to pay at the ensuing meeting among processors, as the company brass who had taken part in the secret meeting had to justify going behind the backs of their bargaining agent. At least we didn't have that problem. After a no-holds-barred discussion, the rank-and-file members of the union's negotiating committee voted to recommend acceptance of the tentative agreement. That recommendation was critical to the outcome.

The well-attended ratification meetings that followed were among the toughest I have experienced. While some areas were overwhelmingly in favour of the proposed prices and conditions of sale, others were just as overwhelmingly opposed. The overall vote would determine the outcome. The committee recommendation passed by a narrow margin. But many members were willing to give up the season rather than fish for the prices on offer.

The first crab was not landed that year until about July 21. This is treacherous timing for a crab fishery: it's getting close to moulting time, and once a crab sheds its shell, the new soft shell that replaces it makes it initially unacceptable to markets, and it takes several months before it regains prime quality. Such a late start also means missing out on the July 4 holiday in the largest market, the US, which is the prime time for crab consumption in that country; compressing landings into too short a period of time for best handling in the plants; and leading to more product being landed during the warmer summer months. None of these are acceptable outcomes.

A market-driven approach would aim to spread out the catch, get product in the market as early as possible to take advantage of any inventory shortfalls, and catch more in the spring and less in the summer than had been achieved in the 1990s. If we were to get out of the vicious cycle of low prices, strike votes, tie-ups, compressed landings, resulting quality challenges, and another round of low prices, something had to give.

Once the fishery was over, Tobin appointed the task force he had promised, with former deputy minister of fisheries David Vardy as chairperson. Among other things, the task force reviewed dispute settlement systems in various jurisdictions with fisheries at least somewhat comparable to ours, and organized visits with small industry delegations to a couple of jurisdictions.

The provincial government also organized a government-industry delegation to Japan that included the task force chair, the minister of

Icing down crab. Crab has paid the bills for many fishing enterprises in the province; crab negotiations have always been hotly contested.

fisheries, processors, and a union delegation that included me as well as leaders from both the plant worker and fishing sectors. What we saw was sobering. The delegation split into smaller groups and visited various crab plants and markets. Our Japanese hosts were courteous, but they were also blunt in telling us that our crab did not come close to the quality of finished product delivered by our main competitors, Alaska and New Brunswick. They didn't just tell us; they took us into their plants and showed us.

Noting that late starts and the resulting compressed fishery had given us this poor reputation for quality, Vardy recommended a system in which the parties would negotiate more or less as usual, but in the absence of a settlement, the price and any other outstanding issues would be settled by a form of arbitration known as final offer selection (FOS) instead of the previous strike/lockout regime. Under FOS, each party would submit its final offer in writing to an independent arbitrator. The arbitrator had no flexibility but had to pick the union's position or FANL's position—where is, as is.

Government eventually adopted the system proposed by Vardy's task force. An advantage of this system was that if buyers representing the majority of purchases of a particular species were involved in representations to the arbitrator, the ensuing decision would be binding on all buyers of that species. Vardy also proposed that the parties eventually move to an auction system for setting fish prices, but this never got off the ground.

From 1998 to 2003, 56 sets of negotiations were conducted under the sole arbitrator system. More than half of these—31—were settled by the parties without referring the matter to the arbitrator. The fact that an arbitrator was lurking in the background helped, no doubt, in reaching some of these agreements. Of the remaining 25 cases, the arbitrator selected the union's final offer 14 times, and FANL's 11 times. For the most part, these fisheries started on time, helping to rebuild the industry's reputation in the market as a reliable supplier. But the processors didn't like an outside party having the power to decide the price of fish, and they resented some of the decisions. It wasn't long before trouble came calling.

The legislation that implemented the arbitration system gave each party (FFAW and FANL) an opportunity every two years to veto the continuation of the system, provided they notified government by a specified date that they were withdrawing. Late in 2002, FANL officially advised government that they were withdrawing from the program, effective December 31, 2002. To the disgust of the processors, the provincial government extended the program anyway, to expire at the end of 2003, unless both FANL and the union agreed to extend it further.

As their first bid had been foiled, the processors tried another tactic. In the latter part of May 2003, virtually all crab processors abruptly stopped buying crab, claiming they couldn't afford the bonus payments they had promised to pay to harvesters. Far from being independent actions taken by processors on an individual basis, this manoeuvre had all the characteristics of a coordinated group action. To me, it was a clear violation of the collective agreement, which prohibits strikes and lockouts while the agreement is in effect. I called our lawyer, Randy Earle, and said it seemed to me that if a union did something like this, the employer would be in court in jig time looking for a court injunction ordering the union to cease its violation of the agreement. So, I asked, why can't we go for a court injunction against the processors?

Earle said it was worth a try, but we would have to establish three core elements in court: that the processors had violated the collective agreement, that they had done so in concert, and that they had done so with the objective or expectation of getting a better deal than they were getting at the time they closed their doors. If we could convince a judge that all three of these elements were in place, we'd have a shot at getting an injunction.

For both strategic and practical reasons, we decided to pick five companies and go forward with an application for an injunction against them—a manageable number that would allow us to move quickly but still sufficient to make the case to the court that the closing of the plants had been a coordinated effort in violation of the collective agreement.

After several days of hearings, the judge ruled in our favour, declaring that the companies had implemented an illegal lockout, and ordered them to stop. The plants re-opened more or less immediately.

Harvesters later reported that the buyers reneged on bonus payments they had promised. These payments were not covered by the collective agreement, which stipulates minimum prices which can be exceeded by individual arrangements between processor and harvester.

The processors didn't let it go at that. Apparently, they weren't prepared to take a chance on government's extending the FOS system beyond 2003, so that fall they announced the dismantling of their organization, FANL, which traced its roots to 1936. It was replaced a few months later by a new organization, the Association of Seafood Producers (ASP), which they structured with no collective bargaining mandate. That meant there was no one with whom the union could negotiate, other than to deal with companies one by one, which would have been a challenge.

The processors were clearly banking on the union being unable to achieve such a difficult task in the short time frame available. They also knew that the demise of FANL would eventually terminate the province-wide master collective agreement that provides important rights for fish harvesters, including crucial grievance and arbitration rights that enable the union to enforce fish prices and other conditions of the agreement. It seemed clear to me that the objective of the processors was essentially the same as it had been back in the 1980 strike/lockout—to put the union out of business in the inshore sector.

The one species which the processors were interested in negotiating with the union in 2004 was shrimp, so they hired a lawyer to negotiate on behalf of several shrimp buyers, but they made it clear that ASP, their new organization, was not a party to the negotiations. In the case of crab, we had to tackle the companies one by one. While the big companies stuck together, slowly we managed to get a few small- to medium-sized companies signed up, establishing a floor price that others would have to match if they wanted any crab. Fortunately, the market was reasonably strong, and we were able to negotiate a price that got the fishery started. In due course, the same lawyer who represented the shrimp buyers negotiated a crab agreement with the union on behalf of most of the large crab buyers, and it appeared that we had survived the challenge, for the time being at least. It wasn't long before ASP added a collective bargaining mandate.

As the crab buyers went through these manoeuvres, they had quietly been lobbying hard behind the scenes for a long-held dream. Underlying the dismantling of FANL and the setting up of ASP was a desire on the part of many processors to set up a system of plant production quotas, later given the harmless-sounding name "raw material shares" (RMS), whereby percentage shares of a particular species would be divvied up among the processors in advance. No wonder the processors wanted RMS—it would effectively eliminate competition for raw material: money the processors had previously used to compete for raw material could be used instead to buy and sell one another's production quotas. Following representations on the matter from ASP, fisheries minister Trevor Taylor, a former harvester who had previously been an executive board member and later staff member of the union before going into politics, promised in the spring of 2004 to hold a substantive debate on this matter before the following fishing season.

The stage was set for a showdown of epic proportions.

RMS: "Any Independence We Had Would Be Gone"

RMS was a poorly conceived idea that Danny Williams thought he was going to shove down our throat. I think he grossly underestimated the power of the union.

— Jack Greenham, inshore harvester, Comfort Cove, Notre Dame Bay

A provincial government news release on February 4, 2004, came with an ironic headline. The release, accompanying a report on fish processing policy by retired DFO official Eric Dunne, was titled "A Framework for Stability." But what unfolded was one of the most destabilized periods in the fishery in the past 50 years—which is an understatement.

Dunne was tasked with looking into several policy matters. By far the most controversial of these was the processors' dream of plant production quotas. Dunne's report recommended that a pilot project be considered along these lines, but subject to specific conditions.

Dunne's report clearly summarized the response he had received on the subject of plant production quotas from plant workers and harvesters during consultations: "Most plant workers who met with the Commission expressed grave doubts about the merits of such a system and the motives of the processors in seeking them. The most common view was that this was an attempt by the companies to concentrate control of the industry, to reduce the number of plants and jobs, and to create an asset that many operators would immediately sell off ... Fishermen are convinced that this is simply an attempt to drive down prices by gaining control of the source of supply. Fishermen will be told when to fish and where and to whom to sell their catch."

Dunne recommended that the development of an RMS pilot project "should proceed when at least 3/4 of the active processing license holders involved agree to such an arrangement, and they can satisfy the minister that there are or will be no substantive and reasonable objections from plant workers and harvesters."

That latter condition seemed to be the kiss of death for the scheme. On April 21, 2004, the chair of the Association of Seafood Producers, Herb Clark, and I received a letter from fisheries minister Trevor Taylor saying that "further rational and informed debate" was required before a pilot project could proceed. He committed to "a substantive debate on the issue in the fall of this year." That debate didn't happen, in the fall or winter, and it certainly wasn't in our interest to pursue the matter.

Given this background, I was flabbergasted when, on March 2, 2005, Taylor announced a two-year RMS pilot project in the crab fishery, even though the promised "substantive debate" had not taken place, nor had Dunne's pre-conditions been met. There was no prior notification to the union of this decision whatsoever. Put simply, it was a double-cross.

It's hard to imagine, considering the union's track record of fighting back on major issues, what could possibly have led the Danny Williams government, usually quite shrewd, to such a disastrous decision. But whatever it was, we knew we had to respond quickly

The union's campaign against RMS began with a demonstration at Confederation Building on March 9, 2005.

and decisively. Apart from a round of media interviews, the first significant pushback event was a large demonstration the following week at Confederation Building, with an excellent turnout of both harvesters and plant workers.

This latter point was particularly important. My sense was that both government and the processors thought they could drive a wedge between the harvesters and plant workers on the RMS issue, and put the union in a tough spot. But this is another example of the value in having both groups in the same union. The union leadership had held extensive discussions on the issue with both sectors, and as Dunne pointed out in his report, plant workers weren't buying the bland assurances of their employers that RMS would protect their jobs. In fact, they saw it the other way round.

"Everyone was scared at the transferable part," recalled Helen

Evans, who had worked for years at P. Janes and Sons crab plant in Hant's Harbour. "If the company decided to shut down, they could transfer that quota."

Mike Noonan, a crew member on a longliner which sailed from Bay de Verde to St. John's to participate in a protest against RMS, said, "The big one was RMS. That was going to do the job on all of us."

And Tony Doyle, who had campaigned assiduously to get access to the crab fishery for small-boat operators, spoke for all crab fleets when he said, "Any independence we had would be gone."

It was necessary for the union to come out quickly with a demonstration to unify our members and make our opposition to RMS clear, but we were under no illusions that would be enough. With the FOS model of settling fish prices scrapped because of the actions of the processors, collective bargaining was back on the strike/lockout system. On March 17 we started a round of meetings to vote on a unanimous recommendation of the crab negotiating meeting for a tie-up.

While these membership meetings were ongoing, the union brought more than 100 members opposed to the RMS scheme into the House of Assembly, each wearing a T-shirt with the slogan "A promise is a promise." This was a reference to a line Premier Williams had used effectively against the federal government in connection with a dispute over offshore oil revenues, and also to the broken promise that meaningful consultations would take place before any decision was taken to implement RMS. The House of Assembly does not allow the display of banners or political messages, so eventually the protestors were kicked out of the gallery. This was the first of what would turn out to be 10 consecutive sitting days in the House of Assembly in which proceedings were disrupted—often noisily— by our members protesting against RMS.

By the end of March, more than 2,500 harvesters had participated in 30-plus membership meetings, with 84 per cent voting to tie up the boats. Meanwhile, protests continued across the province. Over the next month or so, these included fishing vessels slowing down oil tankers in Placentia Bay, a rally by about 500 members in St. Anthony, a floating protest at the mouth of St. John's harbour that played havoc with marine traffic, a symbolic "fishermen's arrest" of a Portuguese fishing trawler on the eve of an international fishing conference, and a "women's protest day" at Confederation Building when about 60 union women cornered the premier outside the Legislature and gave him an earful. By this time, I was on a first-name basis with the bailiff who served injunctions for the Supreme Court.

During these protests, Williams took a hard line in the media, saying, "I would suggest to the FFAW, to the fishermen, that they get back out on the water, that they start fishing. Let me make it clear. The decision has been made. The decision is done."

But the relentless pressure eventually created cracks, both in the ranks of processors and in the corridors of power in Confederation Building. First Quinlan Brothers and Quinsea, and later the Daley Group—all major crab buyers—resigned from ASP, Quinlan Brothers saying the RMS proposal could harm their relationship with harvesters and prevent them from providing stable work to their plant workers. It appeared from my vantage point that dissatisfaction with their share under the scheme proposed by ASP might have contributed, but in any event, it was the first split on the ASP side.

On April 29, the premier blinked for the first time, offering to reduce the pilot project from two years to one and appoint an independent panel to review and evaluate it. With momentum on our side, we quickly rejected that proposal and announced plans for a major demonstration at Confederation Building on May 2.

Knowing parking was going to be a problem, I walked to Confederation Building that morning, and my spirits were boosted when I rounded a corner and saw a crab pot at the top of the flagpole—a good sign that our creative protesters were ready. At the time, there were four access points for vehicles to get to Confederation Building, and our staff had assigned different groups, on a regional basis, to blockade each of these entrances. They all did their job and by the time the scheduled start time arrived, there was a lineup of parked yellow school buses and other vehicles on hand, and the building was on lockdown. The media estimated that 5,000 or more people were present, again a good balance of plant workers and harvesters, from as far away as Labrador. Riot police were also on hand, apparently expecting trouble.

FFAW staff know how to organize a demonstration. There was music blaring and banners, flags, and entertaining placards, and as usual union members responded enthusiastically. You can always count on a few leather-lunged members to lead the hooting and hollering, and this was no exception. After several brief speeches from harvesters, plant workers, the Federation of Labour president, an assistant to the CAW president, and a few others, it was my job as cleanup hitter to finish off the rally, so I gave it my best shot, and the buses began the long trek home.

But the fisheries department building, just a short distance from Confederation Building, was an inviting target for many members, and several hundred headed that way. By the time I'd finished a few media interviews and made my way over, the building was locked, police officers were on the parking lot, and I was told that several

Boats in Placentia Bay stage a protest against RMS.

hundred people had made their way inside the building. About two hours later, a union member alerted me that he had seen riot police gathering on a nearby parking lot, some on horses, all in riot gear, with police dogs on hand for good measure. I could see this getting out of hand, so I asked around and found the Royal Newfoundland Constabulary (RNC) officer who was in charge on site. Our experience, whether dealing with the RNC or the RCMP in volatile situations, is that they want to know if there's a spokesperson they can deal with, to try to avoid a violent confrontation.

I was fortunate to be joined by Bob Chernecki, an assistant to CAW president Buzz Hargrove and a labour veteran who had been through his share of tough situations. Bob and I talked to the young RNC representative. I don't recall exactly what I said, but this is close: "I understand you have the riot squad in formation and ready to move in. Before that happens, let me give you my assessment of the situation. We have monitors in the building on each floor, and there's nothing serious going on. I suggest you just sit tight. I can tell you that our guys won't back down, riot squad or no riot squad. Someone who spends his working life on a 45-foot boat on the Grand Banks is not going to be all that worried about a night in jail. If you decide to move in, so be it, but I don't see the point of it. Some of your guys will get hurt, some of our guys will get hurt, and we'll be the lead item on the national news. I don't see much sense in that."

Of course, this officer wasn't the decision-maker—he had to report to his superiors—but he seemed to get it. While he was gone to report in and get instructions, I called both the deputy minister of fisheries and his counterpart in the department of justice with a similar message. The RNC officer came back to me a few minutes later and said they'd hold off for the time being. After a few more hours, we went into the building and squeezed everyone into the boardroom and adjoining corridor to assess our next move. Some people favoured sticking it out; others, noting that the evening newscasts had come and gone, felt we'd made our point and should call it a night. Kevin Slaney, a harvester who had spoken in favour of staying in the building, suggested a show-of-hands vote to decide the matter. Seeing many nodding heads, I took his suggestion and called the vote. A clear majority felt it was time to go home. Everyone agreed that the campaign against RMS would continue.

The momentum of our fightback had government on the run. On May 5, school children in St. Bride's and Ferryland walked out in support of their parents—a brilliant idea, whoever came up with it. That same day, Fabian Manning, Progressive Conservative MHA for the fishing district of St. Mary's-The Capes was kicked out of caucus for speaking out against RMS. Manning told the news media that a Progressive Conservative caucus meeting "was derailed in the first five minutes when a message arrived from the premier in Houston,

Texas. The message was an ultimatum to caucus. They had a choice between me or the premier, but that either way, next week both of us would not be sitting at the same caucus table."

By this time, Williams had obviously had enough—a few days later he announced a three-person panel to examine the RMS issue, but all the power was placed in the hands of Richard Cashin as chair; the other members were window-dressing. The premier was clear about how much authority Cashin would have: "It will be Mr. Cashin's decision that will be accepted. We will not colour it, we will not taint it, we will not amend it under any circumstances."

To me, this amounted to a white flag. The co-founder and long-time president of our union would have full authority to decide the matter. Confident of Cashin's response, I recommended to our negotiating committee that we seek an immediate resumption of negotiations with ASP. The committee agreed. When we reached a tentative agreement on price, our committee recommended we go fishing based on that price schedule and continue to fight any attempt to resurrect RMS beyond that season. More than 4,600 members voted at 28 ratification meetings squeezed into three days. It was an excellent turnout, with 73.6 per cent voting to go fishing. The ballot included an option to accept RMS. That option received 50 votes.

Cashin's report was released by government a few months later. The RMS concept, he said, "is now seriously flawed and damaged as a possible instrument of fisheries policy." Recommendation No. 1 of his report was that government "terminate the project and abandon the concept totally unless first agreed in the collective bargaining arena."

Government also asked Cashin to recommend a new system of settling price disputes in the inshore fishery. His eventual recommendation in this regard was the creation of a price-setting panel, with the authority to set binding fish prices if collective bargaining between the parties failed to produce an agreement.

The outcome on RMS was a major union victory. At the time the dispute started, Williams was riding high in the polls, with the highest popularity rating of any premier in Canada. But our members were equal to the task, and the fact that plant workers and harvesters stuck together was critical. Jim Porter from Port de Grave had been a regular visitor at the House of Assembly protests and spent hours phoning members about the various demonstrations and other events, as he had done for many years as a union activist. As he put it: "That's why I believe in a union—there's strength in numbers."

Hundreds of kilometres away in Shoe Cove, Green Bay, another activist from the inshore sector, Glen Newbury, recalled: "One morning during the RMS dispute, four of us left at 4 a.m. and drove for seven hours for a protest in St. John's at 11, then drove back that night. The next evening, we drove in again."

There were many Jim Porters and Glen Newburys who joined the fightback against RMS from all over the province. Their collective strength and determination fought off a policy that would have rolled back the clock on decades of progress, if it had been implemented. Millions of dollars were at stake in the long run, and the union's success, with the militant backing of the membership, made sure that those millions ended up in our members' pockets, and in circulation in coastal communities.

When the Newfoundland Salt Codfish Association was the only industry organization advising government on fisheries policy, such an outcome would have been unthinkable. But those days were long past, and the union now represented a strong counter-balancing presence to the power of the corporate sector.

Owner-Operator: Linking the Resource to Coastal Communities

We've lost most of the licences in our smaller communities. That's the backbone of the community ... It's an investor's paradise rather than a fisherman's paradise.

— Bob Grant, retired British Columbia fish harvester

Most communities in Newfoundland and Labrador were settled for one reason only—their proximity to productive fishing grounds. By the 1880s, about 90 per cent of the male workforce was engaged in the catching and production of fish, and the limited technology led people to settle as close to the fishing grounds as possible—often on small islands. The link between the resources and the adjacent communities was clear. A fish harvester had to live close to the fishing grounds to be able to prosecute the fishery; those adjacent fish stocks in turn were the lifeblood of the communities.

But changing technology made it feasible for people to gain access to fish stocks from greater distances, either by fleets from other countries or larger vessels from far-flung locations within the province or elsewhere in Canada. The challenge to traditional fishing communities—not only in our province but around the world—is how to maintain the link between the fishing communities and the nearby fish stocks upon which they have traditionally depended. As the abundance of stocks has declined and technology has made it feasible to fish from much greater distances than in the past, fisheries policy has become the critical means of maintaining these vital links.

Some countries have destroyed the links between coastal communities and adjacent fish stocks by surrendering themselves to privatization. Deep-pocketed interests all over the world have campaigned to allow fishing licences and quotas to be bought and sold. One of the most extreme examples is New Zealand, where the government bought the privatization sales pitch hook, line, and sinker. This ultimately led to a situation where fish quotas were bought and sold by anyone who wanted to enter the bidding.

That the inshore fishery in Atlantic Canada has so far managed to avoid the fate of the New Zealand fishery is due in no small part to Romeo LeBlanc, the minister responsible for fisheries in Ottawa in the late 1970s and early 1980s, who recognized the vital importance of fishing communities and small-scale fisheries.

Limited entry—controlling the number of people permitted to fish in a particular fishery through the issuance of fishing licences—was a relatively new concept in LeBlanc's day. It started in the lobster fishery in the late 1960s and gradually spread to other fisheries, gaining momentum under Jack Davis, an MP from British Columbia who was the federal minister responsible for fisheries in the late 1960s and early 1970s.

LeBlanc, an Acadian from New Brunswick, wore his allegiance to the inshore fishery on his sleeve. In a 1975 speech, LeBlanc said that he listened closely to what he called "the bona fide fishermen": "But I would remind the fishermen we can't consult every single one of them. In a word: organize. Be sure your voice is heard."

In a 1977 speech to a Rotary Club in Yarmouth, Nova Scotia, LeBlanc, foreshadowing what was to come, sent shock waves through the corporate sector: "I propose that in future we separate the fishing fleet from the processing companies in Atlantic Canada ... Fishermen should own their own boats and be able to sell where they want ... Creating a truly independent fleet should improve the efficiency of vessel operations, improve the match of fishing and processing capacity, raise fish prices and fishermen's incomes, increase the fishermen's bargaining power, create a healthier balance of forces in the industry, and invigorate fleet development by the fishermen."

LeBlanc never went as far as requiring that ownership of the offshore trawler fleets be separated from the fish processing companies. But in 1979, he made one of the most far-reaching fisheries policy decisions in the history of fisheries management in Atlantic Canada, shaping the inshore fishery in Atlantic Canada for decades. To the dismay of the processing sector, LeBlanc announced a new fleet separation policy, which prohibited fish processing companies from acquiring the licences of vessels less than 65 feet in length. An owner-operator policy requiring inshore vessel owners to operate their own boats came into effect in piecemeal fashion, until DFO minister Tom Siddon made it an Atlantic-wide policy in 1989. Together these policies became the lynchpins of inshore fisheries policy in Atlantic Canada and greatly strengthened the vital link between fishing communities and the adjacent fish resources.

Unfortunately for fish harvesters in British Columbia, these key policies were not extended to the Pacific fishery, which has cost them dearly. By failing to extend these core policies to the British Columbia fishing fleets, government succeeded in concentrating the wealth of that province's fishery in the hands of a few people.

Over the years, many powerful forces in Canada, including in Newfoundland and Labrador, have advocated aggressively for a New Zealand-type model for Canada's fishery. These interest groups include fish processing companies, some politicians, high-ranking DFO officials, right-wing think tanks, and editorial writers. Since LeBlanc's momentous decision in 1979, these interest groups have attempted to have these policies eliminated.

One of the most concerted attacks on LeBlanc's policy foundation for the Atlantic fishery was launched in 1994 by the Fisheries Council of Canada, the corporate fisheries lobby organization headquartered in Ottawa, representing both the processing sector and the corporate offshore fleets. Their main policy demands included a "rights-based fishery," vertical integration, and "freedom of fishing technology." While these propositions were framed in terminology that sounded benevolent—after all, who is opposed to "rights" and "freedom"?—it is important to understand the real, underlying meaning. It was nothing less than a demand for a total reversal of the policy LeBlanc had put in place 15 years earlier. The FCC was demanding a privatized, corporatized Atlantic fishery: New Zealand in the North Atlantic.

What the FCC meant by "rights-based fishery" was essentially the privatization of the resource—managing fisheries by a scheme of individual, transferable quotas which could be "traded freely among economic units ... allowing any quota-holder, whether individual fish harvester or fishing enterprise or processing company, the right to hold a vessel licence." Vertical integration would eliminate the fleet separation policy and allow processing companies to accumulate licences and quotas in all sectors of the fishery, and freedom of technology would eventually enable them to use their offshore trawler fleet to fish what had previously been fixed-gear inshore allocations.

Owner-operator and fleet separation policies are the crucial link between coastal communities like McCallum, shown above, and adjacent fish resources.

For a model to guide the management of the Canadian fishery, the FCC manifesto pointed specifically to the New Zealand fishery.

The FCC and its representatives could claim that their proposal would also allow inshore interests to buy out the big companies' stake in the fishery, but the economic reality was that it was the big corporate sector that had the economic might to control the entire industry if the policy pillars of the community-based, owner-operator fishery came crashing to the ground.

It was imperative that the union respond strongly to the FCC. I called the FCC policy paper their "letter to Santa." When a Fisheries Broadcast interviewer asked me what I thought of the FCC's description of their manifesto as a "vision statement," I replied, "There's a fine line between vision and hallucination."

Among other things, the FCC report said that the fishery "does not have to be a ward of the state and a burden to taxpayers." They told the world that their own industry "consistently represents a substantial net drain on the Canadian economy." At a time when the fishing industry was suffering through the demoralizing crisis of the moratorium and was widely depicted in media reports and elsewhere as an economic basket case, the last thing we needed was a prominent national fishing industry organization talking about their own industry being a drain on the economy. Their talk about "moving away from a largely social fishery" came only a few years after a massive government bailout of the large corporate sector of the industry.

"It's a wish list," I told the *Evening Telegram*. "For Christmas this year they'd like to have much greater control over the fishermen ... These proposals would very dramatically change the rules in the fishery ... We believe the fishing should be left to the fishermen."

But the FCC initiative was a serious threat, and we knew we would need more than a few media interviews to fight it off. The big fish companies were well-heeled and well-connected, with a strong national lobby organization headquartered in Ottawa. Inshore fish harvesters, on the other hand, had no national organization, and in many regions of Canada, the inshore sector was splintered into a multiplicity of small, local associations with limited resources. In fact, at the time, the inshore fishery was probably the largest occupational sector in Canada without a national organization.

This suited DFO Ottawa bureaucrats. As longtime DFO Ottawa employee Joe Gough put it in his history of fisheries management in Canada: "Department officials were sometimes more comfortable with the better organized, better educated representatives of the FCC than the fragmented, hard-to-handle fishermen. To many people in the department, the words 'fishing industry' meant large processing companies, particularly in Atlantic groundfish and Pacific salmon."

If the inshore sector was to have a chance of surviving and prospering, we knew this fundamental weakness had to be addressed. FFAW worked initially with the Alliance des Pecheurs Professionels du Quebec (APPQ, the Quebec Fishermen's Alliance) as well as with other inshore and midshore harvester organizations to form the Canadian Council of Professional Fish Harvesters (CCPFH) under the federal government's sector council program.

Every now and then, coincidence can be a friend. As it happened, the FCC's attack on the policy pillars underpinning Atlantic Canada's inshore fishery coincided with an FFAW initiative to address a long-standing sore point in the Newfoundland and Labrador fishery. Since the early days of the union, the issue of "moonlighters"—those who dabbled in the fishery as a sideline but did not depend on it for a livelihood—had been a major sticking point with inshore members. The union had succeeded in building language into the inshore collective agreement that gave priority in the sale of fish to "bona fide fishermen"—those who depended on the inshore fishery for their livelihood. But pressures to downsize the fishery in the wake of the cod collapse made it clear to the union that a more structured and substantial foundation governing access to the fishery was needed to protect the rights of those who depended on fishing to support their families.

To this end, the union leadership had undertaken a province-wide consultation of its inshore members to create a "professionalization" program. A plan was developed to recognize those who had achieved a defined combination of fishery-related training and time at sea as professional fish harvesters. The plan proposed two categories of professional fish harvesters, replacing the full- and part-time categories that had been in place under the DFO regime. Those who had been fishing for many years and already possessed the fishing skills and know-how were "grandfathered" into the program upfront, and a training regime in areas ranging from safety to navigation was developed for future entrants into the fishery in co-operation with the Fisheries and Marine Institute.

In the first of three rounds of consultations conducted by the union, more than 5,200 inshore harvesters attended 250 meetings across the province and ratified the proposed professionalization regime by a margin of more than 90 per cent. This was a remarkable level of engagement. The overwhelming mandate eventually gave rise to the Newfoundland and Labrador House of Assembly passing legislation in 1996 giving legal authority to a new Professional Fish Harvesters Certification Board (PFHCB), with a significant presence of professional fish harvesters on its board of directors. The board took over the registration of fish harvesters in the province from DFO. After years of being managed under rules created by the Ottawa bureaucracy, fisheries registration in Newfoundland and Labrador would now be based on criteria developed and ratified by fish harvesters throughout the province.

FFAW led the move toward professionalization, which was later taken up by DFO and by other fish harvester organizations. Professionalization became the initial focus of the CCPFH. It worked with harvester organizations, fisheries training institutions, and relevant government departments and agencies in developing training programs, conducting major research projects including a comprehensive occupational study of the fish harvesting sector in Canada, as well as other work aimed at developing respect and institutional recognition for the occupation of fishing.

DFO assigned a senior official from their Moncton office, Jim Jones, as DFO lead on professionalization, and a model for professionalization was developed at a large regional conference in Moncton. By this time, Father Des McGrath had moved from parish duties back to the FFAW, where he was education director. In that role, he became a champion of professionalization, which he saw as another vehicle for fish harvesters to take control of their own destinies.

A logical extension of the CCPFH mandate was to coordinate a vigorous defence of the community-based policies which were the foundation of the inshore fishery. The CCPFH served as a focal point for organizing representations to relevant Cabinet ministers, government departments, agencies, and parliamentary committees on a variety of matters, ranging from fisheries policy to unemployment insurance. In fact, when the Chrétien government launched a major attack on the UI program in 1995, particularly as it related to fish harvesters and other seasonal workers, the CCPFH was the first national organization to speak out. Coincidence worked in our favour once again: government's announcement happened to be made on the same day that the CCPFH board of directors was meeting in St. John's. The Council's press conference blasting the cutbacks was televised live on the CBC national news channel from the FFAW boardroom in St. John's. Human Resources Development Department officials were not amused.

On the matter of the Fisheries Council of Canada's attempt to get rid of the owner-operator and fleet separation policies, the pushback from the member organizations of the CCPFH, together with other allies, was successful in fending off the attack for the time being, but those who wanted to privatize the fishery by undermining these key policies weren't about to give up the fight.

In 1999, DFO launched the Atlantic Fisheries Policy Review, which again put the issues of fisheries access and allocation back on the table in what DFO said was an attempt to "modernize the fisheries policy framework." I see nothing modern about turning back the clock 50 or 100 years and jeopardizing the link between coastal communities and adjacent fish resources, but once again the key fisheries policies were in jeopardy. This time, the CCPFH was in full swing from day one, and we made sure that member organizations and individuals supporting the owner-operator and fleet separation policies showed up at every single one of the 19 or 20 Atlantic-wide public meetings, with a consistent message in defence of coastal communities.

At the end of the process, DFO officials involved in the consultations remarked off the record that the coordinated defence of coastal communities spearheaded by the CCPFH had made a strong impression. The "policy framework" document that eventually emerged in 2004 recognized the owner-operator and fleet separation policies as "integral elements" of fisheries policy, but it also opened the door to changes in the name of "providing resource users with the flexibility they need." The document also made it clear that the DFO minister would retain the right to make what it called "best use decisions" in allocating fish resources among competing user groups—commercial, Aboriginal, recreational, aquaculture, marine tourism, and other sectors—after weighing "the relative benefits for Canada of these legitimate uses of fisheries resources, which may change over time."

In other words, the inshore sector survived the immediate threat of the policy review, but the final document contained enough weasel words to leave the critical policy issue open to further challenge. The cornerstone policies were not removed, but those of us with some experience recognized in harmless-sounding words like *flexibility* and *best use* loose threads that, if pulled, could unravel the policy foundation of the owner-operator fishery.

Another round of changes came in 2007, tied to what government described as rationalization objectives. This time FFAW armed itself with the results of two mail-in surveys conducted among its inshore members. About 1,500 members, including both owner-operators and crew members, completed the detailed surveys. Of these, 84 per cent endorsed a proposed statement of principles that had been drawn up by the union's Inshore Council. A key principle: the benefits of any fisheries rationalization program should flow to the people who catch the fish.

Both levels of government talked about rationalization—by which they meant reducing the number of people in the fishery—as a goal in itself: that somehow the fishery would automatically be better if fewer people were engaged in it. Their plan was essentially to reduce the size of the fleet by having licence holders buy one another out and accumulate quota. The government's rationale for this plan fell short because they assumed that doubling and tripling individual shares would automatically make enterprises more viable. They took no account of the critical impact that the increased debt incurred in acquiring additional quota would have on enterprise viability. The union was open to the concept of fleet reduction, but only insofar as it was voluntary for those who left the fishery and improved the economic circumstances of those who remained.

The 2007 announcement included a policy called Preserving the Independence of the Inshore Fleet in Canada's Atlantic

Fishery (PIIFCAF). The announcement gave licence holders up to seven years to get out from under "controlling agreements"—agreements between inshore licence holders and others (usually fish processors, but sometimes other third parties) to get around the clear intent of the fleet separation policy. Under this approach, processors used financing arrangements with licence holders to gain effective control over licences and quotas which government policy prohibited processors from holding directly. Ottawa's stated intention to gradually get rid of these arrangements was encouraging, but decisive action was needed.

Before that seven-year time frame for eliminating controlling agreements had expired, DFO again opened the door to significant policy changes with another round of "consultations." St. John's was the location of the first meeting. Attendance was by invitation only. The union was invited to send two representatives. When I looked around the table, I saw virtually every corporate licence holder in Atlantic Canada represented, in complete imbalance to the tiny representation from the owner-operator fleets.

Despite all the previous policy reviews that had taken place, there was no underlying framework of principle to this latest round, and it became abundantly clear that everything was on the table. I asked a direct question at the St. John's meeting as to whether the owner-operator and fleet separation policies would remain as pillars of the inshore fishery. I received a fuzzy answer. Corporate executives argued openly to eliminate the owner-operator and fleet separation policies, as did others at the meeting. Knowing that further meetings were scheduled for elsewhere in Atlantic Canada, I immediately sounded the alarm to other inshore and midshore fish harvester organizations through the CCPFH.

Union president Keith Sullivan stirs up the crowd at a public meeting opposing the LIFO policy in the northern shrimp fishery.

The truck system had allowed merchants to dominate the industry and control the fish harvesters. As that system fell out of favour, the processing companies were constantly looking for other ways to control the fishery. It was difficult for them to do so under a competitive fishery, so they favoured fisheries with individual transferable quotas that could be bought and sold. When DFO implemented what was initially a limited "combining" policy, which allowed one owner-operator to buy out the quota holdings of another in his fleet, the processors lobbied to expand the extent of combining that would be permitted. At the so-called consultation in St. John's, one corporate representative expressed the view that there should be no limit on the number of quotas that could be accrued under a single licence. What he and others were advocating was the total privatization of the fishery. This placed the link between coastal communities and adjacent resources in peril, because unlike the inshore owner-operators who live in the coastal communities, the quota holdings of a company like OCI could be bought up by just about anyone, regardless of where they lived or based their operations. Anyone who doubted that need look no further than New Zealand, whose fishery was the very model that the privatizers wanted enshrined in the Canadian fishery.

The union's view was that a fishing licence provided the right to fish—not the right to peddle the right to fish. The privatizers felt that fishing rights should be allowed to be bought and sold by whoever had the deepest pockets, irrespective of any connection to fishing communities.

This time the inshore sector took an important further step to protect the community-based fishery. The CCPFH had done yeoman work in defence of the inshore fishery, but it was limited by its reliance on federal funding for professionalization and training initiatives, and there were gaps in the areas and fleets that participated in the CCPFH, notably in the midshore sector.

Bill Broderick attempted to address the funding issue at a CCPFH meeting in Vancouver, proposing that all organizations agree to contribute $10 a year per member to sustain the organization. When this failed, he organized a follow-up meeting with Christian Brun of the Maritime Fishermen's Union (MFU) in New Brunswick, and O'Neil Cloutier of the Alliance in Quebec. This was a first step toward the formation of what became the Canadian Independent Fish Harvester Federation. This federation eventually included 31 inshore and midshore fisheries organizations representing the majority of the owner-operator fleets from across Canada, including some associations that had traditionally been rivals of one another.

Brun, then executive secretary of the MFU, was the founding president of the Canadian Independent Fish Harvester Federation, and Marc Allain, an Acadian fisheries policy analyst with a strong allegiance to the inshore fishery, provided coordination and maintained day-to-day communications with and between the leaders of the various organizations as its executive director. It was particularly helpful that both Brun and Allain were fluently bilingual and thus able to facilitate communication among organizations with both English- and French-speaking memberships.

The federation has continued to meet over the years with DFO ministers and their officials and has played an important role in convincing DFO to continue to defend the owner-operator and fleet separation policies. The fish companies financed a legal challenge that, if successful, would have legitimized a controlling agreement between a Newfoundland-based processing company and an individual inshore licence holder in Labrador, but the Federal Court upheld DFO's decision to take back the licence. This court decision essentially said that DFO had acted within its constitutional powers in enforcing the owner-operator and fleet separation policies. Policy, however, is easy for a government to change, and the Federation pushed hard to strengthen these policies by having them enshrined in the *Fisheries Act*. In 2019, the federal government passed Bill C-68, which gave the federal Cabinet the authority to enact regulations to strengthen these policies. The DFO minister was Dominic LeBlanc, son of Romeo LeBlanc who had brought in the critical fleet separation policy a generation earlier.

"The owner-operator, fleet separation, and PIIFCAF policies ... exist to ensure inshore and midshore harvesters remain independent, and that the benefits of inshore and midshore fishing licenses flow to the fish harvesters who hold them and coastal communities that depend on the resource," LeBlanc said in a speech to the Canadian Independent Fish Harvester Federation. "These policies are helping to generate stable and long-term economic prosperity in Atlantic Canada."

But the battle is far from over. Those who want to undermine the policy basis of the inshore fishery continue to design legal constructs intended to circumvent the intent of these policies, and the FFAW as well as other members of the Federation will need to continue to be vigilant in defending the foundation of the owner-operator fishery.

Jack Greenham, an inshore owner-operator from a fishing family in Comfort Cove, Notre Dame Bay, has for years delivered fisheries training programs through the Fisheries and Marine Institute. "Professionalization is the key," Greenham said. "Without professionalization there's no checks and balances. Processors are just waiting to get their hands on product. In the absence of professionalization, fish harvesters would lose the fishing rights. That's the important thing—the fishing rights are key."

Ivan Lear, a young harvester representative on the FFAW inshore council who is the latest in several generations of his family to operate a fishing enterprise in Port de Grave, points to the spinoffs for fishing communities of the owner-operator fishery: "Every enterprise is a small business. The money stays in the province. There are definitely big spinoffs when you land a trip—dockside monitors, truck drivers, plant workers all benefit."

Probably the clearest illustration of the importance of the owner-operator and fleet separation policies is the experience in Canada's Pacific fishery, where these policies do not apply. Bob Grant, a former fish harvester and representative of the British Columbia Council of Professional Fish Harvesters, described the situation in a CBC Fisheries Broadcast interview in 2008:

> Large fishing companies had a huge number of vessels sitting on the beach ... They squeezed out the small operator, some of the smaller communities as well. Licence stacking—it's all paper. There's no fishing licences or anything attached to these quotas, they're completely transferable. Anyone can buy one and anyone can lease one out.... So we've got outside investors and the more successful fishing companies controlling these quotas ... Too much money is going into paying for access to fish. There's not enough money left to pay the person to catch the fish.

Ten years after Grant's interview, Stephanie Lights, a Port de Grave harvester who also took over her family's enterprise, participated in a young harvesters' panel at the 2018 FFAW convention. The union arranged for her participation in a British Columbia Young Harvesters Conference in January 2019. "The difference between their fishery and ours is night and day," Lights recalled. "They look at our problems and wish they were us. In BC their issues are a lot more than we have to face. The biggest difference is the owner-operator policy."

In December 2020 and April 2021, DFO implemented regulations in two stages designed to ensure strict enforcement of the owner-operator and fleet separation policies. The challenge as the union heads into its next 50 years is ensuring that DFO enforces these regulations.

"The biggest challenge I see is to the owner-operator policy," said Albert Wells, an owner-operator in Wild Cove, White Bay. "The big corporations have got the fishery taken over. They're driving prices to the point where individual harvesters can't compete."

FFAW secretary-treasurer David Decker agreed, arguing that strict enforcement of the regulations was needed to meet the intent of Bill C-68. Corporate concentration in the fishery and the recent entry into the Newfoundland and Labrador processing sector of a Danish company, Royal Greenland, have highlighted the need for tight enforcement of these regulations. "The companies are out to squeeze out the harvesters. The Fogos and Twillingates won't survive without an independent fishing fleet. It's absolutely critical that the provincial government pass legislation that dovetails with the federal legislation and forbids corporate ownership of inshore fishing enterprises," said Decker. "Fish processor investment in controlling agreements is a cancer that will destroy our communities."

Promoting Safety in a Dangerous Industry

The Safety Association is the best thing yet. It makes people aware of a lot of stuff. A lot more people are wearing life jackets, especially on smaller boats. You see people wearing hard hats when they're unloading boats; you never used to see that. It's very worthwhile.

— Mike Noonan, crew member, Bay de Verde

In 1999, a division of the United Nations based in Geneva, Switzerland, issued a report that described fishing and related occupations as among the most dangerous in the world. The International Labor Organization estimated that, worldwide, 24,000 people who work in fishing, fish processing, and fish farming lose their lives annually. The fishery in Newfoundland and Labrador has had its share of tragedy. FFAW's focus has been to develop organizational structures aimed at education, appropriate regulation, and, above all, prevention.

For centuries there was no one to develop a safety culture in an industry with a history of being fatalistic about whatever the elements might bring. One of the union's earlier safety initiatives came in the deep-sea sector, when the old, notoriously dangerous, side trawlers were still in use. Ches Cribb, who for years was vice-president of the union's deep-sea division, recalls the days before the trawler fleets joined the union: "I don't know if safety conditions entered anyone's mind. When the union got involved, Guy Hackett and I went to see Jimmy Anderson (Director of Ship Safety for Transport Canada). We laid out our issues. He set up the Large Fishing Vessel Safety Committee. Through that committee is how progress happened. Hard hats came through that committee. It met three or four times a year."

Frank Strickland, a trawlerman from Burgeo, describes some of the issues the union had to tackle: "We had to get crew to wear hard hats and flotation vests. Then emergency floater suits. We had nothing before. We used to have old dories instead of life rafts. The side trawlers had no flotation suits, no lifeboats, no hard hats."

It took a three-week strike in 1978 to nail down in the collective agreement a systematic joint approach to safety issues, with full participation by the companies as well as the union.

Barbara Neis is a sociology professor at Memorial University who has taken a major interest in fishing issues generally, and safety issues in the fishery in particular. She notes that when trawlers went north to fish northern cod through the ice in the late 1970s, "They weren't designed for it. The decision was made without consideration of health and safety." This prompted her, along with others, to start the Fishery Research Group, which was successful in obtaining funding to study technological change in the deep-sea plants and trawlers and to issue a report with recommendations.

This led to a request from the union's women's committee to study repetitive motion in fish plants. But while the union was anxious to do this research, the companies—or, some of them—were less enthusiastic. "A manager of one non-union plant on the Northern Peninsula got in trouble for bringing health professionals into the plant," Neis recalled.

An emerging issue in the 1980s and 1990s—one that continues to this day—was shellfish asthma, a form of occupational asthma that has serious health effects on some crab-plant workers. Symptoms include chest tightness, wheezing, coughing, and breathing difficulty. A major study was done on this problem in Quebec in 1984, and Neis was involved in the first study in Newfoundland at the crab plant in Bareneed, Conception Bay.

In the early 1990s, Neis and her colleagues' report, called *Invisible*, was forwarded to the provincial government. The union brought worker representatives from unionized crab plants to a conference on the subject. Participants included the author of the Quebec study and representatives from Workers' Compensation and the provincial government. "Plant worker after plant worker spoke about their experience," Neis said. "By the end of the workshop, nobody in the room could pretend there wasn't a problem. We got funding then to set up Safety Net and do a major study."

Research has shown that about 18 per cent of the workforce in a crab plant will develop crab asthma. When there was still a cod fishery and many of the plants were multi-species operations, one option was to have affected workers move out of the crab-processing area of the plant and work on other species, but because recently the plants are specialized crab plants, that solution is no longer available.

Articles in FFAW's 2018 *Union Forum* highlighted the severity of the problem. Donna Beck, a crab-plant worker in St. Lawrence, documented the misery she experienced, including multiple trips to the hospital with lung infections, chest tightness, and other severe breathing problems. "I found it so hard to get up and down the stairs to the lunch room," she reported. But it was only when the research group from Memorial University tested plant workers in the plant that she discovered that "lo and behold, I was allergic to raw and cooked crab." Advised to quit her job before it killed her—a tough choice for any worker—she then had to live below the poverty line on meagre Workplace NL and CPP disability benefits. At the time of the article, she suffered serious health complications, including a 24/7 oxygen requirement.

Another article paid tribute to Noella Fitzpatrick, a plant worker in the same facility who had died from respiratory failure at the age of 57. Her daughter said that her mother was so seriously affected by her work that when she came home from work, "she'd have to lie down to rest for a few hours until she built up the strength to take a shower."

Neis says that, in 2017, the world's leading researchers on the subject came to St. John's for a conference and published a paper. "They found that shellfish was one of the world's worst sources of occupational asthma. There should be presumptive coverage [for workers' compensation, meaning those presenting with the symptoms would be deemed to have gotten them through workplace exposure]. At least they wouldn't have to pay for their meds."

Neis has made a point of co-operating with the union over the years. "I've also done work in places with no union. You can just see the gaps and vulnerabilities. In a way, you don't know what you have [with a union] until you go somewhere that doesn't have it."

Employers whose workers experience these hardships from their work should be expected to go the extra mile to work with the union to find solutions. But FFAW's industrial director Greg Pretty said the processors' association has "stonewalled for years" union efforts to establish a joint employer/union safety council in the fish processing sector, similar to the safety association in the inshore sector, as well as in three or four other sectors of the economy.

Eventually, after pushing for years, the union was partially successful in that fish processing is now a subset of a broader manufacturing safety council, with a separate working group for fish processing.

Before that was implemented, in 2019 four workers at the OCI plant in Fortune had a close call: they were taken to hospital with carbon monoxide poisoning that workplace inspection authorities traced to a poorly functioning forklift emitting excessive exhaust. Inspectors issued nine safety directives to the company following the ensuing investigation.

"The seafood processing industry still has a lot of work to do to ensure their employees and our members come home safely at the end of each shift," Pretty said.

"Safety is my issue," said Doretta Strickland, who works at the Triton crab plant. "We all deserve to come home safe. For the last 10 years, when we've been talking about shellfish asthma, and talking about forming a safety association, OCI (the plant owner) has been dead opposed to it. Why would you be opposed to the safety of your own workers?"

In the union's inshore sector, Jimmy Anderson of Transport Canada worked closely with the union to set up a Small Fishing Vessel Safety Committee around the time that the large vessel committee was getting under way. The common links were Anderson and union staff representative Matt Murphy, who played an active role on both committees. For years, harvesters Charlie Roberts from St. John's and George Chafe from Petty Harbour were key participants in the inshore committee.

Challenges in the inshore sector included motivating harvesters to follow best safety practices and working with Transport Canada to ensure that any regulations they brought in were practical and helpful.

Keith Sullivan and assistant Tina Pretty present a wreath on behalf of the union at the annual April 28 National Day of Mourning honouring those who had lost their lives or were injured at the workplace.

But an appallingly high frequency of fatalities in the inshore fishery pointed to the need for something beyond committee members and representation at Canadian Marine Advisory Committee meetings. In the early 1990s, the union developed an inshore safety program called "Lifeline." At the heart of the program was the concept of peer training. Step one: train the trainers. This was done with the help of the CAW local union discussion leader program. The first class of 16 Lifeline trainers-to-be took a three-week course that included public speaking as well as training in the safety curriculum. They went out into the communities and delivered a five-day safety program—three days of basic training and a two-day first aid component.

Safety awareness and enhancement became a signature area of responsibility of the PFHCB when it became operational in 1997.

"The Professional Board is accepted by fish harvesters and by government," said board chair Bill Broderick. "From a safety perspective, it's the best avenue we've got for training. Thousands of people have Fishing Master qualifications now. That was unheard of twenty years ago."

The equivalent of the original Lifeline course is now part of the board's mandatory certification training for new entrants.

Harvester Stephanie Lights said she was "shocked at how much was involved" when she took the professionalization program. "I sat at the kitchen table for two or three hours a night. Navigation and safety—there's a lot involved. It gives you a better understanding of what to do in certain situations—stuff I never thought of before."

Sometimes the solution to serious safety problems lies in sensible regulations. For years, I dreaded opening day of the lobster season, because that was the most likely time for a tragedy to occur. Pots could not be set until opening day, and because the first haul of the year was often the best one, there was pressure on boat owners, who fished mainly from small boats, to set their pots and get a trip in, even if the weather was less-than-ideal. Weather conditions and potential overloading of boats with lobster pots were safety risks.

The union set up a meeting with DFO regional officials, explained the problem, and proposed a simple solution—allow lobster harvesters to set their pots up to 48 hours before they were permitted to fish them. We made the argument that this would have no adverse conservation consequences (which should be DFO's main concern) but would create a much safer situation for the harvesters. To their credit, DFO officials moved quickly to implement this change, and Broderick reports that there hasn't been a loss of life on opening day of the lobster fishery since the new regulation came into effect.

Workplace NL, the arm of government that deals with worker safety and compensation, developed a program of sector safety councils to encourage best safety practices in various industries. The inshore fishing sector was one of the first industries to get on board, with the formation in 2012 of the industry-led Newfoundland and Labrador Fish Harvesting Safety Association (NLFHSA), with a mandate of promoting safety awareness and working to reduce workplace injuries, illness, and fatalities in the fishery. It now holds annual safety conferences as well as hundreds of community meetings.

In 2019, the NLFHSA, with financial assistance from FFAW, Workplace NL, and the PFHCB, developed a fish harvester safety logbook which contains, among other things, skipper's standing orders, emergency contact and reference information, safety drills, a list of hazards associated with fishing, fishing vessel safety legislative requirements, safety procedures, and general information.

The Safety Association and the FFAW were tested in the spring of 2020 with the outbreak of the COVID-19 pandemic. The NLFHSA executive director, Brenda Greenslade, said the association worked in conjunction with the union and the PFHCB, with input from other fish harvester safety organizations in Canada and the provincial Chief Medical Officer of Health. "It is challenging to develop safe work practices that can be applied to all fishing vessels, given the type of vessel, vessel size, and crew size," she said.

Eventually the NLFHSA in conjunction with the union and the PFHCB developed a COVID-19 Safe Work Practice to serve as a guideline for fish harvesters to prevent the spread of the virus on their boat and among their crew. "The intention," said Greenslade, "was that harvesters would apply what they could from the document to ensure the safest work environment possible for themselves and their fellow crew members."

Keith Sullivan said the processing companies "started a not-so-subtle campaign to open our province's two biggest fisheries—crab and lobster. They wanted to put harvesters on the water, where social distancing and face masks are impossible, with no regard to the consequences of how an outbreak would affect rural Newfoundland and Labrador. These same companies wanted thousands of people, mostly women, to work on a line in a plant, where social distancing is difficult, where ventilation is a concern, and where underlying lung issues like shellfish asthma are common. A COVID-19 outbreak in a fish plant in this province was a terrifying, but possible, prospect in April."

David Decker said that while governments adopted rigorous COVID-19 protocols for most sectors of the economy, they left the fishing industry to its own devices: "Government was giving out firm directions on just about everything. In the fishery, it was all put on us. It was up to us when we would give it a go, and we were trying to look at the risk. We delayed the fishery five weeks, until our leadership people felt it was safe. In the meantime, we had our provincial fisheries minister saying there shouldn't be a problem—they're fishing in other provinces."

Decker said that the Association of Seafood Processors was "saying we didn't want a fishery, we just wanted a government cheque, that kind of thing. At the same time, they weren't willing to meet with us with five people each in a room. They said it was too risky."

Plant workers were extremely concerned about having to go to work. Food processing plants of various kinds in North America—meat processing facilities, in particular—were experiencing significant outbreaks of the virus.

"Those were scary times," said Doretta Strickland. "There are people who never went outside their homes for weeks on end. The company wasn't ready. If it wasn't for the union, we would have been in there with nothing done. The company should have contacted the plant safety committee to get our views. The union told us we didn't have to go in if we didn't feel safe. People began feeling safer when there were fewer cases."

Eventually the fishery went ahead and the plants opened as the COVID-19 risk diminished significantly in the province. In a year when many sectors of the economy struggled because of the pandemic, the fishery once again provided work and economic vitality in hundreds of communities around the province.

The fishery is an inherently dangerous occupation. A significant amount of personal risk comes with it, and the job of promoting best safety practices never ends. At least now the structures are in place to systematically address these challenges.

"More Than Just a Union"

*The men and women who built the NFFAWU ... did more
than build a union. They wrote an important chapter
in the history of Newfoundland, and of Canada.*

— Gordon Inglis

As an associate professor of anthropology at Memorial University, Gordon Inglis was interested in social change, which he defined as "the forces that cause people to act and react in ways that alter the circumstances of their lives." He thought that the NFFAWU story, which was 15 years old at the time of his comment, "seemed to provide a neat case-study" and "academic considerations apart, it is a rattling good tale, full of real-life drama, and excitement, and humour." Inglis's book, published in 1985, is entitled *More Than Just a Union: The Story of the NFFAWU*. Here is his explanation for the title:

> The NFFAWU has been remarkable not only for its rapid and successful growth, but also for the unique place it has held in the political consciousness of the province. From the time that it first came to public attention as the NFU, it has been identified not merely as a labour

organization, but as a political phenomenon. It is this, more than anything, that has justified its existence as "more than just a union." No other organization since the FPU (Fishermen's Protective Union) has had its activities so closely watched, so widely commented upon and speculated about.

The new union didn't take long to stake its ground on matters beyond the collective bargaining table. In 1972, Richard Cashin led a small union delegation who made a wide-ranging presentation, dealing with various aspects of fisheries policy, unemployment insurance, and other matters, to a House of Commons Standing Committee. The union has continued the practice of making representations to appropriate House of Commons and Senate committees ever since.

In his keynote speech at the union's constitutional convention in 1978, Cashin elaborated on his vision of this expanded role when he told delegates that the union "has to go beyond the collective agreement, beyond the price of fish. It has to deal with the type of society we have. You can start with the collective agreement, but it has to go beyond that."

Inglis summed up the ongoing significance of the fishery, despite its decline as an economic engine: "By the time the NFFAWU began, the fishing industry had long since lost its role as the centrepiece of the economy … It retained, however, a central place in the consciousness of the people—in their collective, historic sense of what Newfoundland was, and meant. For the fishing and plant-working families, the struggle for recognition and contracts were bread-and-butter issues of work and wages, but their struggles struck deep and powerful chords in the whole society. They took on an aura of mythic drama; cultural significance far beyond their purely economic meaning."

Lana Payne, in 2021 the national secretary-treasurer of Unifor, said the FFAW "changed the power structure" in the province and had "a big impact on the broader labour movement ... The union needs to be a political force as well as a collective bargaining agent. You can't make gains for workers without that. Our lives don't stop at the bargaining table. The fishing industry is interwoven with our identity. Everyone fancies themselves as an expert on the fishery. It's a threat to the power structure when working people do these things."

I have described in earlier chapters some of the particular areas in which FFAW achieved success beyond the conventional activity of a union—the creation of the LFUSCo to provide hope and stability for people in coastal Labrador; access to crab for small-boat owner-operators and their crews, and to shrimp for midshore owner-operators, crew members, and plant workers; a comprehensive strategy to build the lobster fishery from a fringe fishery in some areas to its current status as the mainstay of many inshore enterprises; shaping government's response to the moratorium; the development of a professionalization program in the inshore fishery; and the establishment of 15 education centres to provide learning opportunities for people in fishing communities. These are significant achievements. In some cases, toes had to be stepped on to achieve them.

Joe Gough worked for many years in DFO's communications branch, including during Romeo LeBlanc's term as minister. In *Managing Canada's Fisheries from Early Days to the Year 2000*, he sums up the union's track record: "Helping to shape the Kirby restructuring, and the special aid programs, consistently backing limited entry and the 'real fishermen,' defending the owner operator and fleet separation rules, negotiating prices with companies and allocations with DFO, pioneering the professionalization and certification of fishermen—on these and other matters, the union wielded great influence, while also carrying out extensive educational and other programs for fishermen. The union lost on some issues, for example the shrimp allocation granted by Minister Herb Dhaliwal to Prince Edward Island. But on major points it usually prevailed."

One area where the union had a significant positive impact on the livelihoods of inshore members popped up out of nowhere in 1978. The story starts with staff representative Bill Short: "One Saturday evening I was alone in the union office. A strange man came into the office looking to buy mackerel. He said he had a fish plant on the Black Sea, and a big ship tied on at the time in Nova Scotia." The "strange man"—a Bulgarian named Nikolov—proposed to have this vessel, along with several others he owned, buy mackerel and squid directly from inshore fishing boats.

Short promptly reported the call to Cashin, who sent Short to Nova Scotia to look at the ship to assess its suitability for the task. Meanwhile, Cashin negotiated a contract that called for the Bulgarian company to provide five ships that would anchor in various locations in the province to buy mackerel and squid under what became known as over-the-side sales. Inshore boats would have their catch hoisted aboard the big ships, where it was weighed under the supervision of union weighmasters. Although the union did not actually take possession of the fish, for the purposes of the contract the union was deemed to be the buyer, and subsequently sold the fish to the Bulgarian company. To oversee the project, the union hired Kevin Carroll, who later worked for the union as a staff representative. Squid and mackerel were in much greater abundance in 1978 than in the preceding years, so there was little market for squid, and only a fish meal market at 1.5 cents a pound for mackerel. Under the contract with the Bulgarians, the harvesters were paid 6 cents for mackerel and 9 cents for squid. In all, the union wrote 7,800 payroll cheques that fall to 2,300 fish harvesters.

"Over-the-side sales put a lot of extra money into communities," said Cyril Dalley of Twillingate. "Twillingate and New World Island were busy spots. It had a very positive impact on the economy, no question."

Predictably, the fish companies howled in protest. Cashin couldn't resist having fun at their expense, telling the media, "For years they've accused me of being a socialist. Now we've engaged in a little free enterprise, and they're screaming bloody murder."

In addition to the Bulgarian company, a Swedish trading company with access to Russian factory ships also contracted with the union. In 1979, over-the-side sales put $6 million in the pockets of fish harvesters. After 1979, the abundance of squid and mackerel dropped off almost as quickly as it had materialized, but over-the-side sales were used for a few years to handle an over-supply of cod during the trap fishery and to provide a badly needed outlet for turbot on the coast of Labrador.

On one occasion, inshore plants on the Southern Shore and the St. John's area had more cod than they could handle, so trap crews were unable to sell their catch. An available foreign vessel would buy surplus fish, but the union couldn't get approval from the provincial government. Early one morning, I received a call from Bill Short, who told me that fish harvesters from Petty Harbour, Torbay, and other communities in the area were bringing pickup loads of fish to the provincial fisheries office, which was in Atlantic Place, a large retail/office complex in downtown St. John's.

"What are they going to do with the fish, Bill?"

"I don't know," said Short.

"They're going to dump it on the steps of the Atlantic Place, aren't they?" I surmised.

"Probably."

I wasn't sure this plan would help us fix the problem, but when members are ready to fight, it's the union's job to find a way to produce results. I came up with an idea that I thought would reflect better on our members, while at the same time ramping up the pressure on the provincial fisheries minister. I told Short that if he could persuade the fish harvesters to stand by at the fisheries office but hold off on doing anything with the fish, I would call the news media and the open line radio programs (there were two at the time) to encourage members of the public to take a bag or some other kind of container down to Water Street to get a free meal of fish, compliments of the inshore sector. Short sold the idea to the fish harvesters, St. John's residents came scurrying downtown in droves, senior citizens who were delighted to get a free meal of fish told the media what fine people they thought the fish harvesters were, and the event was the lead item on CBC national news that night. The following day, the union received permission from the provincial government to engage the foreign vessel to buy fish that was surplus to the capacity of the local plants.

Catches available for sale to foreign vessels petered out in the early 1980s, but by that time the program had not only provided much-needed income for fish harvesters but it had also created a fund from which the union established a voluntary health and

Keith Sullivan, David Decker, and a group of inshore harvesters meet with officials from the regional DFO headquarters in St. John's. Over the years, the union held hundreds of meetings pressing for resource management policies that make sense for the harvesting sector.

welfare program that benefitted participating inshore members for several years at bargain rates.

Another aspect of the health and welfare of fish harvesters needed the union's attention at around the same time. The inshore fishery was still operating without proper coverage for primary producers under the province's workers' compensation legislation. Coverage was not mandatory, and it was a challenge to get thousands of enterprises to engage with the cumbersome Workers' Compensation Commission bureaucracy. Most inshore fish harvesters had no coverage at the time.

Nearly 25 years earlier, when the federal government dealt with the challenge of finding a workable way for inshore fishing benefits to function under the UI program, they created a special form of UI benefit called fishing benefits, in which the fish buyer was deemed to be the employer and the fish harvester the employee for the purposes of the *Unemployment Insurance Act*. The union felt that this was a useful model for tackling the workers' compensation issue, so in 1980/81, the union launched a vigorous campaign calling on the provincial government to treat the workers' compensation issue as the federal government had with UI decades earlier.

The campaign kicked off with a press conference, followed up by membership meetings to educate and enlist the support of inshore members, a province-wide petition, a postcard-writing campaign to members of the House of Assembly, bumper stickers, newspaper advertisements, and meetings with ministers and MHAs. Fish harvesters filled the galleries of the House of Assembly on the day their petition was being presented. The next day, government announced in the House that they would act on the union's demand and amend the *Workers' Compensation Act* to make coverage mandatory as it was in other occupations and to deem fish buyers the employers of people who sold them fish, for the purposes of the Act.

If the buyers weren't pleased with this development, they were even less impresssed to learn that they would be responsible for paying the workers' compensation premiums. But it's important to note that inshore fish is the lifeblood of most plants and fishing is one of the most dangerous occupations in the world. In this context, the requirement for the buyers to pay the premiums and submit the paperwork for workers' compensation coverage was not unreasonable.

I have outlined in previous chapters the events that led to the closure of so many key groundfish stocks in Atlantic Canada. The overwhelming challenges this catastrophe created were magnified in 1996 when the federal government increased its effort to reduce the country's debt and deficit.

As Joe Gough put it: "After years of budget pressure, DFO had few big and easy targets for cost reduction. Rather than trimming fat, the knives sometimes had to slice into muscle and bone. Science took a one-third cut in personnel."

This was part of a 25 per cent overall cut in the DFO budget under the government-wide program Program Review. Program Removal would have been a more apt description. The government talked about "co-management" with industry groups and "the generation of new trust between the department and its clients," Gough reported, but "Rhetoric failed to transform reality ... Officials talked more and more about getting back to the 'core mandate' of conservation, sometimes forgetting that it had almost as strong a tradition of intervening in other matters. As the department tried to do less, it asked fishermen to do more."

David Decker, then FFAW staff representative for the southwest and west coasts and Labrador, recalls the impact of this decision and responsibility it downloaded on the union: "Before 1996, DFO was more localized. Newfoundland region had a huge amount of autonomy and used to meet more with fishermen. When their budget was cut, they pulled back. As they did that, who was talking to the fishermen?"

The short answer is that the union had to fill that void. DFO brought in a new requirement for fishing fleets to submit Conservation Harvesting Plans acceptable to the department before a fishery would be permitted to open. These plans cover a wide range of fisheries management elements, including type and amount of gear permitted, mesh size, and opening and closing dates. DFO essentially abandoned its regulatory role on these matters. The union's challenge in putting together CHPs for the various fisheries is that there are often widely differing opinions among members of a particular fleet as to what measures should be proposed, and the union needed to find a solution that everyone could live with.

The magnitude of the challenge is highlighted in the case of the 4RS3Pn cod stock, which ranges from LaPoile on the southwest coast to the tip of the Great Northern Peninsula, including the Labrador side of the Strait of Belle Isle. "DFO did nothing," Decker recalled. "We had to try to get a consensus among all those people, scattered over that huge area. It was very difficult."

Compounding the problem in recent years is that while DFO has been interacting less and less with industry, decision-making within DFO is becoming more and more centralized in Ottawa. "It boggles my mind that someone who doesn't understand our province or our culture or our people has the power to make those decisions," Decker added.

This is a giant step backward from the helpful collaboration that took place in the late 1990s and early 2000s when Max Short ran the fisheries minister's regional office in St. John's. He would convene regular, off-the-record meetings at least once every few weeks, and more frequently when necessary, between key players in the industry. Participation was limited to the presidents of FFAW and FANL, the deputy minister or his assistant from the provincial department of fisheries, two senior representatives of DFO fisheries management branch, plus Short and one of his assistants. These were not decision-making meetings. No formal minutes were kept. Individual comments were confidential. But the meetings kept industry leaders jointly informed on key issues, with a regular opportunity to provide input and to identify and consider possible solutions for looming problems.

Unfortunately, when Short left the regional office, these meetings were discontinued, and there has been nothing remotely similar, or as useful, since then. Meanwhile, the downloading continued, and harvester organizations had additional responsibility for dockside monitoring, safety programs, professionalization and registration, and countless other responsibilities that DFO once considered part of its mandate.

Rick Williams, a progressive academic from Nova Scotia with a strong history of supporting fish harvester organizations, has worked closely with the CCPFH and has studied the fishery extensively. In his 2019 book *A Future for the Fishery*, Williams called the ability of the FFAW and other harvester organizations to take on the downloaded responsibilities "a major accomplishment." "Democratic harvester organizations now carry a huge load for fisheries management and conservation," he observed. "Harvesters are now the primary stewards of resources."

Concomitant with tackling these responsibilities was the creation, under the leadership of FFAW, of separate entities to provide direction: the PFHCB to handle the professional registration regime; the Fish Harvesters' Resource Centre (FRC), a not-for-profit dockside monitoring company; and the Newfoundland and Labrador Inshore Fish Harvesters Safety Association (NLFHSA) to deal with safety issues. Fish harvesters play a key role on the governing boards of each of these organizations.

FANL, the processors' organization, had been operating a dockside monitoring company up to the time of the moratorium, but dropped it when quotas were slashed, in some cases to zero. The union stepped in and set up a not-for-profit organization whose mandate was to operate a dockside monitoring program that would meet DFO's requirements while keeping member costs as low as possible.

After occupying various office accommodations for its first 40 years, the union, in 2010, considered buying its own space instead of renting. By this time, the PFHCB was well established, operating out of an obscure location in an industrial park, and the union was occupying rented accommodations in downtown St. John's, where parking for visiting members was virtually non-existent. The union approached the PFHCB and suggested a joint purchase of suitable office premises. It agreed, and the search was on.

After looking at potential sites—both existing buildings and lots that could be developed—I was tipped off about a former supermarket building that might soon hit the market. The union engaged a structural engineer who reported that, although the premises were dilapidated inside and out, the building was structurally very sound; it needed recladding on the outside and total gutting and rebuilding inside. It was also easily accessible for members coming from outside

St. John's, and it provided ample parking.

So the union had a building, a partner, and a plan to provide "one-stop shopping" for union members. Not only were the union and PFHCB offices set up in the new premises on Hamilton Avenue in midtown St. John's, it also became home to the Safety Association and the FRC. Over the years, the union had participated in efforts to defend the province's seal hunt, but generally deferred to the Canadian Sealers' Association, which was the lead organization on matters related to the seal hunt. The union and the PFHCB agreed that it made sense to provide an office as a home base for the CSA to continue to do their good work, which brought another important organization under the Hamilton Avenue roof. It wasn't just about convenience. Having all these organizations operating in the same building allowed for a much greater level of interaction, collaboration, and exchange of ideas than when the offices were scattered.

Both the FFAW board and the PFHCB approved my recommendation that the new building be named the Richard Cashin Building in recognition of Cashin's central role in starting the union and building it into a dynamic organization.

The five organizations now housed in the Richard Cashin Building provide a variety of services for inshore harvesters and a union home for plant workers and other FFAW members. As Bill Broderick, PFHCB chair and retired FFAW inshore director, put it: "The union spawned the FRC, PFHCB and the Safety Association. The union had to come first before these other entities could be created."

The building also provides a home for union staff working on science projects. One of the great frustrations fish harvesters experienced in the buildup to the moratorium was that their years of experience and intimate knowledge of fish stocks and the natural environment of the ocean were dismissed as "anecdotal" by scientists. Long before scientists sounded the alarm, fish harvesters were experiencing declining catch rates, a smaller run of fish, and other signs of trouble in the fish stocks that they relied on for a living, yet they were assured that the stocks were just fine. As the moratorium became a grim reality, there was a growing demand from the harvesting sector for meaningful input into the assessment of fish stocks that had been their lifeblood.

A Comprehensive Science Program

The sentinel program came about because the union listened to the fishermen. The buzz words before the moratorium were that science should listen to fishermen. If fishermen's input was there before the moratorium, perhaps it wouldn't have turned out so bad.

— Cyril Dalley, retired inshore harvester, Twillingate

The "buzz words" Dalley referred to grew into a clamour once the moratorium on northern cod was called. DFO's main tool for estimating the abundance of vital fish and shellfish stocks was a multi-species otter trawl survey conducted in the fall, entirely beyond 12 miles from shore. For some fisheries, the only information the department had from inshore waters came from the fishery, but once the moratorium was called, there was no fishery on northern cod.

FFAW tackled this shortcoming through the creation, in 1995, of the cod sentinel program. This survey, a collaboration between harvesters, the union, and DFO scientists, provides DFO with annual data on catch rates, geographical distribution, biological characteristics, and the like. This information is collected by harvesters at sites around the province. This program has not only created a vehicle for gathering information on provincial cod stocks in a systemic way, it also facilitated a much broader program

Dr. Erin Carruthers, a research biologist with FFAW-Unifor since 2014, designs research projects that address the priorities identified by harvesters and assists with scientific presentations to DFO.

of identifying the priorities of harvesters and developing science-driven projects to address them. Once such project focused on the snow crab fishery, the fishery that has produced the most overall value in the province since the moratorium on northern cod and other fisheries.

Harvesters, not convinced that otter trawl technology was an accurate measuring stick of crab abundance, pushed for a program which would use crab pots—gear designed to catch crab. This led the union to work with DFO on a post-season crab-pot survey that would measure the residual biomass of crab—the amount left over after the fishery was completed for the year. To measure "pre-recruits"—crab too small to be caught in a pot using regulation mesh—the survey design included the use of some pots with undersized mesh.

Unlike most fish population surveys developed solely by DFO, the crab survey was developed jointly by DFO scientists and the union, with harvester participation. In this respect, it followed the sentinel cod program. The joint effort eventually produced an ambitious survey, starting in 2003, which involved 88 vessels fishing in about 1,500 different locations, from inner bays to outside the 200-mile limit.

An index cannot be developed overnight. By its nature, this tool requires several years of comparative data before it can provide useful information. But it must start somewhere, and the union's sentinel program now has 25 years of comparative data, and the crab survey 17 years.

Following the introduction of the crab survey, the union initiated a host of science projects, many involving the collection of data to be forwarded to DFO. Miranda McGrath, a science coordinator with FFAW at the time, said the science team "takes on the issues the harvesters believe are not being served by DFO and further push DFO to dig deeper in their research."

The union's role in science started with data collection, followed by some input in survey design. But there was still a missing element—involvement in stock assessment. Harvesters brought not only data but endless hours of observation and a personal understanding of the natural environment. The union needed its own scientist to add a layer of formal scientific training to this vast collective knowledge. In November 2014, research biologist Dr. Erin

Carruthers was hired to head up the union's science team. As David Decker put it, she was "someone who can speak both languages."

By this time, the union science program had been involved in developing, implementing, and managing more than 50 research projects involving cod, snow crab, Atlantic halibut, lobster, lumpfish, seals, capelin, turbot, and the invasive green crab. Specific projects included sampling, measuring, and tagging various species, survey design, habitat stewardship, gear design, and survey questionnaires among harvesters. The FFAW science team grew over the next few years to six year-round employees and involved hundreds of harvesters annually.

By late 2020, Carruthers said that harvesters had a role in the assessment process for cod, snow crab, and redfish, "but capelin, squid, herring, and mackerel remain challenges." Science, she said, "needs to evolve and improve," adding that the harvester role is important because of knowledge gained from their "on-the-water observations" that they bring to the assessment process. "All models have to make assumptions. Knowledge of the fish and the fishery is needed to challenge whether these assumptions make sense. Fisheries management and science are about fisheries as well as about fish."

The Atlantic halibut fishery is one in which the union's involvement is critical. DFO's multi-species trawl survey operates with 30-minute tows, but powerful Atlantic halibut can outswim the tow. This renders DFO's primary stock assessment tool nearly useless for this species which is so important to harvesters in the Gulf and the south coast in particular.

Carruthers described catch rates of Gulf halibut as "through the roof," yet DFO, lacking the basis for biomass estimates that they

Mildred Skinner measures cod as part of the union's ongoing research efforts.

normally use as the basis of quota decisions, were exceptionally cautious about any quota increases. The union collaborated with DFO, along with fish harvester organizations from other parts of the Gulf of St. Lawrence, in developing a longline survey—gear much better suited to developing an abundance index for this species. The International Council for the Exploration of the Sea (ICES), the oldest intergovernmental organization in the world concerned with marine and fisheries science, called the Gulf halibut project "a unique academic-government-industry collaboration that sheds light on movement ecology of Atlantic halibut."

FFAW also became involved in an existing longline survey in the "alphabet soup" stock—so named because of the numbers of letters in the various management zones that make up this stock, believed by scientists to be a single stock covering the Scotian Shelf, the southern Grand Banks, and 3Ps off Newfoundland's south coast. The survey was conducted throughout 3Ps, and the union was also given access to half the surveys on the southern Grand Banks.

Once a time series has been established for the Gulf halibut stock survey, this should allow for the development of biomass estimates, which in turn should allow for quota allocations that better reflect the extraordinary abundance in this resource.

Another stock for which DFO's multi-species trawl survey has proven problematic is 3Ps cod; the results have been notoriously erratic. According to Carruthers, the cod sentinel results have been more consistent over time than the research vessel survey: "For this reason, while sentinel results are factored into the stock assessments in all areas, in recent years they have been given greater weight in 3Ps."

Summing up the overall FFAW science program, Keith Sullivan, who started his work with the union on science projects, said, "We are focused on bringing harvester views to the table in the science and management process. There is no major species that the union and our members hasn't gotten involved in. Challenging the status quo of government policies and decisions like we did with the crab quota fightback in 2019 requires evidence—the kind of evidence our science program provides. The union's capacity and in-house expertise give fish harvesters a bigger voice through their union."

The driving force behind the systematic growth of the union's science program has been Secretary-Treasurer Decker, who observed:

Technician Scott Smith measures lobster.

"Before we started, DFO Science designed and conducted surveys and presented them to harvesters. Harvesters' information was dismissed as 'anecdotal.' Now, harvesters are in on survey design and they carry out the survey. It's all about getting their knowledge into the assessment of the stocks."

As owner-operator Andy Careen put it, "With what we're dealing with over at DFO, it's a must to have somebody. We'll educate her, and she'll know what the fishermen are thinking."

The union will need its full resources to deal with a fundamental challenge from DFO. As of the time of writing, the department had a strategic objective—if it can be called strategic—to rebuild the northern cod stocks to the average biomass level of the 1980s, while using abundance levels of the late 1990s as reference points for crab and shrimp stock management.

"The DFO rebuilding plan on the Newfoundland Shelf is doomed to fail," said Jim Baird, who worked for 15 years in DFO's science branch before moving to a series of fisheries management positions, including three and a half years as regional director-general, the top position in the region. "You can't rebuild cod, crab, and shrimp stocks to the target levels."

Scientist George Rose explained in *Cod: The Ecological History of the North Atlantic Fisheries* that in the early 1990s, "shrimp and snow crab numbers grew in part because their dominant predator, the cod, was virtually gone. Strong cod stocks are unlikely to co-exist with abundant shrimp and crab stocks; hence, the rebuilding of cod will almost certainly be accompanied by a decline in these invertebrates."

Lobster: Creative Solutions to Difficult Problems

If it wasn't for the union and the tie-up we had that time, we'd still be getting two or three dollars a pound for our lobster. That was the making of our lobster pricing. The union showed it had the gumption to do something for this part of the island.

— Joan Doucette, inshore harvester, St. George's

The growing strength of crab and shrimp stocks, small-boat access to crab, and the development of an inshore shrimp fishery created fishing opportunities in the aftermath of the closure of all cod fisheries adjacent to Newfoundland and Labrador. But few of these opportunities were available to small-boat operators west of the Burin Peninsula along the south, southwest, and west coasts, where crab stocks have never been abundant.

One fishery that had proven durable in a portion of the south coast and most of the west coast—and, to a lesser extent, the northeast coast—is lobster. George Rose described the lobster fishery as "one of the best examples of a fishery that has been sustainable. The lobster fishery is managed by effort limits rather than quotas; perhaps more importantly, management invokes considerable responsibility at the local level."

For many years, annual lobster landings in Newfoundland ran

consistently in the 4- to 5-million-pound range. But as the years passed without a meaningful cod stock recovery, fishing pressure on lobster populations increased. Harvesters were anxious to avoid having restrictive measures imposed unilaterally by DFO, so the union organized meetings in the various Lobster Fishing Areas to discuss options for a conservation harvesting plan that would be acceptable to licence holders in each area, while meeting the requirements laid down by DFO for conservation measures to protect the resource. Measures including trap reductions, a ban on Sunday fishing, a shorter season, and the implementation of V-notching were considered, and different combinations emerged in different Lobster Fishing Areas (V-notching involves cutting a notch in the shell of a roe-bearing lobster; harvesting V-notched lobster is illegal).

Conservation measures were controversial, but necessary. "Incomes really started to improve when the union helped us get conservation measures in place," said Loomis Way, an inshore harvester from Green Island Cove on the Northern Peninsula. "We had a difficult time convincing people about V-notching and trap reduction, but it paid off."

Even with conservation measures in place, significant barriers made lobster the foundation of small fishing enterprises in non-crab areas, in the way the crab fishery has been for so many enterprises on the northeast coast. Because DFO had been cutting back on its limited science work on lobster, there was little science on which to base fisheries management decisions. The resource, while reasonably stable with the new conservation measures in place, was not plentiful enough to provide a reasonable income for the thousands of licence holders that were fishing it, as well as for their crew members. Marketing was a major problem: there was a lot of lobster hitting the market from competing states and provinces in New England and the Maritimes, there was no coordination of marketing effort to maximize the return, and there was no transparency to ensure that harvesters were getting a fair share of the market returns.

Licence buyouts during the TAGS and post-TAGS programs helped to a degree, but when the global financial meltdown hit in 2008, there were still too many licences for the size and overall market return from the lobster resource. The union pushed hard for another round of licence buyouts under the infamous Memorandum of Understanding which had been entered into by the union, the Association of Seafood Producers, and the provincial government in 2009/10, only to have the provincial government effectively halt the whole endeavour.

A combination of the recession and exceptional lobster catches in Maine and other areas had created an oversupply and a price collapse. Average prices in our province, which had ranged from $4.50 to $5.25 a pound from 2002 to 2007 crashed to $3.25 in 2008 and 2009. This is not close to being a sustainable price for fishing enterprises, and a crisis ensued in the Atlantic lobster fishery. As is often the case, crisis spawned opportunity, but a healthy dose of creativity was required. The union supplied it.

As the lobster fishery makes up a much larger proportion of the overall value of the fishery in Prince Edward Island, New Brunswick, and southwestern Nova Scotia than it does in Newfoundland and Labrador, the market troubles had a major impact in those provinces. David Decker was familiar with the importance of lobster to many of the hardest hit enterprises in Newfoundland, having served as staff representative on the southwest and west coasts,

Branding lobster is an important aspect of improving value.

and he had extensive contacts with fish harvester organizations throughout the Gulf of St. Lawrence. In 2009, by then the FFAW secretary-treasurer, Decker organized a meeting in New Brunswick with colleagues from other harvester organizations to put together a coordinated response. There was widespread agreement on the need for a voluntary buyout program, such that the available landed value would be shared among fewer enterprises, but there was no desire on the part of either level of government for another round of licence buyouts. Political pressure would be needed to force government's hand.

Decker proposed an Atlantic-wide tie-up. Representatives of other organizations were not confident that their members would support such a drastic step, but various organizations agreed to participate in protest action. Once again, our members were in the forefront. FFAW lobster harvesters tied up their boats for four days. Some occupied DFO offices; other protests took place in other provinces, ramping up the pressure on both federal and provincial governments.

Once again, the protests were effective. It helped that the DFO minister was Gail Shea from Prince Edward Island, where lobster is the dominant fishery. The push from harvester organizations in the five eastern provinces eventually led to the announcement of a federal-provincial program called Atlantic Lobster Sustainability Measures, which made funding available for programs linked to conservation, stewardship, restructuring, and rationalization in the lobster fishery. But there was a serious catch. To be eligible for federal and provincial funding, fleets applying for funding had to share the cost, which for a program to be worthwhile would have to run in the millions of dollars. The economics of the industry had just collapsed. Where was this money supposed to come from?

Decker met this challenge by drafting an ingenious proposal to attach a deemed dollar value to trap reductions in any Lobster Fishing Area where licence holders agreed to reduce their trap limits and to accept this as the fleet's contribution to the funding for the buyback program. The federal government eventually, if reluctantly, accepted this proposal. Union officials then held meetings with licence holders and conducted votes in each Lobster Fishing Area. Once licence holders in a particular area voted to accept the trap reduction, this triggered financial contributions from the two levels of government for the buyback.

When I joined new DFO minister Keith Ashfield and provincial fisheries minister Darin King at a press conference in November 2011 to announce the details of a lobster sustainability project, I was probably the only one of the three of us in front of the cameras who really wanted to be there. Both levels of government had strongly resisted putting money into a further buyout program, but here they were, announcing a contribution of $9 million each to the new program. Some of the funding went to lobster science, but of the total of $18 million, $16 million was targeted to licence buybacks. Those who chose to sell back their licences received the benefit of the buyout payments. Those who remained in the fishery benefitted from having the available resource divided among fewer participants.

Environmental factors as well as the impact of trap reductions and reduced pressure on the stocks were all at play, and by 2018, province-wide landings were at their highest level in many years. Kevin Hardy from Burnt Islands on the southwest coast, not traditionally a lobster area, said landings in the area doubled over a three-year period. "People are making money now at lobster," he said. Down the coast in Burgeo, Bill Bowles said catches averaged around 1,000 pounds a day in a fishery which used to amount to about 1,000 pounds for the whole season. In Bay St. George, Darren Boland said lobster harvesters were "benefitting big-time from license retirements, trap reductions, and V-notching," while in Trout River, Blaine Crocker called the buyback program "a big bonus," saying that average catches in the area had gone "from 30 or 40 or 50 crates to 150 crates" (100 pounds per crate).

Parallel to the union's efforts with the buyout program was the development of a strategy to attack the lack of transparency in raw material pricing for lobster. Lobster is a tough species to deal with in that regard because there are many minor buyers with traditionally little or no organizational structure. Earlier attempts to negotiate lobster prices fizzled out, although for a brief period there was an agreement with National Sea Products in the 1990s when they were still a significant lobster buyer. Amendments to the *Fishing Industry Collective Bargaining Act* arising from the creation of the Price-Setting Panel in 2006 following the RMS battle created a window of opportunity. But we needed information.

Prior to the establishment of the Price-Setting Panel, lobster pricing was done in much the same manner as FANL had done back in the pre-union days. The minor buyers who dominated the lobster scene tended to be seriously under-financed and were essentially at the mercy of the middlemen who bought from them. On a Saturday, they would be told by the middleman what he would pay them the following week; on Monday morning, the Newfoundland buyers would get together on a conference call, subtract their cut from the price quoted by the broker, and announce the raw material price based on what was left over. The minor buyers didn't join the Association of Seafood Producers, but eventually formed the

Harvesters line up to join a lobster co-op that the union established to take on a boycott by lobster buyers in 2012.

Seafood Producers of Newfoundland and Labrador to represent them on some matters, notably lobster.

To help build a database, the union needed to make a convincing case to the Price-Setting Panel. Allies from various Maritime regions agreed to provide the union with weekly pricing information, and FFAW members in different lobster fishing areas around Newfoundland volunteered to provide weekly pricing reports. This gave the union—and through the union, the Price-Setting Panel— the correlation between wharf prices and published market prices that had been the foundation of the lobster-pricing formula since 2011. In 2012, the Seafood Producers of Newfoundland and Labrador tried every imaginable stunt to avoid having a price agreement in place for lobster. They refused to negotiate. When they did show up for negotiations, they refused to make an offer. They refused to make a price position to the Panel. And when all else failed, they stopped buying lobster in the middle of the season.

Keith Sullivan, then a market analyst for the union, was pressed into service as a lobster salesman. Seafood Producers of Newfoundland and Labrador had said publicly that they would not buy lobster until they got rid of the pricing formula that tied the raw material price to independent published market and currency indicators. The union had support from the harvesters, but there was pressure to find an alternative outlet for their lobster, and apprehension about making it work. The provincial government refused the union's request for a buyer's licence—they didn't want to take sides, although turning down the request effectively came down on the side of the buyers. Fortunately, the Fogo Island Fish Producers Co-op co-operated with the union. One of the most successful co-operatives in the history of the province, the Fogo Co-op was created in the late 1960s to fend off resettlement and provide an economic foundation for the island. It's still going strong more than 50 years later. The Co-op agreed to allow the union to buy through their lobster buyer's licence and use the Co-op's payroll facilities to get cheques out to harvesters. With the traditional buyers refusing to buy, the union was in business, at least temporarily.

"The buyers spent two or three years just fighting the Panel," said Kevin Hardy. "They didn't want anyone telling them what to pay for lobster. They were used to looking down the wharf and telling you the price was down 25 cents. When the buyers stopped buying, the union really stepped up to the plate buying the lobster. There was a lot of risk. A lot of fishermen bought into it."

The union set up a new entity, Lobster Harvesters Inc., to work essentially as a sub-agent for the Fogo Co-op and set up several buying stations. The arrangement: have harvesters bring their lobster to these stations, where union staff organized trucks to pick up the lobster and get it to the ferry in Port aux Basques and on to market in the Maritimes. It was a major risk for the union, but as Sullivan said, "We were not going to be held captive by the processors. I was on the phone trying to sell the lobster. We were looking at the forecast—would Marine Atlantic be running tonight? Fishermen were holding a lot more lobster than they normally would. They weren't equipped to do it, and some places were not suitable to hold lobster."

The risk paid off. After several days of watching lobster they would normally handle being shipped across the Gulf, the buyers backed down and advised the union that they wanted to resume business. An agreement was quickly worked out, nailing down the price-to-market formula that has been the mainstay of lobster pricing ever since.

Blaine Crocker from Trout River calls the lobster pricing formula "the backbone of the west coast," while Nancy Bowers of Beachside on the northeast coast deems it "the saviour for lobster harvesters."

It is a major step forward from the previous system of the buyers meeting among themselves and announcing the price every Monday morning to the current system where the wharf price is tied to independently verified market indicators and both buyers and harvesters find out the current price from the union website, where it is posted once a week. Because of the authority the *Fishing Industry Collective Bargaining Act* confers on the Price-Setting Panel, this price is binding on all lobster buyers in the province.

The combination of enhanced conservation measures, reduced pressure on the resource, a fair and transparent share of the market, and favourable environmental conditions has produced an explosion of lobster landings and landed value in the province. Province-wide landings of around 5 million pounds and total landed value of about $25 million was the norm for many years up to 2014, when things started to look up. Then, in 2017 and 2018, annual landings exceeded 6 million pounds and landed value shot up to $44 million in each year, before skyrocketing to just over 10 million pounds worth $65.1 million to harvesters in 2019.

Lobster is still a tricky market; it is highly vulnerable to outside forces like the 2008 economic and the COVID-19 pandemic that threw many markets into turmoil in 2020. But there is now a plan for the management of the fishery and a level of transparency in pricing that point to a much brighter outlook for the primary producer.

David Decker observed that the pricing outcome "would not have been possible without the Panel." It introduced a decision-making authority into the price-setting process that forced companies who wanted absolutely nothing to do with the harvesters who supply the raw material they need to operate. This in turn led to a sharing formula in which both parties benefit as the market return improves. As noted earlier, lump and halibut are also good examples in which the collective bargaining process has brought about greater transparency and a formula to provide fair sharing of market returns, but work still remains. Decker notes that in several of the major species—notably crab, shrimp, and cod—processors resist disclosing actual market prices, processing yields, and other important information.

"It's ridiculous that public money has to be spent to pay consultants in Europe and the United States to tell us what prices we're getting in the market," Decker said. "It should be a condition of a buyer's licence to disclose on a confidential basis what prices they are getting and what their yields are. This information could then be consolidated and made available to all parties, including the Panel. Currently, the Panel is expected to decide when it doesn't even know what the production yields are in the plants. We should all be working toward stability, increased value and sharing the wealth. That's what's best for everyone, but it won't work without transparency."

Sullivan expressed a similar view in a *Union Forum* column: "Processors operate in near total secrecy, not just from harvesters but from each other. For some reason, they think that is good—that maintaining secrecy in how they operate gives them an advantage. It does not. It actually holds everyone down because there is no exchange of ideas to foster improvement."

CHAPTER 24

"Where the Power Comes From"

We try to do the best we can for everyone in the union—all sectors. When we fight DFO, we're all together. In the crab demonstration in 2019, we were all together supporting one another. We got one another's backs.

— Doretta Strickland, Triton plant worker, IRO vice-president

In 1971, when delegates gathered at the Newfoundland Hotel in St. John's for the founding convention of NFFAWU, one of the first items they dealt with was a fundamental issue in the union's structure. The proposed constitution that was debated by delegates called for two sectors—a fishing and an industrial sector—with an overall provincial council.

The Memorial University Extension Service record of the proceedings at that convention noted that when one area staff representative questioned whether the industrial section supported the fish harvesters, another area representative, Lawrence Mahoney from Harbour Breton, "reported that as Chairman of the Industrial Group at the panel discussion, he had witnessed the expression of support by the plant workers for the fishermen. He felt that it was important that the Government know that the Convention, as a whole, was firmly behind the legislation that would affect the bargaining rights of fishermen."

There were no further challenges, and the constitution was adopted as presented. The union was under way with provision for membership in all sectors of the fishery. Ever since its founding, the diversity of its membership base has been challenging, because of the controversial nature of the fishery, but it has also been a source of strength.

Lew Hann of Burgeo put it in a nutshell: "The fishery will always be contentious." Decisions in the fishery will be complicated and controversial whether people are organized into one union, or two, or 10, or none.

Tony Doyle from Bay de Verde spoke of the "foresight" that went into the initial decision to include both the fishing and plant sectors in the union: "It gives you more political clout. We're all entwined. I'm a fisherman. I can't do without plant workers, and vice versa."

Helen Evans, who worked for years in the P. Janes & Sons plant in Hant's Harbour, said: "You don't need division. I've always preached—we all must stick together. The majority of our members, either the husband and wife both work in the plant, or the husband fishes and the wife works in the plant."

Al McCarthy from Highlands on Newfoundland's west coast put 60 years' fishing experience into his explanation for supporting the industry-wide structure of the union: "To make the union strong, you have to represent everyone. That's where the power comes from."

But there have always been some who don't buy this logic. After losing bargaining rights in most of the bargaining units they had previously represented, United Food and Commercial workers attempted to separate the inshore sector from the rest of the union with a card sign-up in the late 1990s, but they were unsuccessful.

Another effort to divide people in fishing communities came from a group calling itself FISH-NL, which announced in 2016 that it would be conducting a card-signing drive among fish harvesters aimed at getting them to leave FFAW in favour of their group. There appeared to be two aspects to their campaign—to try to convince harvesters they would be better off in a smaller, weaker organization and to spread negativity about FFAW and its leadership.

The problem they encountered was that harvesters weren't buying their message, at least not in anything close to the numbers needed for them to meet the requirements of the *Fishing Industry Collective Bargaining Act* to trigger a vote. They weren't even close. When FISH-NL applied to the Labour Relations Board at the end of 2017 for certification to represent inshore harvesters, by their own admission they had fewer than 2,400 signed cards. The existing bargaining unit had more than 9,000 members. Under the *Fishing Industry Collective Bargaining Act*, the board has no authority to consider an application for certification unless the applicant claims to represent at least 40 per cent of the proposed bargaining unit.

To attempt to get around this obstacle, FISH-NL understated the size of the bargaining unit, claiming it had only 4,500 harvesters. The Association of Seafood Producers, no doubt preferring to deal with a weaker adversary, also tried to downplay the number of fish harvesters in their representations to the board, although it is really none of their business who the harvesters choose as their bargaining agent.

The board wasn't fooled. FFAW provided documentation to the board's investigating officer showing a dues-paying membership in excess of 9,400. This was consistent with information available publicly on the PFHCB's website, which showed that from 2013

M&M Offshore, one of many workplaces the union has represented over the years apart from the fishery.

to 2019, the number of fish harvesters registered annually ranged between 9,000 and 10,000.

The board dismissed the FISH-NL application out of hand. Instead of accepting this outcome, FISH-NL announced it would be launching a second sign-up campaign. But by December 2019, they had discontinued the sign up and dissolved their organization.

One of the reasons FISH-NL fell far short of the mark, as David Decker pointed out, was that virtually none of the FFAW's elected rank-and-file leadership supported FISH-NL. These were the council members, committee members, the unpaid volunteers who took on the responsibility of representing the fleets who had elected them. They were familiar with the give and take that was often needed when views on a particular issue differed. They also understood the advantage of a large, powerful organization with the kind of resources that FFAW possesses. They had no interest in the kind of conflict FISH-NL was peddling or the bare-bones operation it was proposing.

"It is clear that this group has done nothing but create turmoil and unrest in our coastal communities, pitting fish harvesters against plant workers, skippers against crew," Keith Sullivan said in reaction to the announcement. "They kept it going for years even though they knew they didn't have the support."

Constant negativity can take its toll on any organization. In his media reaction to the demise of FISH-NL, Sullivan was quick to extend an olive branch to those harvesters who had supported it. "Our union needs you," he said, "and if we want to advance our industry and improve the lives of our members, we need people moving forward together."

FISH-NL talked nonstop about potential conflicts between plant workers and harvesters, but they didn't appear to understand the difference between conflict of interest and difference of opinion. The inshore membership includes both large- and small-boat operators, skippers, and crew members. The most controversial policy issues over the years tended to be within the inshore sector, not between inshore and industrial. Despite any differences of opinion that might exist on policy matters, whenever the union called for a public show of support on a particular issue—TAGS, EI, RMS, LIFO, the 2019 crab quota cuts, or any of the issues described in previous chapters—members from all sectors showed up in support: plant workers and harvesters, skippers, and crew members, large- and small-boat operators.

Mike Noonan, a crew member on a 65-footer who has represented crew members on both the inshore council and the executive board, recalled an incident when the union was taking a vote on the RMS issue, and a vessel owner stood up at a meeting and said that crew members shouldn't be allowed to vote on the matter. As chair of the meeting, I sharply responded that crew members were union members as much as he was and were absolutely entitled to vote. In fairness, it's not a comment I often heard, but I felt it was important to put it to rest, pointing out that we had always been able to count on crew members to support union demonstrations and other events. That individual left the meeting, and everyone else participated in the vote.

The following comment from Woodrow Philpott, an early driving force in the union's inshore sector from Cottlesville, New World Island, is a good description of the mutual reliance between skipper and crew: "On a boat, you can have the best crowd of men in the world, but you won't go nowhere without a good skipper. By the same token, you can have the best kind of skipper and he won't go nowhere without a good crew. The union's had both—a good skipper and a good crew."

Philpott's comment was in response to a question concerning the relationship between union leadership and membership, but in doing so with a nautical metaphor, he put his finger on the importance of having skippers and crew members together in a single organization.

The union has also represented various non-fishing industry units. At the founding convention, NFFAWU took in bargaining units in the province previously represented by the Canadian Merchandising Union, including retail shops in St. John's and central Newfoundland. Since that time, the membership has included workers in a variety of sectors, including hospitality, brewing, metal fabrication, dockside monitoring, aquaculture, and oil tanker crews.

Keith Sullivan rallies the troops from the plant and fishing sectors in the fightback against proposed crab quota cuts in 2019.

But as Reg Anstey put it, "It was the fishery that captivated the public."

Despite the challenges, or maybe because of them, the union has been trying to find solutions that work for as much of the membership as possible.

"No one else in Canada has the kind of multi-species enterprises that we have," said David Decker. "It's based on an inherent sense of fair play versus a system of winners and losers. That's the role of a strong organization."

When the FFAW executive board supported small-boat access to the crab fishery in a meeting with DFO minister Brian Tobin in 1994, two crab supplementary licence holders at the meeting—Bill Broderick and Hedley Butler—supported the move, even though as holders of supplementary crab licences it was in their self-interest not to do so. That's the kind of inherent sense of fair play Decker was talking about.

"A great way to have it" is how Andy Careen, an owner-operator from Point Lance, described the industry-wide structure of the union. "The plant workers have stood on our picket line more than once. They supported the fight against RMS. Down through the years, the union did things that didn't make me happy. But it's not about Andy. You have to do what's best for the whole group."

Constitutional conventions provide an opportunity once every three years for leaders in the various sectors of the union to come together to deal with union business and to debate policy direction. But many decisions need to be made between conventions, and the union's executive board and councils often meet to debate controversial issues and find compromise.

An important starting point is to ensure that these bodies are representative of the diversity of the membership. The IRO Council includes representatives of large and small plants, non-fish as well as fishing industry units, offshore and onshore bargaining units. In addition to regional representation, the inshore council makes specific accommodation for women, young harvesters, crew members, and skippers, with a balance between small- and large-boat representatives.

Calling the council structure the "heart and soul" of the union, Albert Wells of Wild Cove links the future of coastal communities to the work of the union. "My take is, do you want to live in a community by yourself? I'm a firm believer in the fishery. Do the right thing. Be fair to everyone. Everyone must give and take a little. The numbers make us stronger. The role the union plays fighting for fishermen and plant workers—that's a fight for the community. Without the support of the union, a lot of those communities would have died a long time ago."

That Blasty Bough Is Still Burning

*You never forget what the union done for the people
in the community. Everything changed when the union came.
Things didn't come on a silver platter.
We had to fight for everything.*

— Frank Strickland, trawlerman and oil tanker worker, Burgeo

I've addressed the dynamic activity that has taken place over the past 50 years, much of it aimed at improving the sharing of the wealth of the fishery to the benefit of those who work in the industry, at sea or on land, and through them to the economy of the communities in which they live.

The outport communities of Newfoundland and Labrador are priceless assets. They are built on co-operation and shared values, where people survived over the generations by working together. One need look no further than the province's highly touted tourism advertisements to see how a rural lifestyle, the spectacular coastal scenery, and the uniqueness of a fishing society are used to sell people who live outside the province on Newfoundland and Labrador as a tourist destination.

The 2020 provincial budget underlines the importance of the fishery in the provincial economy, especially in rural areas. The

Stable leadership has been one of the union's strengths. This photo, taken the day Keith Sullivan was elected president, shows the only three people who held the position in the first 50 years: me, Keith Sullivan, and Richard Cashin.

document reports that 2019 was the fifth consecutive year in which the production value of fish products exceeded $1 billion. The fishery directly employed 15,800 people in 2019, living in 400 communities. This does not include the many spinoff jobs—truck drivers, dockside monitors, graders, inspectors, as well as indirect jobs in the service sector. It is difficult to put a number on the financial impact of the fishing industry on the tourism sector, but there is no question that the presence of fishing boats, premises, and all the activity that goes with a vibrant fishery is a photogenic draw for visitors. No one wants to visit a ghost town or a community with a stagnant economy. For many of the 400 communities referred to in the budget, it's the fishery that makes the economy tick.

The last 50 years have been marked by extraordinary challenges. Some factors are beyond the control of the union or its members. Climate change can bring about dramatic changes in populations of marine life, as we have seen. Broader economic circumstances, such as the great recession in 2008/9, can cause havoc, and any export industry is highly vulnerable to fluctuations in foreign currency exchange rates. Although prevailing interest rates in the overall economy have not been a prohibitive problem in recent years, they were a major factor in the near-death experience of the deep-sea sector of the industry in the early 1980s.

Over the past half-century, while coping with the often severe impact of these and other external factors, the union methodically put in place the building blocks for success—democratic structures within the union; affiliations with other like-minded organizations; creation of compatible entities to deal with areas like professionalization, safety, and dockside monitoring; an emphasis on promoting high quality and achieving maximum value for seafood products; and a legacy of

This photo, also taken the day Keith was elected, includes two long-time secretary-treasurers, David Decker (third from right) and Reg Anstey (second from right). At right is Keith's father Lloyd, who served for many years as a member of the inshore council and later the executive board.

fighting for a better deal for union members and greater vitality for the province's coastal communities. In Labrador, the union had the singular accomplishment of being the driving force in the formation of the LFUSCo, which has been the salvation of coastal Labrador for more than 40 years.

With occasional bumps in the road since its founding convention in 1971, the union made steady progress until the devastation of the moratorium, on the northern cod stock and then on other key groundfish stocks. The future of our communities and our union, not to mention our members and their families, was in peril. But by employing its fightback instincts and ensuring that adjacent harvesters and plant workers received the benefits of the shellfish stocks that blossomed as groundfish stocks declined, we were successful in coping with this existential challenge and helping our members re-invent their livelihoods.

When people think of unions, collective bargaining is generally the first thing that comes to mind, and that remains the number one priority. But as we saw in the battle for benefits for people thrown out of work by the moratorium, the continuing fight for EI benefits, and the ongoing and ultimately successful struggle to rid the shrimp fishery of the iniquitous LIFO policy, to name just three examples, much work is needed outside the conventional collective bargaining arena with employers.

In most sectors of FFAW, collective bargaining with employers is done in a traditional manner, employer by employer, contract by contract, with the IRO Council serving as the voice of the membership, meeting regularly with the top leadership of the union.

In the inshore sector, with its own council, more equitable sharing of the wealth was achieved in a variety of ways. Innovative strategies linking price agreements to fisheries management plans and raw material prices to actual market returns produced a better share of the value of the product for the primary producer in fisheries such as lump, lobster, and halibut.

The union also played a pivotal role in gaining access to northern shrimp for midshore fleets and the plants they supplied. Overall returns from the northern shrimp fishery have diminished significantly in recent years because of the sharp decline in stock abundance, but the union was successful in blunting the impact of the decline by means of a relentless and ultimately successful campaign to get rid of the LIFO policy. In the absence of this campaign, LIFO would have eliminated any inshore presence in this fishery, despite the adjacency of the people who fish inshore and the plant workers who produce the finished product.

In the case of crab, there was the normal push and pull of collective bargaining over the years. Expanded entry into this fishery for supplementary and small-boat fleets ensured that the wealth derived from this valuable resource was distributed widely. When the provincial government and the crab processors attempted RMS, a play that would have greatly increased the processors' share of the value of the crab resource, the union staged an unprecedented fightback, and forced government to back down. This would have been beyond the wildest dreams of fish harvesters in the days Richard Cashin described when paternalism, the truck system, and the St. John's elite ruled with no meaningful challenge.

The book has highlighted some of the union's major activities over the years, including milestone collective bargaining achievements in all sectors, as it grappled with the low incomes described in Chapter 1.

Some changes in landings and landed value in the fishery are listed in Appendix A. Table 1 shows the landings by major species group at five-year intervals, from 1955 to 2015, with an update in 2019, the latest year for which comparable information was available. This table shows the dramatic shift over the years from an industry dominated by groundfish at the time the union was founded to one in which groundfish is still significant, but shellfish is dominant.

Table 2 uses the same time intervals but tracks the total landed value in the various species groupings. Whereas more than 70 per cent of the value was derived from groundfish in 1970, by the 2000s shellfish accounted for 80 per cent or more of the landed value of the fishery. The union's work to broaden access to shrimp and crab for people adjacent to the resource paid huge dividends.

FFAW staff representative Ben Baker from Carbonear hams it up with a plant worker in L'Anse au Loup. Baker passed away in 2009.

While there have been ups and downs from year to year, there is a clear and substantial upward trend in the value of our industry, which suggests the ongoing growth potential of the industry as an important part of the economy of the province in the future, just as it has been in the past. It puzzles me why the fishery's potential as a significant growth centre in our economy has been overlooked by provincial governments, who tend to issue hollow platitudes about the fishery but give policy and funding priority to areas like tourism and aquaculture.

As the union moves into its second half-century, several challenges present themselves, in addition to the usual struggles to get a fair share of the value of the fish resources in the pockets of those who work on the boats and in the plants:

- Pressuring DFO to enforce regulations intended to strengthen owner-operator and fleet separation policies.
- Challenging the increasing trend toward corporate concentration and foreign ownership in the Newfoundland and Labrador fishery.
- Tackling the human resource challenge of gradually replacing an aging workforce in all sectors of the industry.
- Taking on DFO's peculiar view that groundfish stocks can be rebuilt to their 1980s levels and shellfish stocks simultaneously rebuilt to their late 1990s levels.

A major responsibility will be dealing with a changing marine environment, as shrimp stocks decline while some groundfish stocks are showing signs of a significant rebound.

In this regard, as with so many other challenges previously dealt with, the union didn't wait to be overtaken by events; rather, it anticipated and planned, as the driving force in the formation of the Groundfish Industry Development Council. This council, whose membership includes the union and several groundfish processors, has committed to a new approach in how the groundfish industry conducts its affairs—what it calls "a better way of doing business."

The council's agreement-in-principle recognizes conservation and sustainable use of groundfish stocks as its priority, followed by economic viability and sustainability of the province's owner-operator fishing fleets and onshore fish processing plants. It also added the following, often-overlooked objective: "A sustainable and economically viable groundfish industry will also establish stable local economies in coastal communities and thereby contribute to a vibrant and sustainable rural society."

Building on lessons learned, the council's plan is based on a sustainable, quality-driven industry that will extract maximum value from world markets and provide improved incomes for fish harvesters and plant workers. It envisages a management plan that would supply high quality raw material to plants for eight to 10 months a year, while avoiding fishing on spawning aggregations.

This book has highlighted the first 50 years of the organization created from scratch by the people who work in the province's fishery, at sea and on land. Through their union, they challenged the power structure in the fishery—what Cashin called the "paternalism" in which a "St. John's elite" held all the power—and by so doing, gained a greater and more equitable share of the wealth of the industry made possible by their hard work and know-how.

The union's first 50 years have proven that rural Newfoundlanders and Labradorians can accomplish a great deal by sticking together. The union's recipe for success was a combination of solidarity, militant action, experienced and decisive leadership, and the support of professional union staff, unbelievably dedicated rank-and-file leaders and, whenever called upon, a membership that rises to the occasion.

No instruction manual exists for how to deal with the many challenges the union faced over the past half-century, but we always found a way.

The events described in this book include, as Irene Ploughman so aptly put it, "some good times and some hard times." The union didn't win every battle it faced—who does?—but it always took up the challenge, and remains a force to be reckoned with, 50 years after Richard Cashin and Father Desmond McGrath and their supporters started out with an idea, a passion, and thousands of Newfoundlanders and Labradorians who enthusiastically joined them on the voyage.

Appendix A

Changes in landings and landed values in key fish products in Newfoundland and Labrador in five-year intervals, 1970 to 2019.

Table 1

Volume of fish landed, by species or sector (tonnes)

	1970	1975	1980	1985	1990
Cod	152,930	77,523	250,056	270,693	219,286
All Groundfish	306,597	193,977	380,575	366,313	298,088
Lobster	1,455	1,698	2,452	2,920	1,427
Shrimp	159	1,372	3,808	3,579	17,723
Snow Crab	890	2,011	9,427	7,964	10,952
All Shellfish	3,323	8,290	50,863	17,901	43,284

Table 2

Value of fish landed, by species or sector ($000s)

	1970	1975	1980	1985	1990
Cod	$11,847	$14,821	$18,941	$91,632	$118,941
All Groundfish	$25,940	$31,975	$111,845	$121,516	$154,872
Lobster	$2,511	$3,913	$9,954	$17,787	$6,589
Shrimp	$53	$724	$2,700	$4,141	$44,695
Crab	$145	$497	$5,257	$6,880	$13,035
Shellfish	$2,843	$5,415	$22,165	$32,454	$69,298
Total	$36,141	$45,571	$161,286	$168,670	$251,895

Volume of fish landed, by species or sector (tonnes), continued

1995	2000	2005	2010	2015	2019	% Change
914	30,216	16,274	12,228	10,271	9,234	-94%
25,004	69,109	59,382	39,663	34,075	30,424	-90%
2,544	1,759	2,616	2,597	2,751	4,464	207%
29,157	83,917	114,851	112,061	84,965	24,314	15,192%
32,342	55,513	43,956	52,229	47,099	29,579	3,223%
91,406	162,961	190,085	198,601	154,503	137,138	4,027%

Value of fish landed, by species or sector ($000s), continued

1995	2000	2005	2010	2015	2019	% Change
$908	$43,059	$17,168	$12,122	$13,812	$12,801	8%
$19,866	$74,706	$72,756	$75,399	$107,251	$86,233	232%
$24,595	$19,282	$31,222	$18,851	$32,797	$42,569	1,595%
$79,283	$183,986	$176,498	$181,963	$387,718	$224,815	424,079%
$176,207	$268,002	$104,252	$155,448	$256,469	$224,815	154,945%
$313,559	$490,839	$383,969	$399,920	$721,154	$408,780	14,278%
$349,299	$584,319	$515,206	$510,699	$860,684	$523,654	1,349%

Key points to note:
- Devastating impact of groundfish collapse and moratorium in 1990s.
- Rapid development and growth in economic dominance of shellfish fisheries (shrimp and snow crab) after groundfish collapse.
- Levelling off in value of shellfish landings in 2015 to 2019 period. Preliminary evidence suggests the crab sector sector has rebounded in 2020 and 2021 seasons.
- Recent growth in value of lobster landings reflects both higher landings and improved market prices.
- Strong long-term growth trend in fishery despite ups and downs in landed volumes and market prices. In current dollar terms, total value of fish landed rose from $36 million in 1970 to a high of $860 million in 2015, followed by some decline due to a reduction in shellfish landings.
- Tables from Department of Fisheries and Oceans data, as tabulated by Canadian Council of Professional Fish Harvesters.

Appendix B

The Founders

These individuals attended the founding convention of the Newfoundland Fishermen, Food and Allied Workers' Union and adopted the union's first constitution in April 1971.

Labrador
Frank Flynn

West Coast and Northern Peninsula
Byrne, Michael Jr.
Cornick, Margaret
Dredge, Stephen
Elliott, Raymond
Elliott, Samuel
Gould, Jean
Gould, Romco
Herrit, George
Mahar, Michael
Mailman, Stella
Noel, Phoebe
Patey, Francis
Payne, Henry
Pilgrim, Reginald
Skinner, Arthur

South Coast
Brown, Alec
Brenton, Joe
Cox, James
Day, Allan
Edwards, Patrick
Green, Austin
Hann, Lewis
Hunt, Wallace
Marsden, Lynn
Skinner, John

Avalon Peninsula
Ash, Kenneth
Blundon, Frank
Bursey, Ronald
Butt, Tony
Condon, Kevin
Dodd, John
Duggan, Arthur
Everson, Vincent
Gatherall, Leonard
Grace, Carol Anne
Holwell, George
Kane, Albert
Kennedy, James
Kenny, Ambrose
Kenny, Austin
Kenny, Genevieve
Molloy, John C.
Norris, Levi George
O'Leary, Joseph
O'Shaughnessy, Felix
Parsons, Lindy
Power, Michael
Reid, Leslie
Ryan, Maurice
Short, Bill
Sparkes, Clarence
Sutton, Ronald
Tucker, Nelson
White, Frederick

Northeast Coast
Abbott, Maxwell
Best, Sidney
Cooper, Wallace
Curl, Philip
Furlong, Ronald
Hayley, Gerald
House, Peter
Johnson, Simeon
Kean, Lester
Lodge, Raymond
Noble, Harold
Norman, Benjamin
Norris, William
Pardy, Charles
Paul, Murray
Philpott, Woodrow
Russell, Victor
Samson, Albert
Ward, Archibald
White, Philip
Woodland, Raymond
Young, Donald

Executive and Staff
Beck, Ches
Cashin, Richard
Greening, Ray
Locking, Fred
Mahoney, Lawrence
Martin, Mike
Maynard, Ed
McGrath, Desmond
Sutton, Hubert

National Union Representatives
Borsk, Charlie
Bury, James
Dowling, Fred
Falls, William

The Builders

These individuals built on the vision of the founders. Thousands of volunteers have held leadership positions over the years in their workplaces, community committees, or fleet committees—as well as on the union's various boards, councils, and committees.

Apologies to anyone who was missed in this list, either due to records being unavailable (particularly in the earlier years) or to faulty memories. This list is intended to be an indication of the large numbers of leaders it takes to make a union work. A complete list would not have been possible.

Many thanks to these activists and to the many others who served the union over the years, and to the spouses and families who had to contend with family members being on the road, down at the plant or on the wharf, or on the phone attending to union business.

Labrador
Bolger, Norm
Brown, Peggy
Brown, Violet
Cabot, Stanley
Campbell, Harrison
Chubbs, Eric
Clark, Frank
Clarke, Winston
Davis, Chester
Davis, Connie
Davis, Mercer
Dyson, Allan Jr.
Edmonds, Lorraine
Fifield, John
Fillier, Nancy
Fowler, Gilbert
Holwell, Jack
Hudson, Geoff
Hudson, James Jr.
Keefe, Lewis
Kippenhuck, Don
Letto, George
Mangrove, Roy
Martin, John
Martin, Mike
Mesher, Kenneth
Morris, Vicki
Normore, Kevin
Normore, Morley
Notley, Genevieve
O'Brien, Eric
O'Brien, Marcel
Parr, Hayward
Pye, Wallace
Rumbolt, Alton
Rumbolt, Byron
Rumbolt, Claude
Rumbolt, Ray
Russell, Aubrey
Russell, Dwight
Russell, James Sr.
Trimm, Gaius
Turnbull, Wilton
Walsh, Bill
Webber, Clarence

Northeast Coast
Adams, Phyllis
Andrews, Les
Aylward, Jamie
Bailey, Hubert
Barfett, Ellisson
Bath, Lloyd
Batstone, Guy
Blackmore, John
Boland, John
Bowers, Nancy
Boyd, Leonard
Breen, Martin
Brett, Betty
Brett, Reg
Bridger, Guy
Brinson, Aubrey
Broderick, Warren
Brown, Matt
Brown, Shirley
Brown, Steward
Budgell, Wallace
Burton, Fred
Burton, George Sr.
Burton, Roy
Butler, Hedley
Canning, Albert
Canning, Rhonda
Carter, Herman
Chatman, Rick
Chaulk, Dennis
Chippett, Hazen
Clarke, Clayton
Clarke, William
Collins, Marshall
Cullimore, Marvin
Dalley, Cyril
Dalton, Jim
Dawe, Patricia
Dearing, Weldon
Decker, Barry
Devereaux, Mike
Diamond, Cal
Dicks, Pierce
Donahue, Kathleen
Duffett, Bernice
Dyke, Bev
Easton, Edison
Easton, Larry
Eveleigh, Junior
Farrell, Ed
Feltham, Charlie
Feltham, George
Fennell, Jeanette
Fitzgerald, Kevin
Foote, Allan
Fosse, Henry
Fudge, Bryce
Furlong, James
Giles, Lester
Giles, Michael

Giles, Stanley
Giles, William
Goodyear, Basil
Goodyear, Jamie
Gordon, Redmond
Granter, Bob
Greenham, Bernice
Greenham, Frank
Greenham, Jack
Grey, Rodney
Grimes, Claude
Hann, Donald
Hennifent, Edward
Hicks, Ross
Hill, Gloria
Hillier, Gord
Hillier, Manuel
Hollett, Barbara
Hounsell, Gerard
House, Roger
Howell, Kevin
Howell, Sheila
Hoyles, Rick
Hynes, John
Hynes, Ray
Jerrett, Ed
Johnson, Albert
Johnson, Darryl
Johnson, Tracy
Jones, Edgar
Jones, Matthew
Jones, Trevor
King, Ralph
Kean, Les
Kean, Paul
Kean, Rick

Kelly, Loretta
King, Ralph
Knee, Barry
Lander, Linda
Layte, Bernice
LeDrew, Roy
LeDrew, Ruby
Locke, David
Marsh, Darrin
Marsh, John Sr.
Martin, Calvin
Martin, Derm
Martin, Des
Martin, Eric
Mehaney, Bill
Mehaney, Nichole
Melendy, Della
Miller, Gordon
Mills, Flora
Morgan, Joe
Morgan, Tiffany
Morrison, Carmen
Mouland, Harvey
Mutford, John
Newbury, Glen
Newman, Ray
Nippard, Stella
Noble, Fred
Noble, Rudy
Noel, John
Norman, Leonard
Norman, Melvin
Noseworthy, Austin
Noseworthy, Gordon
Nurse, Eric
Oldford, Augustus

Osbourne, Aylmer
Osmond, Arthur
Osmond, Melvin
Pardy, Cluny
Parsons, Joan
Payne, Aubrey
Payne, Chad
Pelley, Bon
Pelley, Lloyd
Penney, Gilbert
Perry, Norman
Pickett, Calvin
Pierce, Shiralee
Pike, Hayward
Pinksen, Larry
Pittman, Ernest
Pittman, Ken
Powell, Karen
Prince, Gerald
Pye, Raymond
Ralph, Albert
Randell, Barry
Randell, Randy
Randell, Warrick
Randell, Will John
Reid, Ray
Reid, Will
Rice, Scott
Ricketts, Beryl
Rideout, Hubert
Rideout, Sandy
Roberts, Everett
Roberts, Nellie
Robinson, Robert
Rogers, Malcolm
Rowe, Phyllis

Ryan, Craig
Ryan, Dorman
Ryan, Jay
Samson, Neville
Seward, Jody
Skinner, Don
Sansome, Calvin
Saunders, Scott
Slade, Hayward
Slade, Walter
Small, Harold
Small, Mark
Snook, Morley
Spurrell, Wilson
Stafford, Winsor
Stagg, Harry
Starkes, Heather
Stokes, Gordon
Stuckless, Gary
Street, Noreen
Strickland, Doretta
Sturge, Bill
Templeman, Lloyd
Tilley, Emma
Tobin, Harold
Tremblett, Larry
Vincent, Derrick
Warren, Lloyd
Warren, Robert
Warren, Tony
Watkins, Cavell
Watkins, Dennis
Watkins, Ted
White, Shelly
Weir, Gordon
Wells, Albert

Wells, Varrick
Welcher, Claude
Welshman, Fred
West, Robert
Wheaton, Vaden
Wheeler, Wallace
Whiffen, Doug
White, Calvin
White, Glenn
White, Velma
Wicks, Arthur
Wicks, Carl
Whalen, Dennis
Williams, Shelly
Wimbleton, Ray
Winsor, Pete
Winsor, Stafford
Winsor, Wendy
Woodford, Eldred
Woodford, Linda
Woodworth, Jim
Young, Dave
Young, Wilf

Avalon Peninsula
Alcock, Hughie
Anderson, Roy
Anthony, Sam
Ash, Allan
Bailey, Wayne
Barrett, Eric
Bartlett, Melvin
Batten, Max
Bennett, Stan
Best, Kevin
Boone, Ed

Boone, Maurice
Bowen, Eugene
Brown, Aiden
Brown, Percy
Brushett, Pat
Bussey, Nelson
Butler, Bev
Button, Bruce
Cahill, Don
Campbell, Andy
Careen, Andy
Careen, Brian
Careen, Henry
Carew, Brian
Carey, Tom
Chafe, George
Chaulk, Mike
Chidley, Gerard
Chidley, Jim
Christopher, Kevin
Clarke, Margaret
Clarke, Terry
Clowe, Tony
Coady, Don
Coady, Jamie
Coady, Junior
Connors, Harry
Connors, Maud
Corcoran, Jim
Corcoran, Julia
Corcoran, Peter
Crane, Paul
Crann, Freeman
Daley, Brendan
Dalton, Gerard
Dalton, Gus

Dalton, Jim
Dalton, Ronnie
Day, Alec
Dobbin, Mike
Dobbin, Pat
Dohey, Phil
Doyle, Joe
Doyle, Tony
Drew, Don
Drover, Scott
Dunne, Kevin
Durnford, Jim
Efford, Harold
English, David
English, Ed
Evans, Helen
Ferguson, Andy
Finley, Robert
Fleming, Joe Sr.
Fougere, Rheal
Frances, Glen
Gibbons, Cyril
Gosse, Charlie
Grace, Dave
Green, Harold
Green, Robbie
Green, Robert
Green, Warren
Greene, Betty
Halleran, Keith
Harnum, Dwayne
Hartery, Harold
Hawco, Dave
Hayden, Bill
Hearn, Donald
Hearn, Mike

Hewitt, John
Hickey, Fred
Hickey, Jim
Hickey, Ron
Hillier, Hector
Hutchings, Nat
Hyde, Linda
Hynes, Glenn
Ivany, Dennis
Kane, Charlie
Kavanaugh, Graham
Kavanaugh, Phonse
Keith, Jim
Kenney, Reg
Kerrivan, Jerome
King, Ken
Lawlor, Bill
Lawlor, Steve
Layman, Pat
Lear, Ivan
Lights, Stephanie
Lockyer, Ed
Lockyer, Melvin
Lynch, Cecilia
Lynch, Levi Jr.
Maher, Peter
Maloney, Maud
Manning, Bernard
Martin, Tom
Mason, Ron
McCarthy, Gord
McCarthy, Robert
McDonald, Ed
McGrath, Ellen
McGrath Kevin
McGrath, Melissa

Melvin, Gerard
Menchions, Albert
Mercer, Alton
Mercer, Kathleen
Miller, Gerald
Milley, Noel
Molloy, Pat
Molloy, William
Morrissey, Don
Mulcahy, Loyola
Mulcahy, Ned
Murphy, Pius
Murphy, Robert
Murphy, Roy
Nash, Lena
Newhook, Doug
Noonan, Mike
Norris, Calvin
Norris, Leonard
Norris, Melissa
Noseworthy, Frank
Nurse, Gerry
O'Leary, Gerard
O'Toole, Derrick
Osborne, Marie
Parsons, Barbara
Parsons, Harold
Parsons, Warren
Petten, Dwight
Petten, Lester
Petten, Matthew
Pevie, Joe
Pevie, Wade
Pitcher, Cec
Pitcher, Lindo
Ploughman, Irene

Ploughman, Sara
Pomroy, Gerard
Porter, Jim
Power, Randy
Quilty, Danny
Ralph, Pat
Reddick, John
Reid, Rose
Rice, Phil
Roberts, Charlie
Russell, Wayne
Ryall, Don
Ryan, Dennis
Ryan, Ralph
Ryan, Wilson
Shugarue, Sherry
Slade, Leslie
Slade, Sam
Slaney, Kevin
Slaney, Mike
Smith, Keith
Snook, Morley
Spurvey, Francis
Squires, Wayne
Stanford, Dave
Stone, Roy
Strong, Scott
Sullivan, David
Sullivan, Lloyd
Sullivan, Ernest
Tapper, Ray
Tuck, Lucy
Vaters, Harris
Walsh, Gerard
Walsh, Kevin
Walsh, Sebastian

Warford, Joey
Warren, Calvin
Warren, Robert
Waterman, Nick
Wells, Alex
Wells, Jim
Whalen, Basil
Whalen, Orman
White, Bill
White, Ray
White, Sharon
Williams, Doug
Williams, Jerry
Windsor, Algy
Winsor, Leonard
Winslow, Glen
Winter, Ramsay
Yard, Joseph
Young, Calvin

South Coast
Anderson, Edith
Augot, Frank
Baker, Charlie
Baker, Dan
Baker, Eli
Baker, Jim
Baker, Maisie
Baker, Wanda
Barnes, Anita
Bateman, Melvin
Beck, Bill
Beck, John
Benteau, Clement
Best, Mike
Blagdon, Tom

Boland, John
Bouzane, Fred
Bowles, Bernadette
Bowles, Bill
Bowles, Edward
Brenton, Frank
Brinston, Edgar
Brushett, Gordon
Buglar, Calvin
Bungay, Charles
Bungay, Harvey
Bygott, Ron
Byrde, Robert
Caines, Karen
Caines, Lucy
Carter, Edward
Chapman, Dan
Clarke, Austin
Cluett, Wanda
Coady, Mike
Coley, George
Collier, Amos
Collier, Bill
Cooper, Ron
Crant, Eric
Curtis, Ewan
Cutler, Wilf
Cutler, Rex
D'Eon, Pierre
Day, Eric
Day, Jim Sr.
Dimmer, Cathy
Dodge, Albert
Dooley, Bern
Drake, Bill
Dunne, Jim

Dunphy, Wayne
Durnford, Arch
Durnford, George
Edwards, Joe
Elson, Don
Ereaut, John C.
Felix, Barry
Feltham, Bruce
Fiander, Stan
Fitzpatrick, Alfred
Fizzard, Eliza
Flannigan, Conrad
Follett, Fred
Foote, Walter Jr.
Forsey, Ross
Francis, John
Fudge, Nat
Giles, Bert
Giles, Cecil
Giles, George
Giles, Roy
Grandy, Marie
Grandy, Wallace
Green, Lester
Greene, Bert
Hackett, Guy
Hann, Lew
Hann, Ross
Hardy, Kevin
Hare, Gord
Hannam, Don
Hannam, Tracy
Hayman, Hartley
Hennebury, Peter
Herridge, Walt
Herritt, Don

Herritt, Guy
Hillier, Bill
Hillier, Denise
Hillier, Frank
Hiller, Freeman
Hillier, Leslie
Hunt, John
Hussey, George
Ingram, Clayton
James, Edward
Janes, Overton
Jarvis, Edgar
Jenkinson, Bridie
Johnson, Earl
Keating, Mike
Keeping, Fred
Kendall, Charlie
Kennedy, Bob
King, Jack
Lake, Jack
Lane, Leo
Langdon, Len
Langdon, Melinda
Lawrence, John
Lawrence, Julie
Lawrence, Kevin
Leonard, Terrence
Lockyer, Peter
Loveless, Wallace
Lundrigan, Donna
Lushman, David
Lushman, Edward
MacKinnon, Dave
Marks, Nathan
Marsden, Lynn
Marsden, Owen

Marsden, Max
Martin, Barry
Masters, Wayne
Matthews, Len
May, Frank
Mayo, Lonas
MacDonald, Doris
May, John
McCarthy, Al
Meade, Gordon
Miller, Eric
Mills, Wanetta
Mitchell, Charlie
Mitchell, Frank
Moore, John
Moores, Wayne
Moulton, Allan Sr.
Moulton, Clayton
Mugford, Harold
Mullins, Bill
Murphy, Melvin
Neary, Gerald
Newport, Howard
Nolan, John
Organ, Roland
Organ, Sam
Pardy, Edith
Pardy, Edward
Paul, David
Paul, Don
Peach, Calvin
Peach, Cecil
Perry, Brenda
Pierce, Fred
Pierce, Gloria
Poole, Sidney

Power, Pius Jr.
Power, Theresa
Price, Richard Jr.
Purchase, Johnny
Purchase, Russ
Quann, Pat
Quirke, Raymond
Reid, Harvey
Rideout, John
Roberts, Wilf
Rose, Fred
Rose, Harvey
Rose, Gerald
Rose, Mike
Rose, Reg
Scott, Howard
Sheppard, Kenneth
Skinner, Mildred
Skinner, Ron
Smith, Albert
Snook, Ambrose Jr.
Snook, Pat
Spencer, Carl
Stacey, Eric
Stacey, Hubert
Stockley, Bill
Stoodley, Jerome
Strickland, Frank
Strickland, James
Strickland, Norm
Strickland, Reg
Swift, Calvin
Swift, Frank
Tapper, Glen
Tapper, Robert
Taylor, Sylvia

Tibbo, Wilfred
Tulk, Harvey
Tulk, Onslow
Walters, Gus
Warren, Eph
Warren, George
Warren, Nate
Warren, Pat
West, Oscar
Whittle, Lorne

West Coast and Northern Peninsula
Allingham, Ralph
Allingham, Terrence
Anderson, Gower
Applin, Joe
Ash, Jim
Bennett, Jerry
Best, Keith
Blanchard, Kevin
Boland, Darren
Bonnell, Norman
Bullen, Ralph
Butt, Stan
Byrne, Cliff
Byrne, Gerard
Byrne, Trudy
Caines, Jayne
Caines, Samuel
Carroll, Herb
Carroll, Ralph
Cassell, David
Chambers, Jacob
Chaytor, Gordon
Coates, Kevin

Coates, Stanley
Coles, Ralph
Coombs, Noah
Crane, John
Crane, Max
Crocker, Blaine
Cull, Norm
Cull, Pearce
Cull, Wilfred
Decker, Glen
Decker, William
Dempster, Shawn
Diamond, Wayne
Diamond, Roland
Doucette, Joan
Doyle, Cliff
Doyle, Henry
Dredge, Leslie
Duffy, Jack
Duffy, Dan
Fennemore, John
Fowlow, Roger
Francis, Candace
Galliott, John Sr.
Gardiner, Robert Jock
Genge, Gary
Genge, Hubert
Genge, Ren
Genge, Selwyn
Goosney, Clyde
Gould, Fintan
Gould, Jean
Green, Seymour
Hann, David
Hann, Roger
Hedderson, Carl

Hedderson, Hedley
Hedderson, John
Hillier, Alec
Hopkins, Harry
House, David
Hughes, Louis
Hughes, William
Hynes, Andrew
Kearney, Frank
Kelly, George
Kelly, Matt
Keough, Roger
Keough, Trevor
Lacosta, Roger
Larkin, Tom
Lavers, George
Lawless, William
Major, Cyril
Marche, Peter
Matchim, Selma
McCarthy, Al
McDonald, Barry
McLean, Manette
Mitchelmore, Terrence
Noseworthy, Lambert
Noseworthy, Stewart
O'Keefe, Ralph
Oliver, Howard
Patey, Eric
Patey, Ron
Payne, Asaph
Penney, Sidney
Perry, Austin
Perry, Pleaman

Piercey, Frank
Pieroway, Brenda
Pilgrim, Stan
Pittman, Herb
Pittman, Hubert
Pittman, Simon
Plowman, Joe
Randell, Stewart
Reardon, Charlie
Reardon, Cliff
Reardon, Mike
Richards, Donald
Richards, Hedley
Richards, Tony
Roberts, Clyde
Roberts, Nelson
Ropson, Baxter
Rose, Lorne
Rose, Margaret
Rose, Rex
Rumbolt, Augustus
Rumbolt, Stanley
Ryan, Anthony
Saunders, Bruce
Saunders, Sherwin
Sexton, Max
Sheppard, John
Sheppard, Ruby
Short, Walter
Simmonds, Mike
Skinner, Edith
Smith, Redmond Jr.
Spence, Bobby
Spence, Dwight
Stevens, Isaac
Taylor, Edmund

Taylor, Roger
Taylor, William
Tucker, Hiram
Tucker, Wayne
Walker, John
Walsh, Bryant
Walsh, Jarvis
Way, Bruce
Way, Garfield
Way, Loomis
Way, Monty
Wells, Morgan
White, Eldred
White, Jack
White, Ron

Full-Time Officers and Staff
Anstey, Reg
Baker, Ben
Baker, Jackie
Benteau, Marlene
Blackmore, Ged
Blackmore, John
Blundon, Alma
Boland, John
Brennan, Bernice
Broderick, Bill
Carroll, Kevin
Carruthers, Erin
Coady, Jamie
Cooney, Madge
Davis, Beverley
Decker, David
Drover, Barbara
Farrell, James

Farrell, Sheila
Furlong, Sharon
Glode, Courtney
Glynn, Sherry
Goudie, Jean
Harvey, Levi
Hedderson, Roland
Jacobs, Darlene
Joensen, Johan
Keenan, Robert
Lee, Robyn
MacDonald, Gerald
Mackey, John
MacKinnon, Dave
McCormick, Jessica
McCurdy, Earle
McGrath, Miranda
Morris, Vanessa
Morrissey, Shelley
Moulton, Allan, Jr.
Murphy, Matt
Murray, Neil
O'Driscoll, Ann
Parrott, Melissa
Payne, Lana
Pennell, Janette
Perry, Guy
Pieroway, Brenda
Pomroy, Patricia
Power, Diane
Power, Pius
Pretty, Tina
Pritchett, Stephanie
Reid, Will
Rideout, Lily
Rosa Bian, Paula
Rowe, Glen
Rowe, Trudy
Rumbolt, Claude
Rumbolt, Perry
Rumbolt, Sylvia
Russell, Simeon
Ryan, Janice
Ryan, Mandy
Sheppard, Barbara
Short, Max
Spingle, Jason
Street, Dwan
Stuart, Alyse
Sullivan, Carol
Sullivan, Keith
Sullivan, Nancy
Swyers, Myra
Taylor, Trevor
Tucker, Angela
Verge, Mabel
Walsh, Rose
Walsh, Sharon
Way, Monty
Waye, Rachel
Whitten, Clara

About the Author

A graduate of Memorial University of Newfoundland, Earle McCurdy joined the staff of what was then known as Newfoundland Fishermen, Food and Allied Workers Union in 1977, serving as editor of the union's publication *Union Forum* until 1980 when he was elected to the position of secretary-treasurer. He served in that position until 1993, when he was elected president. He was re-elected president seven times, retiring from the union in November of 2014.

He also served as president of the Canadian Council of Professional Fish Harvesters, an umbrella group representing fish harvester groups from across Canada, and from 1993 to 2014 as a member of the National Executive Board of CAW, and later Unifor.